Four Plays

Also by

ENID BAGNOLD

Prose:

A Diary without Dates
The Happy Foreigner
Serena Blandish: or the Difficulty of Getting Married
Alice and Thomas and Jane
National Velvet
The Squire
The Loved and Envied
The Girl's Journey (reprint)
Enid Bagnold's Autobiography

Plays:

Lottie Dundass
National Velvet
Poor Judas
Arts Theatre Prize, 1951
Gertie
The Chalk Garden
Award of Merit for Drama, American Academy of Arts and Letters, 1964
The Last Joke
The Chinese Prime Minister
Call Me Jacky

Poetry:
Sailing Ships

Translation:
Alexander of Asia (*Alexandre Asiatique* by Princesse Marthe Bibesco)

Enid Bagnold

Four Plays

HEINEMANN : LONDON

William Heinemann Limited

LONDON MELBOURNE TORONTO
JOHANNESBURG AUCKLAND

This collection first published 1970

The Chalk Garden Copyright, 1953, 1956, by Enid Bagnold
The Last Joke Copyright © Enid Bagnold 1970
The Chinese Prime Minister Copyright © 1964 by Enid Bagnold
Call Me Jacky Copyright © Enid Bagnold, 1968

434 04302 8

The Chalk Garden has been previously published by William
Heinemann, Random House and Samuel French (in both London
and New York); *The Chinese Prime Minister* has been previously
published by Random House and Samuel French, New York.
Call Me Jacky was published in London by Elek in *Plays of the Year*,
Volume 34.

Printed in Great Britain by
Cox & Wyman Ltd, London, Reading and Fakenham

CONTENTS

The Chalk Garden

THE CHALK GARDEN was first presented by Irene Mayer Selznick at the Ethel Barrymore Theatre, New York City, 26th October 1955, with the following cast:

MISS MADRIGAL (First Applicant)	Siobhan McKenna
MAITLAND	Fritz Weaver
SECOND APPLICANT	Georgia Harvey
LAUREL	Betsy von Furstenberg
THIRD APPLICANT	Eva Leonard-Boyne
MRS. ST. MAUGHAM	Gladys Cooper
NURSE	Marie Paxton
OLIVIA	Marian Seldes
THE JUDGE	Percy Waram

The Play directed by
ALBERT MARRE
with Setting and Costumes by
CECIL BEATON

It was presented in London, coinciding with the run in New York, by H. M. Tennent Ltd., at the Haymarket Theatre on 11th April 1956, with the following cast:

MISS MADRIGAL (First Applicant)	Dame Peggy Ashcroft
MAITLAND	George Rose
SECOND APPLICANT	Ruth Lodge
LAUREL	Judith Stott
THIRD APPLICANT	Phyllis Relph
MRS. ST. MAUGHAM	Dame Edith Evans
NURSE	Mavis Walker
OLIVIA	Rachel Gurney
THE JUDGE	Felix Aylmer

The Play directed by
SIR JOHN GIELGUD
with Setting by
REECE PEMBERTON

CHARACTERS

MRS. ST. MAUGHAM
LAUREL, her granddaughter
OLIVIA, Laurel's mother
MISS MADRIGAL (First Lady Applicant)
MAITLAND
THE JUDGE
NURSE
SECOND LADY APPLICANT
THIRD LADY APPLICANT
PINKBELL; unseen but not unfelt

TIME: The present.
PLACE: A room in a manor house, Sussex.

ACT I: A day in June.
ACT II: Two months later.
ACT III: Twenty minutes later.

DEDICATION

TO HAROLD FREEDMAN—friend and agent of thirty years through whose endless patience all plans eventually mature—*you* were the spring that released the Dynamo.

Gratefully,

E. B.

(Rottingdean: May 1956.)

FOREWORD

THE CHALK GARDEN owes its New York production (and therefore its outer life) to the devotion of IRENE MAYER SELZNICK.

In America "producer" is the word for the Management. In this case it is difficult to limit Mrs. Selznick's dynamic activity by a word. For two years she lived with one end—to put on this play. She flew, she cabled, she battled. She "cast". In casting she would have ransacked the Shades.

More imperious than I on my behalf she was filled towards the play with an unfaltering magnificence of loyalty.

These few lines are written with my deep thanks and affection.

ENID BAGNOLD

Rottingdean,
  May 1956.

ACT I

Time: The Present.

Place: A room in one of those Manor Houses which border a Village Green in a village in Sussex. The soil is lime and chalk. The village is by the sea.

The Scene: From one high window in the room preferably downstage Left, the personages on the stage can see, when standing up, the life that goes on on the Village Green.

Back stage there is a wide french window, standing open, that gives on to the garden. On stage Left is a door leading to the main part of the house. A corridor (much grander than the room seen in the Set) leads presumably to the front door, to dust-sheeted entertaining rooms, and to the rooms upstairs. Farther upstage Left is a baize door leading to MAITLAND'S *pantry.*

A small door opens downstage Right to show a narrow flight of stairs leading to Pinkbell's bedroom. If another door to the garden would be useful it can be placed upstage Right.

Beyond the open french window a bosky, be-lillied garden runs slightly uphill. A June gale blows. The room has a look of vigour and culture. The furniture is partly inherited, partly bought in MRS. ST. MAUGHAM'S *young days. It is probably Regency but the owner of this house does not tie herself to anything. She has lived through many moods, and is a jackdaw for the Curious and Strange. The only object necessarily described is her work-table backstage, running the length of the windows. It is a rough table, rather high and long. Under it lie in disorder baskets, garden trugs, a saw, two long-handled grass-cutters, a tin of Abol, a sack of John Innes potting soil, a log basket full of raffia, and rubber clogs, etc. On top of the table are strewn scissors, string,*

7

*gardening books, flower catalogues, gardening gloves, a small
watering can for vases in the room, a trowel, etc.
On Curtain Up there are four chairs drawn out from the ordinary
furnishing of the room, as though for a meeting or an interview.
Three are empty. Over the back of one is draped a small ragged
feather boa, as though it had slipped from someone's shoulders.
The next two chairs are empty. On the fourth sits* MISS
MADRIGAL.

MISS MADRIGAL *is an enigmatical, contained woman, neat
and non-committal in dress—with fine eyes and a high aquiline
look. She has the still look of an eagle at rest upon a rock.
Almost immediately a door opens and* MAITLAND (*in a white
linen serving coat*) *shows in a rapid* LITTLE LADY. *She comes
in like a bird over a lawn, stops quickly, moves on quickly.*

LITTLE LADY (*a-flutter*): Good morning. May one sit?
    *No answer. She sits. She hides her hands, looks at them,
    hides them again. It is a trick of hers.*
Lovely blowy weather.... (*There is still no answer.*) Are you
too here for the interview? (MISS MADRIGAL *looks towards
her.*) (*Flustered by the silence.*) As I came in ... I saw a lady
going out ... (*confidential*) ... in a temper.
    The THIRD LADY (*whose beauty is decayed*) *sails in from
    door Left. She carries a chiffon scarf in her hand.*
MAITLAND (*turning sharply*): Who let *you* in?
THIRD LADY: The front door stood wide open. So humane!
MAITLAND: Have you a letter?
THIRD LADY: I wouldn't have come, dear, if I hadn't had a
    letter! (*Waves it at him.*) Are you the butler?
MAITLAND: I am the manservant.
THIRD LADY: A world of difference! In my days it was
    thought common to wear a white coat. A relic of our
    occupation in India! In those days only worn in Cheltenham!
    MAITLAND *follows her as she wanders round the room.*
THIRD LADY (*suddenly waving a coy finger*): In those days—

in the Hill Stations—I was thought to have extra-*ordin*ary charm! (*Noticing the others with condescension.*) Good morning. How do you do? (*To* MAITLAND.) Is this a house where there are gentlemen?

MAITLAND (*stiffly*): I am not to give information.

THIRD LADY (*looking him in the eyes coyly*): But you have only to nod. (*Fingering things on the table.*) . . . gardening gloves. . . . Nicotine for wood lice. . . . Is your lady going up in the world? Or coming down? (*To* LITTLE LADY.) One has to be so careful.

MAITLAND (*outraged*): Mrs. St. Maugham has a house in Belgrave Square!

THIRD LADY: But you are left in the country, I suppose, when she goes up for the Season?

MAITLAND (*shortly*): Madam is past the Seasons. Take a chair, please.

THIRD LADY: Where are the entertaining rooms?

MAITLAND: They are under dust sheets.

THIRD LADY (*to* APPLICANTS): Not that I am applying for the post, you know . . . not *really*!

LITTLE LADY (*gasping*): Not applying?

THIRD LADY (*moves towards door*): I came . . . I came to have a peep! So nostalgic. . . .

MAITLAND: Where are you off to?

THIRD LADY (*tying the lace scarf round her hair. Mockingly*): Such a wind out! So rough and rude in summer. . . .

MAITLAND: But you're not *going*!

THIRD LADY (*teasing him, but it is the truth*): I could not think of staying in a house—where there is not even a nephew!

MAITLAND: But what shall I tell her?

THIRD LADY (*with ancient mischief*): . . . that people who advertise . . . are never quite of one's world! (*Exits.*)

MAITLAND *follows her out.*

The girl LAUREL *comes in from upstairs. She is sixteen, dressed in a summer dress, and wearing a most unsuitable amount of jewellery. She shuts the door behind her, moves towards them and surveys them with an unruffled, contemplative stare.*

LAUREL: My grandmother had a hundred and seven answers. (*Silence.*) I mean to her advertisement for someone to look after me.

LITTLE LADY (*rising, propitiatory, puts out a nervous hand*): You are the young lady—who requires a companion? (*Her poor nervous hand steals out.*)

LAUREL: I never shake hands. It's so animal.

LITTLE LADY *sinks back.*

So one of you has come to look after me? We were expecting four applicants—the ones my grandmother selected from the letters. And now there are only two to choose from! (*To the* LITTLE LADY.) What are your qualifications?

LITTLE LADY (*anxious, leaning forward*): Frobel-trained. Long ago. But Frobel-trained. (*Almost in a whisper.*) And patience.

LAUREL: Would you have patience with me?

LITTLE LADY: I am so fond of young people.

LAUREL: I set fire to things. I am not allowed alone, except in the garden.

LITTLE LADY (*carrying on bravely*): Such lovely weather for the garden. The advertisement said "with handicraft". I am clever with my fingers. I am fond of making pretty things. (*Coy.*) Now—can *you* make a lampshade?

LAUREL (*insolent*): All the lampshades here are made already.

LITTLE LADY (*confidential*): Will you tell me, dear, of what does the family consist?

LAUREL (*matter of fact; without emphasis*): Of my grandmother. Of me. And Maitland. And the terrible old man upstairs. And his hospital nurse.

LITTLE LADY (*horrified*): Your ... grandfather?

LAUREL: Mr. Pinkbell was always the butler. Now he has a stroke.

LITTLE LADY (*glancing at the door*): Who was that then?

LAUREL: That was Maitland. He wears a grocer's coat. You get them for a guinea. Mr. Pinkbell, of course, used to wear a black one and have a footman.

LITTLE LADY: But is there no one else?

LAUREL: Oh we are rich! If we have only one servant it is part of my grandmother's newest theory about life. She says true devotion is only to be got when a man is worked to death and has no rival. Maitland plays games with me so he has his hands full.

LITTLE LADY: But have you no mother?

LAUREL: My mother married again. She married for love. It has given me an adolescent repugnance to her. My case is practically in Freud. My grandmother will explain it to you.

LITTLE LADY: And where is your father?

LAUREL: My father shot himself when I was twelve. I was in the room. (*Turning immediately to* MADRIGAL.) And what are your qualifications?

MADRIGAL (*turning a frosty eye on her*): I prefer to wait for your grandmother.

LAUREL (*interested in this answer*): Are you Scotch?

MADRIGAL: I was born in Barbados.

LAUREL: Where do you live?

MADRIGAL: In my room.

LAUREL: How do you take to me?

MADRIGAL: You are not what I am used to.

LAUREL: I am fond of painting. Can you paint?

MADRIGAL: What I cannot do is wait much longer.

LAUREL: Oh, she'll come! Grandloo will come! She is working in the garden. She's a great gardener, but nothing grows for her. Do wait. You may be the one we are looking for.

Enter MAITLAND, *hurrying over to the chair for the feather boa.*

MAITLAND: She says she left this behind. ... (*Picks it up distastefully. Suddenly sees* LAUREL.) And what are you doing wearing Madam's necklaces! Off with them! You've been upstairs and I thought I left you happy in the garden. (*Slipping jewellery in sideboard drawer.*) Out you go! I've got a bonfire laid at the top there! You shall light it when I get a minute.

LAUREL *exits into garden.*

He runs back through door Left leaving door open behind him and carrying the boa.

LITTLE LADY (*distractedly, to* MISS MADRIGAL): Do you think it's all true?

MADRIGAL (*indifferently*): I should think it unlikely.

MAITLAND *re-enters.*

LITTLE LADY (*to* MADRIGAL, *and also glancing at* MAITLAND): For the interview . . . when the interview . . . ought we to be together?

MAITLAND: One of you ladies can wait in the drawing room. It's dust-sheeted but there's a chair.

LITTLE LADY (*crossing the room at speed*): One must be fair! Let it be me! This lady was before me! (*To* MADRIGAL.) When you're ready you just call, dear! (*Exits.*)

MAITLAND: Whew!

MADRIGAL: She's a little light-fingered.

MAITLAND (*rushing to look in drawer of sideboard*): That one! Oh!

MADRIGAL: No more than a box of matches or the Tatler.

MAITLAND: Do you know her?

MADRIGAL: No. But I have met those hands before. Many times.

MAITLAND: Met her hands! (*Opens the door a crack so that he can glance across into dust-sheeted drawing room. Flings door wide open.*) She's gone! The room's plum empty!

MADRIGAL (*as to herself*): They were none of them solid applicants.

MAITLAND: But they wrote to Madam!

MADRIGAL: It's how they spend their days. They answer advertisements.

MAITLAND: Not meaning to take the job!

MADRIGAL (*absently*): They are always in two minds. It makes a change for them. . . . (*At her own words she goes a bit off track.*) . . . and then too she has a garden.

MAITLAND: It's you who have two minds, it seems! (*Eyeing*

her anxiously.) Don't *you* be flitting! If there's nobody here
—after all the advertising—who do you think's going to get
the brunt!

MADRIGAL (*to herself*): I cannot hope to be acceptable—at
the first undertaking.

MAITLAND: You don't need to worry! Madam's up a tree!

MADRIGAL (*prim and yet nervous*): There's an urgency?

MAITLAND: She's got her daughter coming. A shy lady. A
nice one. If you ask me—Madam's afraid she'll take the
child—

MADRIGAL (*interrupting*): The *child's* outlandish!

MAITLAND: Only what Madam makes her. I can explain her!
Nurse and Nanny I bin to her!

MADRIGAL: In a house like this—would I be suitable?

MAITLAND: She'll take you! Madam loves the Unusual! It's
a middle class failing—she says—to run away from the
Unusual!

VOICE (*from offstage R. in the garden*): Maitland! (*Coming
nearer.*) Maitland! Maitland!

MAITLAND: Madam!

VOICE (*just outside the garden windows*): Are my teeth on the
table? My bottom teeth. . . .

MAITLAND (*searching*): There's nothing.

VOICE: Then I must have left them in the greenhouse.

MAITLAND (*going out to meet her*): Here! Wait, Madam . . .
here they are—wrapped in a handkerchief!

   MRS. ST. MAUGHAM *appears outside the garden windows
and comes in through the garden door. She is an old, overpowering,
once beautiful, ex-hostess of London society.*
(*Following her in.*) There's a dentist taken the empty house
by the church. He might make you comfortable!

MRS. ST. MAUGHAM (*sweeping downstage*): I've tried all the
dentists! You can't fit false teeth to a woman of character.
As one gets older and older, the appearance becomes such a
bore. (*She sees* MISS MADRIGAL.) Good morning. (*Displeased—to* MAITLAND.) But I expected four applicants!

MAITLAND: Four came. Three have gone.

MRS. ST. MAUGHAM: And one wrote me such a good letter! Gone!

MAITLAND: But I've kept this one.

MRS. ST. MAUGHAM (*to* MISS MADRIGAL, *who rises respectfully and stands*): Shall we sit? You can go, Maitland.

MAITLAND *exits.*

(*With a sudden and alarming charm of manner as she seats herself.*)

Now what questions do total strangers put to one another?

MADRIGAL (*colourlessly*): The name is Madrigal.

MRS. ST. MAUGHAM *selects the "Madrigal" letter from the bunch she holds.*

MADRIGAL: I am the daughter of the late Ronald Bentham Madrigal, Rajputana Hussars, Indian Army. He was the son of General Bentham Madrigal—the Honourable East India Company.

MRS. ST. MAUGHAM: No, no! That you can't be! The Honourable East India Company was dissolved in 1860! I'm an expert! My great grandfather was Tarr Bethune, Governor of Madras, tried for corruption in 1859 and found guilty!

MADRIGAL (*calmly*): My grandfather had my father at the age of seventy-five.

MRS. ST. MAUGHAM (*admitting the point*): *That* might make it possible. What experience have you?

MADRIGAL: I have small private means. I have not taken such a post before.

MRS. ST. MAUGHAM: Why do you apply to me?

MADRIGAL: The advertisement tempted me. I have been somewhat alone.

MRS. ST. MAUGHAM: You will be able, I suppose, to give me references?

MADRIGAL (*coldly*): That will be difficult.

MRS. ST. MAUGHAM: What?

MADRIGAL: In fact impossible.

A hospital NURSE *in full uniform comes into the room, carrying a used tray.*

NURSE (*stiff, reproachful*): We've been ringing, Mrs. St. Maugham.

MRS. ST. MAUGHAM: I heard nothing!

NURSE (*acid*): Our breakfast tray was late again.

MRS. ST. MAUGHAM: One can't have everything!

NURSE: Mr. Pinkbell says one should have a great deal more.
Crosses stage with tray and exits, flouncing.

MRS. ST. MAUGHAM (*shutting her eyes*): One of his cross mornings.

MAITLAND *enters from garden.*
Ask *me* questions, Miss Madrigal.

MADRIGAL: Does one have a room to oneself?

MRS. ST. MAUGHAM (*eyes still closed*): Life without a room to oneself is a barbarity. Luncheon here with me and my granddaughter. Your evening meal served in your room on a tray. . . .

MAITLAND: That can't be done!

MRS. ST. MAUGHAM (*automatically*): Ma'am.

MAITLAND (*as automatically*): Ma'am.

MRS. ST. MAUGHAM: And why can't it?

MAITLAND (*phone rings offstage*): Because I shall be busy serving at Madam's table.

MRS. ST. MAUGHAM: I hear the telephone.

MAITLAND *exits.*
Now—now Miss Madrigal! We are so continuously interrupted. . . . Are you Church of England?

MADRIGAL (*whose mind is only on the telephone*): My religion is private. I should tell you—in case you should ask me to— I don't answer the telephone.

MRS. ST. MAUGHAM (*immediately interested*): For what reason?

MADRIGAL: I prefer not to. (*As though realizing by Mrs. St. Maughan's attitude that more explanation is needed.*) It disturbs me to join two worlds.

MRS. ST. MAUGHAM: Which . . .?

MADRIGAL: The outside . . . and the inside one.

MAITLAND (*returning*): They want you to open the village Summer Festival.

MRS. ST. MAUGHAM: Are they holding on?

MAITLAND: They are.

MRS. ST. MAUGHAM: Ask them what attendance they can ensure? Last time I opened something there was nobody there.

MAITLAND: Madam is so unpopular.

MRS. ST. MAUGHAM: How do *you* know?

MAITLAND: I hear it on all sides.

MRS. ST. MAUGHAM: They tell you that when I send you down to the post. Give me my engagement book.

MAITLAND (*fetching it from table*): That's last year's!

MRS. ST. MAUGHAM: Give it me all the same! The dates are not so different. Have you lived in a village, Miss Madrigal?

    MAITLAND *comes back and hands her the book.*

MADRIGAL (*mumbling*): No, Mrs. St. Maugham. . . .

MRS. ST. MAUGHAM (*as she leafs through book*): All the graces of life here go unvalued. In a village one is down to the bones of things. When I was at my height—though I lived here—I never knew them! They were waiting for my old age like wolves it seems! Tell them I won't open it.

    MAITLAND *exits.*

Ah . . . where were we? My advertisement asks for handicraft. What handicraft do you suggest?

MADRIGAL: I have ornamented a chapel.

MRS. ST. MAUGHAM: With your needle?

MADRIGAL: With my brush. I have painted a twining plant on the altar candles.

MRS. ST. MAUGHAM (*immediately interested*): But—as the candles burnt down the painting must have melted away!

MADRIGAL (*ecstatic*): *That* was the beauty of it! Is this a quiet house?

MRS. ST. MAUGHAM: Absolutely.

Wild screams are heard offstage up the garden. MAITLAND *bursts in, rushes through to the garden.*

MAITLAND: That child again. (*Disappears.*)

MRS. ST. MAUGHAM (*calm*): It's my daughter's child. My granddaughter. She's so fond of screaming.

MADRIGAL: While I was waiting a young girl passed through the room.

MRS. ST. MAUGHAM: That was she! She lives with me. Did she say anything?

MADRIGAL (*colourless*): Nothing of consequence.

MRS. ST. MAUGHAM: Not the suicide of her father?

MADRIGAL: I think she mentioned it.

MRS. ST. MAUGHAM (*delighted*): Oh Laurel—to make a drama . . .! He died—poor man—of his liver! Oh I *knew* there would be something! She has a *need* for fantasy!

MADRIGAL (*as though it were a foible*): She does not care for the truth?

MRS. ST. MAUGHAM: No. But I encourage her. She loves a small limelight! One must be tender with her. Alas, he died when she was three. Rich and a fine estate. Four Van Dykes and unique Sheraton furniture. (*Bitterly.*) Her mother's one success. . . . But why speak of it! She married again.

MADRIGAL: And where *is* her mother?

MRS. ST. MAUGHAM: She follows the drum—as they say— in Arabia. Stationed abroad is the term, but I dislike military language. She is coming by ship. . . . I am expecting her.

MADRIGAL (*half-rising*): Would you sooner postpone. . . .

MRS. ST. MAUGHAM: But she does not come here! . . . *I* should be your employer.

MADRIGAL (*cautiously*): She *is* coming?

MRS. ST. MAUGHAM: In front of the child—we don't mention it! She is coming. One does not know why, though I shrewdly suspect it. (*Pause, looks at photograph on the table.*) I have an unworldly daughter. She was always crying out after being simple. That's hard to understand! It seems such a waste, with all the chances of life, to want to be simple.

Privilege and power make selfish people—but gay ones—
(*Breaks off.*) Forgive me, Miss Madrigal, for being personal.
. . . But irritation is like a rash on the heart!

MADRIGAL (*to change the subject*): The child—is she fond of
her stepfather?

MRS. ST. MAUGHAM (*indifferent*): I never asked. His rank is
Colonel. My granddaughter has developed an interesting
mother-hatred, which is clearly explained in Freud. You
have had experience? You feel competent to deal with such
things?

MADRIGAL (*dreamily*): For the worse . . . or the better. . . .

MRS. ST. MAUGHAM: You seem absent in mind!

MADRIGAL (*pulling herself together again*): Not in mind . . .
but in manner. (*Pursily.*) Your granddaughter is naturally
alienated—that a sex life has broken out again in her mother.

MRS. ST. MAUGHAM: You put it well! Exactly! The child
was frenzied. (*The house phone rings.*) When nothing would
stop the wedding—she ran from the hotel into the dark. . . .

MADRIGAL: There seems to be a bell ringing.

MRS. ST. MAUGHAM (*getting up and talking as she crosses R.
to house telephone*) . . . and by some extraordinary carelessness
she was violated in Hyde Park at the age of twelve. It has
upset her nerves. We are waiting as it were for calmer
weather. (*Picking up house telephone.*) You want me, Pinkbell?
One moment. . . . (*Hand over phone.*) Of course we put it less
strongly to her mother. Apart from certain fixations con-
nected with fire, she is a charming intelligent girl. I should
welcome your impressions. (*Into phone.*) What's that!
(*Listens.*) I did. I ordered it. The Extract of Humus—for the
seed boxes. (*Listening.*) It should have come. I'll ring. I'll
ring and ask him.

Is about to put the receiver from her but is recalled by the
VOICE.

I know! I know! But one can't get perfection, Pinkbell!
(*Replaces receiver on hook. To herself.*) Oh . . . isn't jealousy
terrible!

MADRIGAL (*with surprising force*): Yes.

MRS. ST. MAUGHAM: You made me jump. He's my butler. Forty years my butler. Now he's had a stroke but he keeps his finger on things. (*Rings handbell.*)

MADRIGAL (*automatically*): He carries on at death's door.

MRS. ST. MAUGHAM (*as automatically*): His standards rule this house.

MADRIGAL (*absently*): You must be fond of him.

MRS. ST. MAUGHAM: Alas no. He trains Maitland—but now Maitland won't go near him. But I shall overcome it. He's so good with the garden. (*Rings bell again.*)

MADRIGAL: Maitland?

MRS. ST. MAUGHAM: Pinkbell. He directs mine from his window. All butlers dream of gardening. We spoke of references. Who will speak for you?

MADRIGAL (*indifferently*): No one will speak for me—(*Earnestly.*) Extract of humus is too rich for summer biennials.

MAITLAND *enters from garden.*

MRS. ST. MAUGHAM: Has a bag of humus been delivered at the back door?

MAITLAND: There's a sack there.

MRS. ST. MAUGHAM: When did it come?

MAITLAND: Days ago.

MRS. ST. MAUGHAM: And you walk by it and ignore it! How do you know someone hasn't sent me a brace of pheasants! Mr. Pinkbell says you must always report and at once what comes to the back door.

MAITLAND (*suddenly reaching his limit*): *I won't take orders from the old bastard!*

MRS. ST. MAUGHAM: Am I to have trouble with you, Maitland?

MAITLAND (*breaking*): Oh, if I could please and be sure of myself!

MRS. ST. MAUGHAM (*quiet, menacing*): *Maitland.*

MAITLAND: Oh, if things would go smoothly!

MRS. ST. MAUGHAM (*with deliberation and distinctiveness*):

Maitland! (*He looks at her.*) Bring me the Crème de Menthe and two glasses.

MAITLAND's *chest fills with emotion. He seems about to burst. He obeys and rushes out through his door.* MRS. ST. MAUGHAM *sits back in armchair, fanning her face with her handkerchief.*

Touch and go! How frail is authority. What were you saying?

MADRIGAL: When?

MRS. ST. MAUGHAM: About humus and summer biennials.

MADRIGAL (*tonelessly, sleepwalkingly*): Don't pep up the soil before birth. It leads them on to expect ... what life won't give them.

MRS. ST. MAUGHAM (*leaning forward*): Speak louder!

MADRIGAL (*with awkward and unstable loudness*): What life won't give them!

MRS. ST. MAUGHAM (*suddenly reminded*): What was that plant you painted on the candles?

MADRIGAL (*with inner pleasure as though she were eating a sweet*): Lapagaria. Sub-tropical. With waxy umbels.

MRS. ST. MAUGHAM: Lady Dorchester had it in her wedding bouquet after the Battle of the Marne! I had forgotten it! Could I grow it in my greenhouse?

MADRIGAL (*by rote*): It needs the early actinic rays. Exclude the sun again at midday. Counteract the high lime-content in your soil with potash.

MRS. ST. MAUGHAM: Where did you learn about such things?

MADRIGAL: I was put in charge of. ...

MRS. ST. MAUGHAM: What?

MADRIGAL: ... a garden.

Enter MAITLAND, *carrying everything most correctly—liqueur bottle, two small glasses, silver tray, and even a clean napkin over his arm.*

MAITLAND (*setting down the silver tray with exactitude; then straightening himself*): I wish to give my notice.

MRS. ST. MAUGHAM (*eyes like steel*): If I take it you will not get it back again.

MAITLAND: I am prepared for that.

MRS. ST. MAUGHAM (*terrible*): Are you?

MAITLAND (*immediately broken*): You know I can't stand criticism! Every time a word's said against me a month's work is undone!

MRS. ST. MAUGHAM: We all make mistakes.

MAITLAND (*passionately*): But nothing should be said about them! Praise is the only thing that brings to life again a man that's been destroyed! (*Pacing up and down.*) But oh if I leave ... what will you do without me! (*Another scream is heard from the garden.*) ... and what will the child do! (*Runs off into the garden.*)

MRS. ST. MAUGHAM (*smiling in triumph*): Do you know the secret of authority, Miss Madrigal? Changes of mood. The Inexplicable. The thunder, the lightning, and the sudden sun. He won't leave me! Will you have a Crème de Menthe?

MADRIGAL (*stiffly*): I never touch alcohol.

MRS. ST. MAUGHAM (*drinking hers*): Certainly he makes scenes. But I like them. He has been a prisoner.

MADRIGAL: A prisoner!

MRS. ST. MAUGHAM: Five years. Now that there are no subject races, one must be served by the sick, the mad and those who can't take their place in the outside world. ...

LAUREL *rushes in from the garden and stands looking out of the garden door.*

And served I must be. (*Sees* LAUREL.) Laurel!

LAUREL (*not turning*): One moment, Grandloo! One moment, darling ... I'm watching the bonfire ... I must see it die. ... I put salt on it to turn the flame blue. *Blocks* of it!

MRS. ST. MAUGHAM: Who told you to put salt on it?

LAUREL (*sweet*): The old bastard, Mr. Pinkbell.

MRS. ST. MAUGHAM: Not now, my darling. Superlatives only between ourselves!

LAUREL (*turning round*): Where are the others?

MRS. ST. MAUGHAM: *This* is Miss Madrigal!

LAUREL (*eager*): Have you settled everything? (*To* MISS MADRIGAL.) Do you understand all about me?

MADRIGAL: Not yet.

LAUREL: Oh can't we have the interview together? Shall I go and fetch the book that explains me?

MRS. ST. MAUGHAM: Not so fast. Externalize! Externalize, my darling! She has quaint self-delusions. You mustn't mind them. . . .

    MAITLAND *enters from garden with a black look at* LAUREL *and exits through his door.*

LAUREL: . . . but you mustn't cross them!

MADRIGAL: Are you an only child?

LAUREL: I am Delilah's daughter!

MRS. ST. MAUGHAM: Laurel has a poltergeist! Stones fall in the bedrooms, and words leap and change colour in her mouth like fishes! I too at her age. . . .

LAUREL: Wit often skips a generation!

MRS. ST. MAUGHAM: She is my parchment sheet on which I write! I hope she will remember my life and times! There seems no one else to do it. . . .

LAUREL: *I* am your little immortality!

MRS. ST. MAUGHAM: Those who eat too big a meal of life— get no monument. You will note—how light my finger lies upon her! The child's a flower. She grows in liberty!

MADRIGAL: Weeds grow as easily.

MRS. ST. MAUGHAM: As I was saying. . . .

LAUREL: . . . before the interruption!

MRS. ST. MAUGHAM: Freedom is Captain here! Calm is its Lieutenant!

    The NURSE *rushes in.*

NURSE: The madonna lilies have blown over!

MRS. ST. MAUGHAM: Oh—great heavens—this mule of a garden!—*Maitland!* . . . He was to order the bamboos and he forgot them! . . . Are they all down?

NURSE (*with triumph*): All. And not for want of warnings! (*Exits.*)

MRS. ST. MAUGHAM: Oh my lilies! My lilies! One waits a
year for them! ...
> *Exits fast into the garden.*
> *Enter* MAITLAND.

MAITLAND: What was that I heard?

LAUREL: The calm of Grandloo.

MAITLAND: But what's happened?

MADRIGAL: There's been an accident in the garden.

MAITLAND (*to* LAUREL, *denouncingly, he starts for garden*): Fire!

LAUREL (*stopping him*): Wind. You didn't stake the lilies!

MAITLAND (*frantic, rushing to the window to look out*): Oh are
they down? The nurse told me and I forgot! How the old
bastard will be crowing!

MADRIGAL (*primly*): Stake in May.

MAITLAND (*turning on her fiercely*): They weren't full grown
in May!

MADRIGAL: They should have been.

MAITLAND (*more fiercely*): Is that a criticism?

MADRIGAL: So you are the gardener here as well?

MAITLAND: I'm everything! I'm the kingpin and the pivot
and the manservant and the maidservant and the go-
between (*turning on* LAUREL) and the fire-extinguisher!

LAUREL: Prisoner Six Five Seven Four!

MAITLAND (*jumping to attention*): Sir!

LAUREL: Carry your bed-area and about turn! Through the
corridor second door on the left and into your cell! *March!*

MAITLAND (*marches to* LAUREL, *starts to salute but can't make it*):
I'm all to pieces! I can't play it.

LAUREL (*to* MADRIGAL, *in mock tragic tones as she sits in the
armchair*): He was five long years in prison, Miss Madrigal.

MADRIGAL (*politely*): Was it your first conviction?

MAITLAND: Conviction! It was for my ideals! I was a Con-
scientious Objector!

MADRIGAL (*prim*): And didn't you find it trying?

MAITLAND: She says "Trying!" Five years! Five long years!
Given one chance to live and five years taken from it! An

ant among a thousand ants—and taking orders from ants!

MADRIGAL: If it upsets you better not recall it.

MAITLAND: Not recall it! It's stamped on my skin and at the back of my eyes! It's in my legs when I walk up and down! In my heart that sticks with fright when *she* gets angry!

MADRIGAL (*sententious*): But since you felt you had Right on your side?

MAITLAND: "Right on my side"; *That* didn't uphold me! I went in there because I wouldn't take a life but before I came out I would have killed a warder!

MADRIGAL (*platitudinously*): All acts become possible.

MAITLAND: What can *you* know of life?

MADRIGAL: True, it's been sheltered.

LAUREL (*pouring a glass of Crème de Menthe*): All our lives are sheltered.

MAITLAND (*turns and sees* LAUREL): Don't do that! She'll be furious! (*Rushes to her.*)

LAUREL (*tossing it down her throat before* MAITLAND *can reach her*): Not with me. I'm not responsible.

MAITLAND (*to* MADRIGAL): You'll witness, Miss. I didn't touch it! I have to be on the ready for injustice in life!

LAUREL: From me? From your little Laurel? How touchy you are!

MAITLAND: I have soft ground and hard ground to my feelings. You should mind where you step!

LAUREL (*mock-concern*): Have you taken your Luminol?

MAITLAND: That's it! That's it! Even a child knows a man must take a sedative! But coming from you, Laurel. . . .

LAUREL: *Miss* Laurel. I am a victim and you ought to love me.

MAITLAND (*angrily*): I do love you—like the poor mother who ought by rights and reasons to take a stick to you!

LAUREL: What do you expect of me! A child that's been forsaken by its mother!

MAITLAND: That's as may be! That's as those think it to be! I was found in a field but I don't make a fuss about it! (*Rushes out to kitchen.*)

LAUREL (*soapily*): Poor Maitland likes the Right—even when the Right is wrong.

MADRIGAL (*platitudinous*): He has your interests at heart?

LAUREL (*with interest*): Are you a hospital nurse?

MADRIGAL: Why do you ask?

LAUREL: You have that unmeaning way of saying things.

MADRIGAL (*after a second's pause and with a little formal manner of adapting herself*): Now that we are alone—am I to call you Laurel?

LAUREL: It's my name.

MADRIGAL: And what are you interested in—Laurel? I mean apart from yourself?

LAUREL: What I don't like—is to be questioned.

MADRIGAL: I agree with you.

LAUREL: But I *don't* like to be agreed with—just in case I might argue! And I don't like to be read aloud to unless I suggest it! But if read aloud to—*I don't like emphasis!* And every morning I don't like "*Good* morning" said! I can see for myself what sort of a day it is!

MADRIGAL: You sound as if you had had lady-companions before. How did you get rid of them?

LAUREL: I tell Pinkbell.

MADRIGAL: He tells your grandmother. My mind goes more slowly than yours. But it was going that way.

LAUREL: You see she loves to advertise! She loves what comes out of it. It's like dredging in the sea, she says—so much comes up in the net!

MADRIGAL: I—for instance?

LAUREL: Why not?

MADRIGAL: Doesn't she take a chance—that way?

LAUREL: No, she says you get more out of life by haphazard. By the way, if you want to get on with my grandmother— you must notice her eccentricity.

MADRIGAL: She is fond of that?

LAUREL: She adores it! Oh, the tales I let her tell me when I am in the mood!

MADRIGAL (*musing*): Does she love you?

LAUREL: She would like to! (*Confidentially.*) She *thinks* she does! . . . But I am only her remorse.

MADRIGAL: You try your foot upon the ice, don't you?

LAUREL: I find you wonderfully odd. Why do you come here?

MADRIGAL: I have to do something with my life. . . .

LAUREL: What life have you been used to?

MADRIGAL (*softly*): Regularity. Punctuality. Early rising. . . .

LAUREL: It sounds like a prison!

MADRIGAL: . . . and what are *you* used to?

LAUREL: Doing what I like. Have you been told why I am peculiar?

MADRIGAL: Something was said about it.

LAUREL: If you come here we'll talk for hours and hours about it! And why I hate my mother!

MADRIGAL: I too hated my mother. I should say it was my stepmother.

LAUREL: Oh, that's just an ordinary hatred! Mine is more special.

MADRIGAL: The dangerous thing about hate is that it seems so reasonable.

LAUREL: Maitland won't let me say so, but my mother is Jezebel! She is so overloaded with sex that it sparkles! She is golden and striped—like something in the jungle!

MADRIGAL: You sound proud of her. Does she never come here?

LAUREL: To see me? Never! She's too busy with love! Just now she's in Arabia with her paramour!

MADRIGAL: With her . . .?

LAUREL (*vexed*): If you pin me down he is my stepfather! Have you read *Hamlet*? It tipped my mind and turned me against my mother.

MADRIGAL: Does she know you feel discarded?

LAUREL: I don't. I left *her*! (*Pause.*) The night—before she

married—she forgot to say goodnight to me. . . . Do you
think that sounds a little thing?

MADRIGAL (*passionately*): Oh no! It lights up everything.

LAUREL (*looking at her*): Are you talking of *you*? Or of *me*?

MADRIGAL (*her hand on her breast*): When one feels strongly—
it is always of *me*!

LAUREL: Oh, if you are not a spy sent by my mother I shall
enjoy you! Do you know about crime? Maitland and I
share a crime library. Bit by bit we are collecting the
Notable Trial Series.

MADRIGAL (*looking at her—low*): Don't you like detective
stories better?

LAUREL: No. we like real murder! The trials. We act the
parts!

MADRIGAL (*picking up her gloves, faintly*): Which . . . trials
have you got?

LAUREL: So far—only Mrs. Maybrick, Lizzie Borden, Dr.
Crippen. But Maitland likes the murder*esses* better. He's
half in love with them! Oh—if you come here. . . .

MADRIGAL: Here! . . .

LAUREL: —couldn't we act them together? (*Gets no answer.*)
Maitland is so slow I make him read the prisoner. Why
does the prisoner have so little to say (*waits*) . . . do you
think? (*Pause—no answer.*) What a habit you have—haven't
you—of not answering.

MADRIGAL (*whose eyes have been fastened high up in the air, now
lets them travel down to look at* LAUREL, *low, with difficulty*): I
made an answer.

LAUREL: Only to yourself, I think.

MRS. ST. MAUGHAM (*seen outside garden windows waving the
armful of broken lilies at Pinkbell's window*): All gone! . . .
All! . . . (*As she appears.*) Oh—when things are killed in my
garden it upsets me—as when I read every day in the newspapers that my friends die!

LAUREL: I should have thought as one got older one found
death more natural.

MRS. ST. MAUGHAM: Natural! It's as though the gods went rook-shooting when one was walking confident in the park of the world! and there are pangs and shots, and one may be for me! Natural!

MADRIGAL (*involuntarily*): That is why a garden is a good lesson. . . .

MRS. ST. MAUGHAM: What?

MADRIGAL: . . . so much dies in it. And so often.

MRS. ST. MAUGHAM: It's not a lesson I look for! Take Miss Madrigal into the garden, Laurel.

MADRIGAL: No, I think I must be going.

MRS. ST. MAUGHAM: I want you to see the garden!

MADRIGAL (*nervous*): I'll write . . . I'll let you know. . . .

MRS. ST. MAUGHAM: There is nothing to know yet!

MADRIGAL: I'd better not waste your time. . . .

MRS. ST. MAUGHAM: And that great bag. . . . (*Takes it.*) No one will touch it here!

    LAUREL *and* MADRIGAL *exit, but* LAUREL *darts back.*

LAUREL (*conspiratorially, alone on garden threshold*): Grandloo . . . psst! . . . what do you think?

MRS. ST. MAUGHAM: I never allow myself to think! I have another method.

LAUREL: But. . . .

MRS. ST. MAUGHAM: And while you are in the garden, listen to her! She knows her subject.

LAUREL: But shall you take her?

MRS. ST. MAUGHAM: Certainly not! But before she goes I want her opinion on the garden.

    Vanishes through MAITLAND'*s door with vase and lilies.*

    LAUREL *exits to garden.*

    OLIVIA *enters through main doorway followed by* MAITLAND. *One is just aware that she is pregnant. She wears light travelling clothes, as from the East.*

OLIVIA: I didn't telephone, Maitland, I thought it better just to come. How is my mother?

MAITLAND: She has the health of . . . (*grasping for the un-*

explainable in Madam's health) ... something in Nature!

OLIVIA: And my daughter?

MAITLAND: They're as thick as thieves, Madam.

OLIVIA: Could you look for my mother—

MAITLAND: Madam was here. .... (*He exits.*)

MADRIGAL *enters quickly from the garden and gets her bag from the chair.*

OLIVIA (*sharply*): Who are you?

MADRIGAL: It makes no difference. (*Pausing a second.*) Perhaps I should tell you ... the field is free for you. ....

OLIVIA: To see the child?

MADRIGAL: You have to see the grandmother first!

OLIVIA: Yes.

MADRIGAL: Looking at you I wouldn't come here if there is any other post open to you.

OLIVIA: Why?

MADRIGAL: Because the child will make hay of you!

OLIVIA: She *has* made hay of me!

MADRIGAL: Are you the mother?

OLIVIA: Yes. .... Is she out there?

MADRIGAL: Yes.

OLIVIA: Please ... go out—*keep* her there!

MADRIGAL: But I am a stranger.

OLIVIA: I know but sometimes one speaks the truth to a stranger. I'm not supposed to see her. First I must see my mother. Please, go out—

MRS. ST. MAUGHAM (*from offstage*): Olivia!

MADRIGAL *hesitatingly moves towards garden.*

OLIVIA (*urgently*): Please!

MRS. ST. MAUGHAM (*offstage*): Olivia!

MADRIGAL *exits to garden.* MRS. ST. MAUGHAM *enters from* MAITLAND'S *door.*

(*To* MAITLAND *who has followed her into the room.*)

MRS. ST. MAUGHAM: Maitland ... light a bonfire! (*He rushes off into the garden.*) Olivia! So soon! But you're safe—that's all that matters!

OLIVIA: Mother! ...

MRS. ST. MAUGHAM: Oh—let me look at you! How brown you are! You look like an Arab. How is the desert, darling? I can almost *see* the sand in your hair.

OLIVIA: Mother—how's the child?

MRS. ST. MAUGHAM (*stung*): Ask for *me*—ask for *me*, Olivia.

OLIVIA: I do, I would, but you ran in like a girl! And not a day older! As I came in—the standards *dripping* with roses. ... Oh the English flowers—after the East!

MRS. ST. MAUGHAM: Let me tell you—before we talk—

OLIVIA: —before we quarrel!

MRS. ST. MAUGHAM: No—not this time! I was going to say —that I've missed you! If I'd known you were coming I'd have driven up to see you! Whatever—and in your condition—made you rush down here without a word!

OLIVIA: I flew. I got here this morning.

MRS. ST. MAUGHAM: Like one of those crickets that leap from a distance and fall at one's feet! How do you do it?

OLIVIA: By breakfasting in Baghdad and dining in Kuffra, and taking a taxi in England. We're on a Course. I wrote. Two months at Aldershot.

MRS. ST. MAUGHAM: Aldershot! Oh—who would have thought you would have taken on that look—so quickly— of the Colonel's Lady! What was it they called it—Reveille! How are the bugles at dawn, Olivia?

OLIVIA: We don't live in a camp.

MRS. ST. MAUGHAM: I feel sure you said you did!

OLIVIA: Never mind the camp. I want to talk to you.

MRS. ST. MAUGHAM: But why down here the very second you arrive—and without warning!

OLIVIA: Mother, I've come about Laurel ... don't put me off any longer!

MRS. ST. MAUGHAM (*to distract from main issue*): Did you wear that scarf—on purpose to annoy me! What you wear is a language to me!

OLIVIA (*indignant*): Oh—that's an old battle—and an old

method!

MRS. ST. MAUGHAM: When I've *told* you—in letter after letter. . . .

OLIVIA: It's time I saw for myself, Mother! For nine years I shut the world out for her—

MRS. ST. MAUGHAM: Nine years of widowhood—might have been spent better!

I have asked you *not* to come—but you *come*! I have asked you to warn me—but you ignore it!

—And how can you wear beige with your skin that colour!

OLIVIA: Does it never become possible to talk as one grown woman to another!

MRS. ST. MAUGHAM: The gap's lessening! After fifty I haven't grown much wiser! . . . But at least I know what the world has to have—though one cannot pass anything on! When I count my ambitions and what you have made of them. . . .

OLIVIA: I did what you wanted!

MRS. ST. MAUGHAM: But *how* you resisted me! I was burning for you to cut ice in the world—yet you had to be *driven* out to gaiety! I had to beat you into beauty! You had to be lit—as one lights a lantern! Decked—like a may-tree. . . .

OLIVIA: Oh, can't we be three minutes together. . . .

MRS. ST. MAUGHAM: Even your wedding dress you wore like wrapping paper! And where is it now—the success to which I pushed you? Laurel might have been a child, these four years, playing in a high walled park—

OLIVIA: And I might have been a widow, with deer gazing at me! But life isn't like that! You had for me the standards of another age! The standards of . . . Pinkbell.

MRS. ST. MAUGHAM: Plain, shy, obstinate, silent! But I won! I married you.

OLIVIA: But you won't meet the man *I* married—the man I love!

MRS. ST. MAUGHAM: Love can be had any day! Success is

far harder.

OLIVIA: You say that off the top of your head—where you wore your tiara!

MRS. ST. MAUGHAM: So you have found a tongue to speak with!

OLIVIA: I have found many things—and learned others. I have been warmed and praised and made to speak. Things come late to me. Love came late to me. Laurel was born in a kind of strange virginity. To have a child doesn't always make a mother!

And you won't give up the image of me! Coltish—inept, dropping the china—picking up the pieces. . . .

MRS. ST. MAUGHAM: It was I who picked up the pieces, Olivia.

OLIVIA (*passionately*): *I know. But I'm without her.*

MRS. ST. MAUGHAM: You are going to have another child!

OLIVIA: This child's the Unknown! Laurel's my daughter!

MRS. ST. MAUGHAM: Who came to me . . .! Who ran to me —as an asylum from her mother!

OLIVIA (*desperately*): Oh—you find such words to change things! You talk as if I were a light woman!

MRS. ST. MAUGHAM: No, you are not light. You have never been a light woman. You are a dark, a mute woman. If there was lightness in you it was I who lent it to you! And all that I did—gone!

OLIVIA: Mother! Of a thousand thousand rows between you and me—and this not, I know, the last one—*be* on my side! Oh—for once be on my side! Help me. . . .

MRS. ST. MAUGHAM: To what?

OLIVIA: Help me to find her! Help me to take her back!

MRS. ST. MAUGHAM: Take her back! (*Lighting on an idea.*) What, now?—just now! When I have such a companion for her! A woman too of the highest character! Of vast experience! I have put myself out endlessly to find her!

OLIVIA: She can help you to prepare her. When I come back for her. . . .

MRS. ST. MAUGHAM: You mean before the baby's born? *That* will be an odd moment—won't it—to come for her!

OLIVIA (*passionately*): No! It's *why* I want her! Before I love the baby! I can't sleep! I can't rest. I seem to myself to have abandoned her!

MRS. ST. MAUGHAM: To her own grandmother! I am not a baby-farmer or a headmistress or the matron of an orphanage. . . .

OLIVIA: But she'll be a woman! And I'll never have known her!

MRS. ST. MAUGHAM: It suited you when you first married that I should have her! Laurel came to me of her own free will—and I have turned my old age into a nursery for her.

OLIVIA: And God has given you a second chance to be a mother!

MRS. ST. MAUGHAM: Olivia! . . . Oh, there's *no one* who puts me in a passion like you do!

OLIVIA: And no one who knows you so well. And knows today is hopeless— (*Makes to go.*)

Enter MADRIGAL *from the garden* (*on a high wave of indignation—matching the crescendo of the other two*).

MADRIGAL (*menacing—accusing—pulling on a glove*): Mrs. St. Maugham—there must be some *mistake!* *This* is a chalk garden! *Who has* tried to grow rhododendrons in a *chalk garden?*

MRS. ST. MAUGHAM (*taken aback*): Rhododendrons? We put them in last autumn? But they're unhappy!

MADRIGAL (*magnificent; stern*): They are *dying.* They are in pure lime. Not so much as a little leaf-mould! There is no evidence of palliation! (*Passes on across room.*)

MRS. ST. MAUGHAM: Wait . . . wait! . . . Where are you going?

MADRIGAL (*over her shoulder—going*): They could have had compost! But the compost-heap is stone-cold! Nothing in the world has been done for them.

A gay scream is heard from the garden.

OLIVIA (*to* MADRIGAL): Is that Laurel? She's screaming. What's the matter?

MADRIGAL (*withering*): There is nothing the matter! She is dancing round the bonfire with the manservant.

MRS. ST. MAUGHAM: I should have told you—*this* is Miss Madrigal. Not so fast! I want to ask you ... the bergamot ... and the gunnera. ...

MADRIGAL (*over shoulder, on way out*): ... won't thrive on chalk.

MRS. ST. MAUGHAM: There's an east slope I can grow nothing on.

MADRIGAL (*same*): ... the soil can't give what it has not got. *Reaches door.*

OLIVIA: *Don't go!* The wind blows from the sea here and growing things need protection!

MADRIGAL (*suddenly halted by the look in* OLIVIA's *face*): ... and the lilies have rust ... there is blackspot on the roses ... and the child is screaming in the garden. ...

MRS. ST. MAUGHAM: The *roses!* What would you have done for them! Pinkbell ordered ... and I sprayed them!—

MADRIGAL (*turning, magnificent, contemptuous, a few steps towards* MRS. ST. MAUGHAM): With *what*, I wonder! You had better have prayed for them!

They measure each other for a moment.

If you will accept me (*walking up to her*) I will *take* this situation, Mrs. St. Maugham.

OLIVIA *quietly exits.*

MADRIGAL *starts to remove her gloves.*

(*With a dry lightness.*) You have been very badly advised—I think—by Mr. Pinkbell.

CURTAIN

ACT II

Scene: The same.

Two months later. About mid-morning.

The furniture has been rearranged and some of it changed.
LAUREL is seated above a small table. She is painting a flower
which is stuck in a vase in front of her. On a chair to her left is
an old mahogany paint box with tubes of water-colour. On the
table is a glass with brushes and a palette. This table can be used
for the luncheon.

MAITLAND enters carrying a large serving tray which he places
on a console table which serves as a sideboard.

MAITLAND (*with turpentine and oil rag*): All alone? Whose
idea is that?

LAUREL (*who does not look up*): The Boss's.

MAITLAND: And not even burning the curtains?

LAUREL (*with dignity*): I am painting a flower.

MAITLAND (*removing a grease spot from table*): Occupational
therapy?

LAUREL: What was yours? Picking oakum?

MAITLAND: Who would think you were weak in the head?
You've given up screaming.

LAUREL: My madness is older. It's too old for screaming.

MAITLAND (*glancing at her*): Why do you sham mad—
dearest?

LAUREL (*in surprise*): "Dearest"?

MAITLAND: Only in a sad sort of way, I have no dearest.
(*Now polishes table.*)

LAUREL: You shouldn't be sorry for yourself! It unmans you.

35

MAITLAND: It's better than being vain and in love with the glory of one's misfortune! But I'll say this for you! The Boss has changed you!

LAUREL: I'm her business and her vocation.

MAITLAND: Oh—who could imagine that a maiden lady could know so much about life!

LAUREL: She's no maiden lady! (*Looking round at him.*) Might she be a love child?

MAITLAND: That's enough now!

LAUREL: How prudish you are! Look how she came to us— with nothing! A lady from a shipwreck! Her brush is new and her dresses. No box of shells by *her* bed—no mirror backed with velvet. . . . Oh—she's cut off her golden past like a fish's tail! She's had a life of passion!

MAITLAND: What words you use!

LAUREL: *You* have a set of words you keep in a cage! Does she get any letters? Do you spy on her?

MAITLAND: Who?

LAUREL: Our duke's daughter, our hired companion!

MAITLAND: If you are talking of *Miss* Madrigal she never gets a letter.

LAUREL: Don't you get a hint or a sound or a sigh out of her?

MAITLAND: No. Do you?

LAUREL: With me she's on guard. I can't surprise or ambush her. She watches me.

MAITLAND: Whatever she does you're the better for it!

LAUREL: Mr. Pinkbell doesn't think so.

MAITLAND: Poison he is—but influential.

LAUREL: If you ask me rows are coming!

MAITLAND: I don't ask you! You're too set up with yourself and pleased as a peacock to be the bone of contention.

LAUREL: She says he's the devil in charge. He's ordered rhododendrons. It took a *lorry* to deliver them!

MAITLAND: What's that got to do with it?

LAUREL: The Boss reversed the labels. She sent them back again.

MAITLAND: Whew . . . I'm for Miss Madrigal! I've no mercy
on him!

LAUREL: Poor Mr. Pinkbell!

MAITLAND: A man's no better when he's dying!

LAUREL: What's in that bottle?

MAITLAND: Turps. Turpentine.

LAUREL: Give it to me.

MAITLAND (*giving it to her*): How did she take our having a
visitor to lunch?

LAUREL: I was to wear this clean frock. Otherwise nothing.
(*Looking at it disdainfully.*) Straight as an envelope. It looks
so adolescent . . . and with a judge coming!

MAITLAND: How do I call him?

LAUREL: A judge is called, m'lord.

MAITLAND: Oh—I wish I could see it!

LAUREL: What?

MAITLAND: Him in his robes and his great wig and all that
happens!

LAUREL (*rubbing inside paint box lid with turpentine rag*): How
you *dote* on justice!

MAITLAND: It's the machinery and the magnificence! It's the
grandness.

LAUREL (*sly*): In prison—was there grandness?

MAITLAND: No, I was brought up from a cell and saw none
of it.

   MRS. ST. MAUGHAM *enters from garden wearing a gardening
apron.*

MRS. ST. MAUGHAM: Heavens, Maitland! Is this a morning
                 for day dreams!

(*half fantasy,*   The gold toothpicks . . . the green-
  half memory.)   handled ivory knives. . . .

MAITLAND: Locked away.

MRS. ST. MAUGHAM: And the key of the safe! It's years since
                 I've seen it!

                 We used to have celery with the
                 Stilton. . . .

... and the Bristol finger bowls and the épergne. ...

... and the sieve we served the caraque on! ...

... and those glasses for the brandy. ...

MAITLAND: They broke.

MRS. ST. MAUGHAM: There was a gold cigar box that played a tune King Edward gave me. ...

LAUREL: Is it gold? I used to keep a mouse in it!

MRS. ST. MAUGHAM: Go and get it!

LAUREL: I can't remember where I put it. ... But isn't the man who's coming—*old*?

MRS. ST. MAUGHAM: Puppy?

LAUREL: The Judge!

MRS. ST. MAUGHAM: That's what I called him!

LAUREL: Can I wear—?

MRS. ST. MAUGHAM: Wear anything you like! I'm sick of white things and innocence!

The noise of a cricket ball being hit is heard outside the window on the Green.

Oh! Are they playing out there with the hard ball again? Can you identify them?

LAUREL (*jumping up on a chair, looking out*): The one with the bat is the fishmonger's son.

MAITLAND: How do *you* know?

LAUREL: He's looking at me!

MAITLAND: Get down now!

MRS. ST. MAUGHAM: Leave that to me, Maitland.

LAUREL (*getting down*): It's time I looked at boys—or I won't get the hang of it.

MRS. ST. MAUGHAM (*crossing to window taking no notice*): Every summer—the boys with their cricket! Every summer a broken window!

MAITLAND: Isn't it strange that *men* play cricket!

MRS. ST. MAUGHAM (*turning*): And you an Englishman!

MAITLAND: At the Orphanage we played rounders.

MRS. ST. MAUGHAM (*dismissing the whole subject*): We shall want sherry before luncheon. Bring the sweet as well as the dry. (*Looking down at the table he has now laid.*) Shouldn't there be two wine glasses to each person?

MAITLAND: But there's only one wine!

MRS. ST. MAUGHAM: Put two. I forget the reason. Oh—and the spoons *outside* the knives, Maitland!

MAITLAND (*desperately*): You said the opposite last time!

MRS. ST. MAUGHAM: Never! (*A doubt enters her mind as she changes them round.*) Someone must know! I shall ask Pinkbell.

LAUREL: Pinkbell is sulking.

MRS. ST. MAUGHAM: Why?

LAUREL (*mocking*): He is full of jealous rage about his enemy.

MRS. ST. MAUGHAM: What again! And where is she now?

LAUREL (*mocking*): She is urging on the agapanthus lilies.

MRS. ST. MAUGHAM: She is *what*?

LAUREL: She is using diluted cow urine. One in seven.

MRS. ST. MAUGHAM (*ecstatic*): Oh I must go and see at once and watch how *that* is done!

 Quickly exits to garden.

LAUREL: Keep behind the escallonia hedge! Every movement is watched! (*To* MAITLAND.) The nurse came down this morning for the field glasses. Prisoner 6574!

MAITLAND: Sir!

LAUREL: Do you know whose paint box this is?

MAITLAND: Yours.

LAUREL: No. Come here and look at it. *She* lent it to me. The Boss. (*Pointing inside the propped open lid, where she has been rubbing.*) Can you see where the letters are that are burnt in the wood there? Look—under the black mark. Under the smear of paint. Is it C.D. . . .

MAITLAND: And W. It is C.D.W.

 MADRIGAL *is heard coming from garden.*

LAUREL: Take the turpentine! I don't want her to see it! (*He exits.*)

    MADRIGAL *enters from the garden.*

Oh!.... Grandloo has just this minute gone to look for you!

MADRIGAL: I caught sight of her—but I thought it best that we should not be seen together.

LAUREL: She's head over heels with excitement about our guest. Does one still mind when one is old—what men think?

MADRIGAL: One never knows when one is old—for certain.

LAUREL: She calls him Puppy. I think she was once his mistress.

MADRIGAL: Do you know that?

LAUREL (*casual*): No. (*Re-enter* MAITLAND, *carrying a tray.*)

MADRIGAL: Then why do you say it?

LAUREL: Why does one say things? It's more fun!

MADRIGAL: If you pretend—and it's believed—where are you?

LAUREL (*smiling*): Where am I?

MAITLAND: Floating away. The only *hold* we have on this world is the truth. Oh to think I'm to feed him! A man who's got so much power!

LAUREL: We've never had a judge here before.

MADRIGAL (*turning sharply*): A judge? Is the visitor that's coming a judge?

MAITLAND: He's here for the Courts. He's on Circuit.

MADRIGAL: What's his name?

MAITLAND: It's in the newspapers. But the old bastard's got them. They are carried up to him. I only get to read them on the doorstep.

LAUREL: We can talk to him of murder.

MADRIGAL: If you do that it will be a want of tact. It will bore him. You and I will sit at a separate table for luncheon. Maitland will put us a small table here by the sofa.

MAITLAND: Not two tables! Not with a guest! Oh—that can't be managed!

MADRIGAL (*swiftly changing her manner to one of treacherous interest*): You can manage anything! Tell us what surprise you've arranged for us. What are we going to eat?

MAITLAND (*still upset*): Fortnum's have sent the cold cooked chickens. (*But unable to resist.*) I have carved them. I have ornamented them with mint leaves. There's a salad. And salad dressing.

MADRIGAL: Out of a bottle?

MAITLAND: Mrs. St. Maugham doesn't believe so.

MADRIGAL (*treacherously agreeing*): The bottled is *so much* better —but one must never say so!

MAITLAND: Oh, when I have something to do, something to create, everything is clear again!

MADRIGAL: You look ten years younger!

MAITLAND (*at his door about to go*): Oh—if we had guests oftener! The sense of rising to something! (*Exits.*)

LAUREL: Poor Maitland. How you twist him round your finger! (*With a certain suspicious hostility.*) Why do we sit separately from the guest, you and I?

MADRIGAL: It used to be done at luncheon—in the best houses.

LAUREL: Had you a life in them? ... (*Sharp.*) Who is C.D.W.?

MADRIGAL (*taken aback, silent. Then*): My married sister.

LAUREL: I thought you had been born unrelated.

MADRIGAL: Did you?

LAUREL: And now you have a sister.

MADRIGAL: Yes.

LAUREL: Suppose you were to drop down dead. To whom should we write?

MADRIGAL: I shall not drop down dead.

House telephone rings.

LAUREL (*picks up receiver*): Pinkbell! In a rage!

Listening a second, then holding phone at arm's length as though it had bitten her. Rubs her ear.

He has practically stung me! He has asked for you! Would

you be afraid to speak to him? (*Offering phone to* MISS MADRIGAL.)

MADRIGAL (*accepting receiver*): Mr. Pinkbell? (*Listens.*) Yes, it is I, Miss Madrigal. (*Listens.*)

    MAITLAND *enters.*

Ah—but on that I disagree. (*Waits.*) The rhododendrons—*I* sent them back again. (*Listens.*) *I* reversed the labels! And if I could I would reverse everything! And I may yet—we shall see!

    No, I'm afraid on that you are wrong, Mr. Pinkbell. Your facts are wrong—also your deductions! Yes, and alas it is the wrong time of year to plant them. And the wrong soil. (*Listens.*) Not at all. Don't blame yourself. Amateur gardeners very often make that mistake. (*Hangs up.*)

MAITLAND: *Blame* himself!

MADRIGAL: He made use of sarcasm.

MAITLAND: My God, you shall have two tables! You shall have three if you like! And the breast off both the chickens!

    NURSE *enters from* PINKBELL's *door, glares at* MADRIGAL, *and crosses out to the garden as the others watch in silence.*

LAUREL: He's sent the Nurse for Grandloo! Now there'll be ructions!

MAITLAND (*watches* NURSE *exit*): And with the Judge coming! In the newspapers they say it'll be a long trial. Why, Miss! Haven't you read it?

MADRIGAL: Are all the glasses polished? (*Holding up a glass to the light.*)

MAITLAND: D'you think—in Lewes prison. . . .

MADRIGAL (*gently*): There's a cloud on this one. (*Hands* MAITLAND *a glass.*)

MAITLAND (*taking glass from her and holding it*): . . . this murderer, that's lying in his cell. . . .

MADRIGAL (*change of voice*): No man is a murderer until he is tried!

MAITLAND: . . . does the Judge look at him?

MADRIGAL: The Judge never looks up. He seems to sleep. But it's the sleep of cruelty.

MAITLAND (*persisting*): . . . when he first *sees* the Judge. . . .

MADRIGAL: Why do you think only of the Judge? It's the jury they work on.

MAITLAND: But it seems when you read about such trials, that it must be the Judge.

MADRIGAL (*fiercely*): Read more and you'll see it's neither. (*To herself.*) But fate.

MAITLAND: How can that be?

MADRIGAL: Because, when it starts, there's no freewill any more.

MAITLAND (*earnestly*): But they work, don't they, to get at the truth?

MADRIGAL: Truth doesn't ring true in a Court of Law.

MAITLAND: What rings true then?

MADRIGAL (*to herself—trancelike*): The likelihood. The probability. They work to make things fit together. (*Moving.*) What the prisoner listens to there is not his life. It is the shape and shadow of his life. With the accidents of truth taken out of it.

(*Shaking herself free from her trance.*) Time is getting on, Maitland.

MAITLAND (*running to door*): Oh, what would that man in prison give to be as free as I! (*Exit.*)

LAUREL: So you've been to a trial?

MADRIGAL: I did not say I hadn't.

LAUREL: Why did you not say—when you know what store we both lay by it?

MADRIGAL: It may be I think you lay too much store by it.

LAUREL (*relaxing her tone and asking as though an ordinary light question*): How does one get in?

MADRIGAL: It's surprisingly easy.

LAUREL: Was it a trial for murder?

MADRIGAL: It would have to be to satisfy you.

LAUREL: *Was* it a trial for murder?

MADRIGAL (*without turning round to look*): Have you finished that flower?

LAUREL (*yawning*): As much as I can. I get tired of it. (*Wandering to the window.*) In my house—at home—there were so many things to do.

MADRIGAL: What was it like?

LAUREL (*turning*): My home?

MADRIGAL: Yes.

LAUREL (*doodling on a piece of paper, and speaking as though caught unaware*): There was a stream. And a Chinese bridge. And yew trees cut like horses. And a bell on the weathervane, and a little wood called mine. . . .

MADRIGAL: Who called it that?

LAUREL (*unwillingly moved*): She did. My mother. And when it was raining we made an army of her cream pots and a battlefield of her dressing table. . . . I used to thread her rings on safety pins. . . .

MADRIGAL: Tomorrow I will light that candle in the green glass candlestick and you can try to paint that.

LAUREL (*looking up*): What—paint the flame!

MADRIGAL: Yes.

LAUREL (*doodling again*): I'm tired of fire, too, Boss.

MADRIGAL (*as she notices* LAUREL, *doodling*): Why do you sign your name a thousand times?

LAUREL: I am looking for which is me.

MADRIGAL: Shall we read?

LAUREL: Oh, I don't want to read!

MADRIGAL: Let's have a game.

LAUREL: All right. (*With meaning.*) A guessing game!

MADRIGAL: Very well. (*Sitting down at one side of the table.*) Do you know one?

LAUREL: Maitland and I play one called "The Sky's the Limit".

MADRIGAL: How do you begin?

LAUREL (*sitting down opposite her*): We ask three questions each but if you don't answer one, I get a fourth.

MADRIGAL: What do we guess about?

LAUREL: Let's guess about each other! We are both mysterious—

MADRIGAL (*sententious*): The human heart is mysterious.

LAUREL: We don't know the first thing about each other, so there are so many things to ask.

MADRIGAL: But we mustn't go too fast. Or there will be nothing left to discover.

Has it got to be the truth?

LAUREL: One can lie. But I get better and better at spotting lies. It's so dull playing with Maitland. He's so innocent.

MISS MADRIGAL *folds her hands and waits.*

Now! First question. . . . Are you a—*maiden* lady?

MADRIGAL (*after a moment's reflection*): I can't answer that.

LAUREL: Why?

MADRIGAL: Because you throw the emphasis so oddly.

LAUREL: Right. You don't answer! So now I have an extra question. Are you living under an assumed name?

MADRIGAL: No.

LAUREL: Careful! I'm getting my lie-detector working. Do you take things here at their face value?

MADRIGAL: No.

LAUREL: Splendid! You're getting the idea!

MADRIGAL (*warningly*): This is to be your fourth question.

LAUREL: Yes. Yes indeed. I must think . . . I must be careful. (*Shooting her question hard at* MISS MADRIGAL.) What is the full name of your married sister?

MADRIGAL (*staring a brief second at her*): Clarissa Dalrymple Westerham.

LAUREL: Is Dalrymple Westerham a double name?

MADRIGAL (*with ironical satisfaction*): You've *had* your questions.

LAUREL (*gaily accepting defeat*): Yes, I have. Now yours. You've only three unless I pass one.

MADRIGAL: Was your famous affair in Hyde Park on the night of your mother's marriage?

LAUREL (*wary*): About that time.

MADRIGAL: What was the charge by the police?

LAUREL (*wary*): The police didn't come into it.

MADRIGAL (*airily*): Did someone follow you? And try to kiss you?

LAUREL (*off her guard*): Kiss me! It was a case of Criminal Assault!

MADRIGAL (*following that up*): How do you know—if there wasn't a charge by the police?

LAUREL (*pausing a second. Triumphant*): That's one too many questions! *Now* for the deduction!

MADRIGAL: You didn't tell me there was a deduction.

LAUREL: I forgot. It's the whole point. Mine's ready.

MADRIGAL: What do you deduce?

LAUREL (*taking a breath—then fast, as though she might be stopped*): That you've changed so much you must have been something quite different. When you came here you were like a rusty hinge that wanted oiling. You spoke to yourself out loud without knowing it. You had been *alone*. You may have been a missionary in Central Africa. You may have escaped from a private asylum. But as a maiden lady you are an impostor. (*Changing her tone slightly—slower and more penetrating.*) About your assumed name. I am not so sure. . . . *But you have no married sister.*

MADRIGAL (*lightly*): You take my breath away.

LAUREL (*as lightly*): Good at it, aren't I?

MADRIGAL (*gay*): Yes, for a mind under a cloud!

LAUREL: Now for *your* deduction!

MADRIGAL (*rising*): Mine must keep.

LAUREL: But it's the game! Where are you going?

MADRIGAL (*pleasantly*): To my room. To be sure I have left no clues unlocked.

LAUREL: To your past life?

MADRIGAL: Yes. You have given me so much warning. (*Exits.*)

    LAUREL, *taken aback, stands a moment looking after her.*

*Looks around room. Then takes the silver handbell from the table
and rings it.*

MAITLAND (*rushes in from his door putting his jacket on*): Was
it you! You're not supposed to ring it. (*Is about to go again.*)

LAUREL: Maitland!

MAITLAND: I'm busy now! . . . (*Going, but unable to go.*) . . .
Now what is it?

LAUREL (*conspiratorial*): The Boss! We played the game!

MAITLAND (*immediately caught*): You didn't dare! What did
you ask her?

LAUREL: Nothing. And everything. No game would uncover
her! But Maitland—*she knows about life*!

MAITLAND: What sort of knowledge?

LAUREL: Something—intense. Something too dreadful. Something cut in stone over her mind—to warn you when you
walk in.

MAITLAND (*wistful*): I too had something dreadful happen to
me.

LAUREL: But hers is more dreadful! That's why she has no
weakness. Her eyes see through me! I'm a mouse to her.

MAITLAND (*tenderly*): Are you afraid—poor dearest? Let
Maitland speak to her.

LAUREL (*bidding for his co-operation*): You! Oh *you* tell her!
How they brought me back that night—

MAITLAND: Don't talk of it!

LAUREL: So small, such a little thing! How I cried. . . . They
should have called a doctor.

MAITLAND: It's what I said they should! I argued it! Madam's
got her ways! I've got mine! Oh—she would have got the
moon for you! But I was the one who put up with you—
who fetched and carried, who read to you. You had the
right to the best in the world! A lady's child! . . .

LAUREL (*teasing*): "The Colonel's lady."

MAITLAND (*instantly furious*): Not that again. I forbid you!
Your own mother!

LAUREL: Mr. Pinkbell says "Judy O'Grady"—

MAITLAND: I'll have none of it! Out with the devil in you! For shame! And just when I was talking nicely to you!

LAUREL: But I've told you what she is—

MAITLAND: Not me you won't tell! That's got no mother! If your mother's black as soot you don't say so to me, girl!

LAUREL: I shall scream.

MAITLAND: Scream away! Now we've got the Boss to get after you! Oh, the relief of it!

LAUREL (*pleading*): No! No—*be* nice to me! How tough you get—suddenly!

MAITLAND: It comes over me. The Right comes up in me. Like when they tried to make a soldier of me. All of a sudden I *see* how things should be!

Enter MRS. ST. MAUGHAM *from garden carrying a great sheaf of pink Crinum, the nurse following her.*

MRS. ST. MAUGHAM (*to* MAITLAND, *immediately undercutting his attitude*): Cut the stems three inches shorter. Put them in the blue Italian vase and three aspirins at the bottom. ...

MAITLAND *takes flowers lamely and crosses up to his door. The door Right opens and* MISS MADRIGAL *appears.* MAITLAND *remains standing with the flowers awkwardly in his arms.*

(*To* MADRIGAL.) Oh. Oh *indeed*! My ears are filled with poison! What has the nurse been telling me! (*Exit* NURSE.) The poor old man upstairs is crying with rage!

MADRIGAL (*calmly*): I corrected him.

MRS. ST. MAUGHAM: But for forty years Pinkbell has never been corrected! He is the butler who was the standard of all London!

MADRIGAL: Let him take his standard from the garden! (*Fast, ritualistic.*) I corrected his ignorance of detail, dates, fundamentals, application of manure. I spoke—not of his spoons and forks—but of his shallow knowledge of the laws of growth, you can leave the room, Maitland.

MRS. ST. MAUGHAM: *That* should have been said by me! But—go, Maitland!

He exits hurriedly.

Now—now, Miss Madrigal—this is a crisis!

MADRIGAL (*equally severe, majestic*): Yes. *Now* you have to make your decision.

MRS. ST. MAUGHAM: I! I have!

MADRIGAL: Now you have to choose between us.

A moment's silence. Then, taking a step towards MRS. ST. MAUGHAM—*with low ferocious accusation.*

Is Mr. Pinkbell to let the moment pass—when one should layer the clematis? When the gladioli should be lifted? (*Advancing another step, menacingly.*) Has anyone planted the winter aconites? And the pelargoniums? *Who* has taken cuttings? (*Pause. With mounting indignation and on a high enumerating voice.*) And the red tobacco seed and the zinnias and the seeds of the white cosmos for next year? Do you wish—like an *amateur*—to buy them!

MRS. ST. MAUGHAM (*in a faltering tone*): I—always have—bought them.

MADRIGAL (*at the height of her passion*): If that is how you wish to live I am no party to it! It is not possible for me to hold communication with minds brought up on bedding plants—bought at the greengrocer's—dying in shallow boxes! Out there every corner is crying aloud! Must I be dumb when you and I approach together the time of year when all next summer must stand or fall by us! Have you time—before death—to throw away season after season?

Exits on a sweep.

MRS. ST. MAUGHAM (*sinking on to a chair*): *What* have I let in here out of an advertisement!

LAUREL: Oh—we shall lose her, Grandloo! Don't sit there! Go after her! Oh *think* what she knows about the garden!

MRS. ST. MAUGHAM: I *am* thinking!

LAUREL: Oh—she will go if she says she will! You don't want to lose her?

MRS. ST. MAUGHAM: For nothing on earth! I'd sooner strangle Pinkbell—but how is it to be *done*!

LAUREL: With a cord.

MRS. ST. MAUGHAM: How is the *reconciliation* to be done? And with a guest at luncheon!

LAUREL: Weave her in—as you say you used to do in London. Go after her! Promise her the Earth. ... Promise her the garden!

MRS. ST. MAUGHAM: The garden ...? (*A quick glance upwards to the ceiling.*) But ... what shall I say to *him*?

LAUREL (*also a glance upward*): You are not afraid of *him*!

MRS. ST. MAUGHAM: I have always ... always been afraid of Pinkbell. (*Exit.*)

    MAITLAND *enters with vase of flowers.*

LAUREL: If we are to keep the Boss we must fight for her!

MAITLAND: Fight for her! Have *you* upset her?

LAUREL: I haven't. Not I! She and I understand each other.

    Doorbell is heard.

There's the *bell*!

MAITLAND (*ecstatic*): The *Judge*!

    Exits leaving door open. In a few seconds the JUDGE *enters followed by* MAITLAND. *He wears country tweeds and a light overcoat which* MAITLAND *has forgotten to ask him to take off.*

LAUREL (*radiantly*): Oh—the Judge! (*Grandly.*) Oh—we're all expecting you!

JUDGE: All? (*Looks round—but sees only* MAITLAND.)

LAUREL: I am. And Maitland.

MAITLAND (*nervous*): Psssht!

LAUREL: Take his coat. (MAITLAND *jumps to it.*) And my companion, Miss Madrigal. And my grandmother.

JUDGE: So you're the grandchild?

LAUREL: Maitland, bring the sherry! The dry and the sweet—remember!

    MAITLAND *exits to hall.* LAUREL *motions the* JUDGE *to sit.*

JUDGE: Not for me! I never drink at midday.

LAUREL: But my grandmother was telling me this morning you used to glory in your palate!

JUDGE: We change as we grow older. As you'll find, little girl!—(*Looking at her.*) But she *isn't* a little girl!

LAUREL: I am sixteen. But backward.

JUDGE: Bless my soul! What am I to make of that!

LAUREL: Nothing. It's too long a story.

JUDGE: Then you are Olivia's daughter? Shy Olivia.

LAUREL (*finger on lips*): Hush. We don't speak of her.

JUDGE: She is living, I hope, my dear child?

LAUREL: In sin, Judge.

Enter MRS. ST. MAUGHAM *from hall. The* JUDGE *rises.*

MRS. ST. MAUGHAM (*coming in on a swirl*): So you've met her! The little girl of my little girl. No grandmothers today! But *Puppy* ... after twenty years! ... No longer *young*!

JUDGE: What do you expect when you measure me by that unsuitable nickname! Am I late! I lost my confounded way.

MRS. ST. MAUGHAM: But you don't drive yourself!

MAITLAND enters with sherry tray.

JUDGE: I do. I'm so poor. And much too old to be poor. (*Suddenly, snatching his handkerchief.*) Oh ... forgive me. ... (*Is about to sneeze.*)

MRS. ST. MAUGHAM: Have you a cold?

JUDGE: We won't pin it down! A trifle. An allergy. They were threshing in the cornfields. (*Sneezes. Puts on a large pair of dark sun spectacles.*) I can stand London dust—but not the country!

LAUREL: But now we can't see you!

JUDGE: You will! Twenty minutes will cheat my old nose that we are back at the Old Bailey.

MAITLAND exits and brings in the chicken and salad and places them on the sideboard.

MRS. ST. MAUGHAM: Before we talk of the past ... how do you find the present? (*Pours sherry.*)

JUDGE: Too busy. Too busy. One hasn't time to think one's getting nearer to God.

LAUREL (*to her grandmother. Anxious*): Have you made it right with her?

MRS. ST. MAUGHAM (*to* LAUREL): Speak louder. Never whisper. (*Offers* JUDGE *sherry. He refuses. To* JUDGE.) My Laurel has a companion. A charming woman. Able—but passionate. At war, just now, with Pinkbell.

LAUREL (*still anxious*): Grandloo. . . .

MRS. ST. MAUGHAM: The door was closed, sweet. One is not at one's best through mahogany. But I heard no sound of packing.

JUDGE: *Pinkbell.* . . . What it brings back! What incorruptible ritual! How I remember—after the summer glare of Piccadilly—the young man that I was—crossing your hall . . . like a pawn across a chessboard. . . .

MRS. ST. MAUGHAM (*low, aside*): Had you better go and look for her?

JUDGE: . . . and how after the first and second footman . . . one arrived at last at—Pinkbell. *He* stood at the foot of the stairs! The apprehension one had of his sour displeasure. . . .

MAITLAND (*under his breath to* LAUREL): Not him—he's not meaning! (*Lifting his chin slightly at the ceiling.*)

JUDGE: *His* severity, *his* corklike dryness—later on, when I had to rebuke the public Eye, I remembered Pinkbell! (*Discovering the fact with amusement.*) My demeanour on the Bench *is* Pinkbell's.

MAITLAND (*ready to burst—drawing himself up and letting out the words like an explosion, with indignation*): Everything—now—is at your service—Madam! On the sideboard!

MRS. ST. MAUGHAM: Simply. Simply. Times have changed, Maitland!

Hall door opens and MADRIGAL *appears.*

Ah here she is!—our Miss Madrigal!

MADRIGAL *sweeps in, wrapt in an enigmatic mantle of silence, the temporary dressing gown of her anger and offence.*

Let me introduce you! How you have relieved me!

JUDGE *rises.*

My right hand. My *green* hand. The mistress of my garden. (*Apologetically to the* JUDGE *as there is no answer.*) She has a

speciality for the Anonymous! (*Louder.*) Some sherry—Miss
Madrigal?

MADRIGAL: No, thank you.

MRS. ST. MAUGHAM: Then—shall we all sit down?

    MRS. ST. MAUGHAM *glances across as though she had
noticed the other table for the first time. The laying of this second
table for* LAUREL *and* MISS MADRIGAL *can have been accomplished at any time suitable to the director, but the best arrangement is that the* JUDGE *and* MRS. ST. MAUGHAM *should
occupy the centre of the stage and the table for* LAUREL *and*
MADRIGAL *be placed very slightly upstage, Left, so that* MADRIGAL, *with her back to the wall, can be forgotten while the
conversation is carried on at the centre table. It is also more telling
that* MRS. ST. MAUGHAM *should have her back to* MADRIGAL
and be forced to turn when addressing her.

But why this segregation?

LAUREL: The Boss's orders.

    She and MISS MADRIGAL *sit.*

JUDGE (*seating himself. To* LAUREL): Are you below the salt?
Or are we?

LAUREL: Miss Madrigal means this to be the schoolroom.

MRS. ST. MAUGHAM: She is so witty!— Now you can start,
Maitland. You can give us your cold chicken. (*To* JUDGE.)
I don't entertain any more. The fight's over. Even the table
is laid with fragments of forgotten ritual.

JUDGE: Faith is handed down that way.

MRS. ST. MAUGHAM: When Pinkbell is dead we shall not
know why we use two glasses for one bottle.

MAITLAND (*serving chicken to* MRS. ST. MAUGHAM): And
what about the wine, Ma'am?

LAUREL: The Judge doesn't drink.

MRS. ST. MAUGHAM: And I have such a bottle of Chablis on
the ice for you!

JUDGE: Alcohol in the middle of the day disperses the old
brains I try to keep together.

    MAITLAND *serves the* JUDGE.

LAUREL (*leaning across*): But aren't *we* to have any!

MRS. ST. MAUGHAM: If we get flushed, Laurel, and too much at our ease. . . .

LAUREL: I think that will be nice. . . .

MRS. ST. MAUGHAM: The reverse, alas, is the truth. But bring it, Maitland. Bring the bottle. (*To* MISS MADRIGAL, *to include her.*) . . . and after lunch shall we show the Judge our roses? (*To* JUDGE.) Miss Madrigal has soil-magic! (*Leaning round again to* MISS MADRIGAL.) Things grow for you— during the night.

MAITLAND *serves* MADRIGAL.

LAUREL (*as* MADRIGAL *doesn't answer*): You mustn't talk to us. We're invisible.

JUDGE: But you have ears?

LAUREL (*nodding*): We overhear?

MRS. ST. MAUGHAM: You'll overhear the flavour of the past. Life was full of great rules then. And we high women were terrible. Would you have youth back, Puppy?

JUDGE: No. For a man *youth* isn't the triumph.

MRS. ST. MAUGHAM: I'd have it back if I could—even life's reverses! (*Leaning round again to include her.*) Wouldn't you, Miss Madrigal?

MADRIGAL (*high and sharp*): You have spilled the salt, Laurel.

MRS. ST. MAUGHAM: I was asking . . . do you think grief tastes more sharply than pleasure on the palate?

MAITLAND *leaves chicken and dish on sideboard and exits.*

MADRIGAL (*startled*): I beg your pardon. . . .

MRS. ST. MAUGHAM: You can do better than *that*, Miss Madrigal!

Enter MAITLAND *with wine. He starts to open it.*

MADRIGAL: I have not the give and take (*into her plate*) of ordinary conversation.

MRS. ST. MAUGHAM: Show it to me, Maitland.

MAITLAND *shows it to her so that she can see the label.*

Now, open it. (*He takes it to the sideboard.*)

JUDGE (*looking round as* MAITLAND *draws the cork*): In that case ... after luncheon you'll have to let me close my eyes!

MRS. ST. MAUGHAM: What—sleep in the daytime!

JUDGE: That shocks you? In my job old age is part of the trappings!

MRS. ST. MAUGHAM: One gets old—all the same.

JUDGE: Judges don't age. Time decorates them.

You should come and hear me! Learned and crumpled like a roseleaf of knowledge I snuffle and mumble, I sham deaf. I move into Court with the red glory of a dried saint carried in festival. By some manipulation my image bows right and left to the Sheriffs. ...

LAUREL (*to* MAITLAND): Maitland ... psst ... *this* is what you missed!

JUDGE: What?

LAUREL: Maitland and I want to know. ...

MRS. ST. MAUGHAM (*warningly*): And—Miss Madrigal? Talk is a partaking. Not a usurping.

LAUREL: But it's *Maitland* who collects the Notable Trial Series!

JUDGE: Maitland?

MAITLAND (*shamed*): Maitland is myself, m'lord.

LAUREL: We read them aloud together, and we are converting Miss Madrigal.

JUDGE: Ah!

LAUREL: But tell us, in plainer language, how you will enter Court tomorrow!

JUDGE: In ermine. In scarlet. With a full-bottomed wig. Magnificent! Seeing me now as I am— (*Taking off his sunglasses.*) You wouldn't know me!

A wine glass falls, broken, to the ground.

MADRIGAL: Oh!

MRS. ST. MAUGHAM: What's the matter?

LAUREL: She broke the glass.

MADRIGAL: My hand knocked it.

MRS. ST. MAUGHAM: Maitland will get you another. Another glass, please, Maitland.

MAITLAND: There are no more on the sideboard.

MRS. ST. MAUGHAM: There are plenty in the pantry.

LAUREL: Oh—don't make him leave the room while the Judge is talking!

MRS. ST. MAUGHAM: I forgot! (*To* JUDGE.) Maitland has been in prison, Puppy.

JUDGE (*to* MAITLAND): Have you indeed?

MAITLAND: Five years, m'lord.

JUDGE (*blandly*): I hope not too unpleasant?

MAITLAND: It's given me a fascination and a horror, m'lord, if you can understand. A little stage-struck.

JUDGE: Dear me, I hope that's not the usual effect. It's supposed to be a deterrent.

MAITLAND (*waving the bottle a little wildly*): Yes and no. Yes and no. It's hard to explain. . . .

MRS. ST. MAUGHAM: Don't try. Take my second glass and give some wine to Miss Madrigal.

LAUREL: When she had one she wasn't offered any.

MAITLAND: She doesn't drink, Madam.

MRS. ST. MAUGHAM (*conveying a sense of rebuke to* MADRIGAL): One's palate is reborn every morning! Fill the glass!

He takes an extra glass to MADRIGAL.

MADRIGAL: I am not used to wine. . . .

MRS. ST. MAUGHAM (*flinging this to* MADRIGAL): One must dissemble!

MADRIGAL: . . . but today I will have some.

MAITLAND *pours for* MISS MADRIGAL.

MRS. ST. MAUGHAM (*with meaning*): It helps one to hold up one's end—at a table.

LAUREL (*holding out her glass*): And mine! Fill mine! Oh Judge—go on!

MAITLAND *fills* LAUREL'*s glass.

JUDGE: With what?

LAUREL: With tomorrow.

MAITLAND *stops to pick up bits of broken glass and in doing*

so leaves bottle on MADRIGAL's *table. From then on* MADRIGAL
refills her own glass once or twice.

MRS. ST. MAUGHAM: Heavens, Laurel! Talk is a thoroughbred! One does not say "go on!"—as if it were a donkey!

JUDGE: First I am driven to church to pray.

LAUREL: To *pray*!

JUDGE: I pray against my faults. When you are as old as I am
and sit in a high place—everyone sees your faults except
yourself. I suspect I am vain. But I get no corroboration.
I have my likes and dislikes. Nobody should know that—
but everybody knows it.

LAUREL: The Jury doesn't know it!

JUDGE: You are wrong. When the battle around the prisoner
is ended—the relationship is between me and the Jury. *Then*
comes the gamble! Wooden, inscrutable, as they sit hour
after hour—they grow a communal nose. They sniff out
weaknesses. I may speak seldom. But there's no neutrality
even in the rarest words. Even in silence. Long, long before
I come to sum up they will have taken mysterious sides for
and against me. I pray against bias. And against vanity.

MADRIGAL (*low*): And—for charity?

MRS. ST. MAUGHAM *takes her plate to the sideboard.*
MAITLAND *helps her to some salad.*

JUDGE (*smiling, his sharp old ears having overheard*): That's outside my job. (*Direct to* MADRIGAL.) I am sorry ... I have
forgotten how they call you?

MADRIGAL: The name is Madrigal.

JUDGE: I ignore the heart, Miss Madrigal, and satisfy justice.
(*To* MRS. ST. MAUGHAM *as she returns to table.*) Every little
line on my face is written by law, not life.

MRS. ST. MAUGHAM *sits.*

MRS. ST. MAUGHAM: Oh—to be bound up again, Puppy,
as you are! To be involved ... to be back in the hurly-
burly. ...

JUDGE: My life's not the hurly-burly. That's for the Counsel.
I'm the old creature with the memory. I have to remember

the things they *said* they said—but didn't. I have to decide
according to dry facts—when appealed to in a passion.

LAUREL: But *tomorrow*, Judge! *Tomorrow!*

MRS. ST. MAUGHAM: Stop badgering the Judge, Laurel!

JUDGE (*indulgently*): No! Let her be! On to the Law Courts!
At the gate my trumpeters knock three times. Then blow
for my admittance. In a little room behind the Court I
change my great wig for a small one.

LAUREL (*breathless*): Then . . .?

JUDGE (*histrionic, but partly carried away by his own words—
every one of which have an effect on* MADRIGAL): Then—
garbed and toffed with medieval meanings, obscured by
ritual, carrying the gloves of justice and the cap of death—
on a hollow knock—I go in.

LAUREL: . . . and the prisoner. . . .

MRS. ST. MAUGHAM: For the grace of heaven, Laurel, after
such a speech you should have paused and clapped him!

LAUREL: But I want to ask a question!

MRS. ST. MAUGHAM: Not yet! I am trying to weave in. . . .
Oh, *whoever invented* two tables! Can't one join them?

JUDGE: Not across fifty years. Not the Past and the Present.

LAUREL: But can I ask the Judge. . . .

MRS. ST. MAUGHAM: Ask then! And don't leave our friend
out of everything!

LAUREL: I don't know *how* to include her—when I want to
ask my own question!

MRS. ST. MAUGHAM: Ask Miss Madrigal. . . .

LAUREL (*crosses R. to C.*), But it's the *Judge* I'm asking! Judge
—aren't you going to try a murderer tomorrow?

JUDGE (*grim*): That is not a subject for discussion.

MRS. ST. MAUGHAM: You see! You see how stiff he can be!
You see the resemblance!

JUDGE: To whom?

MRS. ST. MAUGHAM (*delighted*): To Pinkbell!

LAUREL: But here, today, you are alone with us! No one will
quote you! (*Pleadingly.*) And we are mad on murder!

JUDGE: Murder is a sordid thing.

LAUREL: Oh—you don't think so! Murder cracks open the lives of people you don't know—like cracking open a walnut! Murder is a crisis! *What* must have gone before to make it so! Isn't it true that to you, Judge, everything is told for the first time?

JUDGE: In principle.

LAUREL: But Miss Madrigal says that the Judge isn't even interested! That he sleeps.

MADRIGAL: I said he *seemed* to sleep.

JUDGE: With one eye open. Like a tiger.

MRS. ST. MAUGHAM (*to* MADRIGAL): Have you been to a trial, then?

LAUREL: She has. She told me.

MRS. ST. MAUGHAM: You defeat my purpose! Let *her* answer.

JUDGE (*to* MADRIGAL, *politely*): Have you heard me in Court, Miss Madrigal?

MADRIGAL (*cautiously*): When I spoke to Laurel of judges it was in a general sense. (*Pause.*) But I heard you on the Bench, Judge.

JUDGE: I trust it was one of my better days.

MADRIGAL (*after a pause—ironic—and high with wine and danger; but must not be played as drunk*): I think, If I remember —I would not have come to your conclusion.

MRS. ST. MAUGHAM (*to* JUDGE): Miss Madrigal has such answers to life! (*To* MADRIGAL, *in quite a different tone, annoyed.*) But *that* was a strange one!

JUDGE: Well, a judge does not always get to the bottom of a case.

MADRIGAL (*loud*): No. It takes the pity of God to get to the bottom of things.

MRS. ST. MAUGHAM: That's enough!

MADRIGAL (*overriding*): You must forgive me. *You* insisted. (*Holding up her glass with a smile.*) It has removed the inhibitions.

MRS. ST. MAUGHAM (*loud*): *Bring the coffee on!*
  MAITLAND *exits.*

LAUREL (*to* JUDGE): When it's a murderer—what do you feel?

MRS. ST. MAUGHAM (*getting up to get cigarette box and to change the conversation*): What should he feel, Laurel! Judges see prisoners by the million!
  JUDGE *gets up too.*

LAUREL (*overriding*): But you've got to say, haven't you, whether the man's to live or die? Do you suffer?

MADRIGAL (*wildly, inconsequentially*): *Nobody* will suffer. They all go into a dream together!

LAUREL: Even the prisoner?

MADRIGAL (*with an air of reasonably explaining*): The prisoner *thinks* he is at the judgement seat of justice. A place where all motives are taken into account.

LAUREL: And isn't it?

MADRIGAL (*loud*): *No.*
  MRS. ST. MAUGHAM *rings the handbell.*

LAUREL: But Judge, while he listens—if the truth is quite different—does he never cry out?

JUDGE: He may write notes to his Counsel.
  MAITLAND *returns with coffee tray and places it on desk.*

LAUREL: Miss Madrigal says that when all has gone against him. . . .

MADRIGAL (*half-rising. Wildly*): I am quoted enough!

LAUREL: . . . that after the verdict—

MADRIGAL (*with a sudden desire for accuracy*): But if quoted, quoted rightly. . . .

LAUREL: . . . when he is asked "Have you anything to say? . . ."

MADRIGAL: The prisoner is punch-drunk. And says nothing.

JUDGE: Not always. Some have said remarkable things. There comes to my mind a woman. . . . Have you the trial, Maitland, of Connie Dolly Wallis?

LAUREL: Of whom?
  LAUREL *seizes flap of* MAITLAND'S *pocket.*

MAITLAND (*stammering, disengaging himself*): I . . . I haven't all the volumes, m'lord. I haven't that one.

JUDGE: It was not one of my successes. But you should read it for what the woman said when she stood before me. It was just before I sentenced her. (*Fingering his chin thoughtfully with his fingers.*) Fine eyes she had. I think I should remember them. A tall woman. With a face like an eagle. "What I have been listening to in Court", she said, "is not my life. It is the shape and shadow of my life. With the accidents of truth taken out of it." Fifteen years ago it must have been. It was my sixtieth birthday.

LAUREL: What was she tried for, Judge?

JUDGE: Murder.

MADRIGAL (*suddenly*): I remember the case. (*Looking at the* JUDGE.) A liar! A liar! (*Going high with the increasing combination of danger and wine.*) A girl who lied and lied! And when she told the truth it didn't save her!

JUDGE (*looking at her, frowning, reminded of something, but baffled*): Have you been to many trials?

MADRIGAL (*gets up with an instinct to escape, which carries her no further than the sofa*): One trial. One. But it isn't the *duplication* that makes the impression! It's the first time . . . the first time . . . the first time. . . .

Crash! A cricket ball breaks a window offstage.

MRS. ST. MAUGHAM (*still at table*): Quick, Maitland! It's the fishmonger's boy! . . . the fishmonger's boy! See if you can catch him!

MAITLAND *rushes out of the hall door.*

MRS. ST. MAUGHAM *crosses to pour out the coffee.*

LAUREL (*to* JUDGE, *but with an awed glance at* MADRIGAL): *Was she hung?*

MRS. ST. MAUGHAM (*handing coffee cup to* LAUREL *to pass*): *Hanged*—my darling—when speaking of a *lady.*

CURTAIN

ACT III

Twenty minutes after luncheon. A light garden awning has been drawn outside garden window. The summer room is faintly shadowed.

The two tables have been cleared. The JUDGE sits in the big chair, covers his face with a handkerchief, pretending to be asleep.

LAUREL enters from the hall door.

LAUREL: Judge ... Judge ... wake up. ... (*The* JUDGE *mumbles behind his handkerchief.*) If you have your teeth out I will turn my back.

JUDGE (*whipping off his handkerchief and sitting up*): My teeth are my own, thank God!

LAUREL: What have you been thinking of—under that handkerchief?

JUDGE: I am an old man—trying to sleep, Laurel.

LAUREL (*urgent*): What did she *do*?

JUDGE: Who?

LAUREL: In that case you were speaking of.

JUDGE: In my days young girls didn't pester old judges about murder.

LAUREL: You are old-fashioned.

JUDGE: You will be old-fashioned one day. It's more shocking than getting old.

LAUREL: Who died—that they should arrest her?

JUDGE: Her step-sister.

LAUREL (*sits on footstool beside* JUDGE): How was it done? And why? Was it jealousy?

JUDGE (*struggling to his feet and moving away*): If you are going to sit down, I am going to stand up.

LAUREL (*rising*): Was she hung?

JUDGE: *Who? What are you saying?*

LAUREL (*smoothly*): I was asking you about the case you were mentioning.

JUDGE (*shortly*): She was reprieved. There was a doubt.

LAUREL: Yours?

JUDGE (*as shortly*): Not mine. Enough has been said, I think.

LAUREL: Where do they go when they come out—all your murderers—when they don't go to the gallows?

JUDGE: One doesn't—mercifully—know.

LAUREL: Do you remember them?

JUDGE: In some strange way they are catalogued. As I get older they don't always come to hand.

LAUREL (*insisting*): But one *would* know them—by peculiar habits?

JUDGE: Perhaps. Some mark might lie upon them.

LAUREL: If they took their country walks, for instance, back and forth, up and down, wearing out the carpet in their bedroom—

JUDGE: What?

LAUREL: With a habit, like a sailor's, of walking in a confined space. Might it be *that*, Judge?

MRS. ST. MAUGHAM *enters from the hall door, softly so as not to disturb the* JUDGE. *She sees* LAUREL.

MRS. ST. MAUGHAM: Laurel! He was to sleep, child! And now you have disturbed him!

LAUREL (*with sly smile from garden door*): I think he was disturbed already!

Exits to garden.

MRS. ST. MAUGHAM: My Original! ... so elegant and gentle. ... What do you think of her?

JUDGE: I am not fond of young girls.

MRS. ST. MAUGHAM: You are not? You used to be! It was unfortunate about her companion.

But your fault, Puppy, for not drinking the wine at luncheon!

JUDGE: How did you discover her?

MRS. ST. MAUGHAM: I advertised. I took a chance and was justified. Miss Madrigal came to me like rain from heaven.

JUDGE: With references?

MRS. ST. MAUGHAM: I never listen to what one woman says of another. References are a want of faith—in one's own judgement! Finish your sleep, Puppy! Since you must have it.

As MRS. ST. MAUGHAM *exits,* MADRIGAL *appears at the garden windows. Seeing the* JUDGE *alone she comes into the room. Crosses herself as she comes in.*

MADRIGAL: I am sorry to disturb you. . . .

JUDGE (*wary, playing for time, needing the last link*): On the contrary . . . on the contrary— (*Waving his small silver box.*) Old men are kept alive on tablets. . . .

MADRIGAL (*attempting to control herself and to speak reasonably*): Of course you think . . . this is not where I ought to be. . . . There would be no difficulty . . . I have private means. . . . But it's an understandable job. So fitted to me. (*Control going.*) Do you believe in God? I thought God had given it to me!

(*Pause. He says nothing.*)

Oh—don't look at me as if I were a sad piece of news! A curiosity! (*Silence.*)

(*In agony.*) Why don't you *say* something!

JUDGE (*with a sudden crack of his fingers—everything has cleared*): That's it!

MADRIGAL (*stopping short*): What?

JUDGE: Well—it has come to me.

MADRIGAL: Oh God . . . I thought you *knew*!

JUDGE (*still to himself*): I must say—the coincidences at luncheon—in retrospect—are distasteful.

MADRIGAL (*aghast*): If I hadn't come in. . . . (*Pause. He makes a wry little gesture.*) So . . . *now* what will you do?

JUDGE: I am an old man, Miss Madrigal, and very learned. I don't know.

MADRIGAL (*ironically*): Judge—I can't wait seven hours—*twice!* You sent me to meet my Maker on a Tuesday—but that was altered. I have done what they call "time". It was a lifetime. I don't know what you *can* do to me! *What* can you do to me?

JUDGE: I do not presume to judge you twice.

MADRIGAL: Oh, you would come to the same conclusion! Cleverer minds than mine could not convince you! But there's nothing to gain by talking! You came here by accident. . . .

JUDGE: I wish I hadn't.

MADRIGAL (*bitterly*): What can it be to you?

JUDGE: Embarrassment. What in the name of heaven made you choose *this* occupation! With *your* history! In *this* family!

MADRIGAL (*satirical*): In "this" family?

JUDGE (*testy*): In *any* family. I remember the young woman! And the lies she told. A Pathological Imaginer.

MADRIGAL: One does not forget the plums in one's speeches!

JUDGE: And now you have planted me—with ethical perplexity! It's most unpleasant.

. . . And *human* perplexity! Old friends . . . and a child to consider!

MADRIGAL: It's the child I'm considering! When I came here I thought I had met myself again. The cobwebs and the fantasies! The same evasions! I could have slipped away. . . .

JUDGE: There are worse solutions.

MADRIGAL! But the child needs me! *If* I stay—will you tell them who I am?

JUDGE: Connie Dolly Wallis—what the devil am I to do with you?

MADRIGAL: The name is Madrigal.

JUDGE (*testy*): Of course you had to take a name!

MADRIGAL: It's more than a name to me!

I come of a stock—who in some insensate way—*cannot* accept defeat!

My father was cashiered. And after forty years of appeal —reinstated.

My grandfather died upright on his feet.

He said God wouldn't give a fallen general houseroom. For fifteen years, and alone, I have hammered out what I am. I did not know I was as dogged as any of them.

JUDGE: But even conceding. . . .

MADRIGAL: You need concede nothing to solitude! It is a teacher!

JUDGE: You were a girl of considerable feeling, if I remember.

MADRIGAL: Not now. I am burnt out white—like the moon —lunar.

JUDGE: Are you not—if I may gently say so—somewhat a stranger to life?

MADRIGAL: The girl I was! *She* was the stranger!

JUDGE: You have greatly changed.

MADRIGAL (*ironical*): At our last meeting I died. It alters the appearance.

JUDGE (*suddenly sorry for himself*): Dear me. . . . Oh deary me. . . . As if there were not quite enough—this week ahead of me.

MADRIGAL: You would have been going. Why not leave?

JUDGE: Because I belong to a guild of men—who feel responsibility. (*Wryly.*) And a deep distaste for situations.

MADRIGAL: What shall you do?

JUDGE: Don't badger me! I can't remember when I was so bothered! (*Sharply—as she puts her hand to her head.*) What's the matter?

MADRIGAL: It is that . . . after being so long unknown . . . it makes my head swim to be known. . . .

OLIVIA *enters from hall door, crossing quickly to* JUDGE.

OLIVIA: Judge! I remember you! You used to be so kind to me when I was little! What was that odd name Mother had for you? Puppy? I used to wonder at it.

JUDGE (*smiling at her, taking her hand*): You were that silent little girl.

OLIVIA: Yes, I was silent. (*Suddenly seeing* MADRIGAL.) We met before—do you remember? I have come back as I said I would to fetch my daughter. . . .

MADRIGAL: To *fetch* her!

JUDGE (*quickly intervening*): I have to go—can my car be of use Miss Madrigal? (*Low.*) It would be simple.

OLIVIA (*breaking in*): Oh don't go—don't go! I'm so glad you are here! It's so lucky.

JUDGE: Lucky?

OLIVIA: For me. For with you here I shall put things better.

JUDGE *looks at his watch.*

JUDGE (*with his own special wry humour*): I ought to go. I am not good out of my setting.

OLIVIA: Surely *you* are not afraid of life?

JUDGE: On the contrary—the Law has made me nervous of life.

OLIVIA: No, Judge! Please stay! It's the influence of a stranger! With a third person in the room my mother hears reason better.

MRS. ST. MAUGHAM (*catapulting into the room*): Don't count on it Olivia! (*Forestallingly.*) I got your letter!

OLIVIA: But you don't read them! You never did! We've had our orders. We leave tonight for Cyprus.

MRS. ST MAUGHAM: Cyprus! Whoever heard of it! It flashed in history and is gone forever! Disraeli—Bismarck—I can't remember! See what comes of marrying an Army Officer! (*Pulls up awning by an inside cord and lightens room again.*)

LAUREL *makes her entry from the garden, stands in the archway, silent.*

OLIVIA: Laurel!

LAUREL: Have you come alone?

MRS. ST. MAUGHAM: We have a guest! No drama!

LAUREL: You haven't been for four years.

OLIVIA (*glancing at her mother in silent accusation*): But *now* I

have come for you! Oh—as I drove down here—all the
hedges and the telegraph poles were saying—Laurel. . . .

LAUREL (*undercutting her*): Are you going to have a baby?

OLIVIA: Yes.

LAUREL: So there's no room for me!

OLIVIA: There's room! There's always been room! A heart
isn't a house—with a room for each person! I can't wait any
longer! Come just as you are. . . .

MADRIGAL (*suddenly, throwing her weight in on the side of the
mother*): I can pack her things!

LAUREL (*turning on her*): What are you up to, Boss!

MRS. ST. MAUGHAM (*satirically*): You are so kind! But there's
no need for packing!

LAUREL (*menacing to* MADRIGAL): Did you speak without
thinking?

MADRIGAL: No.

LAUREL: But I've told you what she is! I've told you. . . .

MADRIGAL: And do you think I have believed you?

OLIVIA: There's a seat taken on the plane tonight. . . .

LAUREL (*furious—but with* MADRIGAL): And fly with you?
Have you thought of the risk?

OLIVIA: On the plane. One doesn't think of that.

LAUREL: The risk that—if you take me—*I might murder my
step-sister!*

JUDGE: Are you mad!

LAUREL: They say so.

MADRIGAL (*to* JUDGE): Don't give her the triumph of your
attention.

MRS. ST. MAUGHAM: Laurel always uses wild words instead
of weeping! (*To* OLIVIA.) I knew that if she saw you we
should have trouble with her!

MADRIGAL (*quietly*): You have missed your effect, Laurel. . . .
The moment is passing. Would you care to let it go?

LAUREL (*menacing*): The sky's the limit, Boss! The sky's the
limit!

MADRIGAL: No time for games.

LAUREL: I mean—*no* limit! I can say anything!

JUDGE (*sharp*): *I would not.*

LAUREL: Shall I go on?

JUDGE: *No*

LAUREL: Shall I?

MADRIGAL: If you want your scene—take it.

LAUREL: How calm you are!

MRS. ST. MAUGHAM: Miss Madrigal has the calm of a woman in a million!

LAUREL: She has the calm of a woman who has been a long time . . . alone.

MADRIGAL (*low*): So we are in for it?

LAUREL: No. It can be played on the edge still.

MADRIGAL: An edge is sharp! One must come down one side or the other. . . .

MRS. ST. MAUGHAM: You see . . . they are always at some amusing invention. They're inseparable! What game, my poppet?

LAUREL: A game that two can play at.

MAITLAND *enters U. L.*

Maitland! Look! It's my mother!

MAITLAND: I know it's your mother.

MRS. ST. MAUGHAM: Must the whole house be gathered!

MAITLAND: I came for the coffee tray. (*He dashes to table, gets coffee tray.*)

MRS. ST. MAUGHAM: Oh no, you didn't! You came for curiosity! You've a nose for a crisis like a basset for a wild hare!

LAUREL: Maitland! *Wait*, Maitland! *How* did you know?

MAITLAND: She has been before. . . .

LAUREL (*suddenly realizing*): How deep you are! (*Looking at her grandmother.*) I did not know that.

MAITLAND: . . . But I am loyal to Madam. (*Escapes.*)

MRS. ST. MAUGHAM (*furious*): Loyal! Loyalty died with Queen Victoria! Disregarded in my own house! Disregarded! I am talking to *you*, Olivia!

OLIVIA: Each time I came you promised you would tell her.

MRS. ST. MAUGHAM: I had my own reasons! You never would listen! You were never like other girls! The Judge will remember—though daughters forget everything! You remember, Puppy, how I tried with her?

JUDGE: I remember only the result. The shy and gentle daughter.

OLIVIA: Thank you, Judge. But I am not staying any longer! (*Crosses to* MRS. ST. MAUGHAM.) I want to go. . . .

MRS. ST. MAUGHAM: . . . but you'll not take Laurel! I have a special knowledge of her! To me she is like a porcelain on a shelf—cracked in some marvellous way for the better!

OLIVIA: My mother uses words in her special fashion! For a phrase—she would make capital of anything!

MRS. ST. MAUGHAM: Charming—for a mother to hear! And in front of an old friend! If—at a luncheon party—you want to have out the damage of a lifetime. . . .

MADRIGAL (*with sudden violence*): Let's have it!

MRS. ST. MAUGHAM: What!

MADRIGAL: I beg your pardon.

MRS. ST. MAUGHAM: Were you objecting?

MADRIGAL: Yes. I think the wine has cut the caution.

The JUDGE *makes a movement of his hands.*

MRS. ST. MAUGHAM: Don't gesture at me, Puppy!

JUDGE: Anything may precipitate. . . .

MRS. ST. MAUGHAM: What?

MADRIGAL: *Anything!*

JUDGE (*to* MADRIGAL): Will you come into another room— and I will advise you?

MADRIGAL: No. Your advice is foreseen! That I must leave here—but it is the child who must leave! Laurel must go, Mrs. St. Maugham, go with her mother.

MRS. ST. MAUGHAM: You take a great liberty!

MADRIGAL: Yes, now I have a sense of liberty.

MRS. ST. MAUGHAM: That is not what I meant!

MADRIGAL: No, but it is what I mean!

MRS. ST. MAUGHAM: This girl of special soil! Transplant her?

MADRIGAL: You have not a green thumb, Mrs. St. Maugham, with a plant or a girl. This is a house where nothing good can be made of her.

MRS. ST. MAUGHAM: *My* house!

MADRIGAL: Your house! Why even your garden is demented! By the mercy of God you do not keep an animal!

MRS. ST. MAUGHAM: You are mad! You are a monster!

MADRIGAL: No, I am a woman who has lost touch with things. With indulgence. With excuses, with making merry over bad things. The light—and the shade—has been hammered out of me. I am as humourless as a missionary.

JUDGE: Why complicate life? The past is over.

MADRIGAL: If the past is useful, I shall not hesitate to use it. What I have been has long been done with— (*To* LAUREL.) What you are is yet to come. Let's *finish* with the charade made here of affection. . . .

MRS. ST. MAUGHAM: Stop the woman, Puppy! Stop her!

OLIVIA: But Miss Madrigal has something to say!

JUDGE: No, she hasn't.

MADRIGAL: Oh! I am not inexperienced! You must allow me a certain bias!

JUDGE: Have a care!

MADRIGAL: I am beyond caring!

LAUREL: Boss, Boss, don't go too far!

MADRIGAL (*crossing to her, taking her by the shoulders passionately*): Don't drive me to it! Who else can tell you that when the moment comes when truth might serve you—you will not make it sound! Or that the clarion note, the innocence will desert you. . . .

LAUREL: But everybody *knows* about me! They *know* what happened!

MADRIGAL: They know what you have told them! You didn't stop the marriage, but you snatched the attention! Shall we now deprive your grandmother of your famous seduction?

MRS. ST. MAUGHAM: At *what* a moment!

MADRIGAL: One has to *find* a moment to say such things.

OLIVIA (*to her Mother*): But is that what she said? Is that what you have believed?

MADRIGAL: *Wait!* Let the child tell you!

LAUREL: You were not there!

MADRIGAL: I did not need to be there. The story can be read backwards! What newspaper did the cook take in, I wonder!

OLIVIA: A child of twelve!

MADRIGAL: An only child is never twelve! (*Crossing to* LAUREL.) Do you cry?

LAUREL: No.

MADRIGAL: I should cry.

LAUREL: I am not near crying.

MADRIGAL: I should cry—with relief—that your mother wants you! (*Pause.*) Be careful! Even a mother can't wait forever.

OLIVIA (*to* MADRIGAL): But *why* did she pretend? Why did she make it up?

MADRIGAL: Odd things are done for love.

LAUREL *runs to garden door, stops and turns at door.*

OLIVIA: Give it up, Laurel! It isn't worth going on.

LAUREL (*to* MADRIGAL): Has it got to be the truth?

MADRIGAL (*half smiling*): One can lie. . . . But truth is more interesting!

LAUREL: . . . and you get better and better at spotting it! You win, Boss!

She looks at her mother. Then exits quickly. OLIVIA makes a step towards MADRIGAL.

MADRIGAL (*softly, urgently, to* OLIVIA): Quick! A straw would break it! (OLIVIA *follows* LAUREL *out.*) (*Calling softly after them.*) Your blue linen dress is folded in the top drawer. Look—for your yellow striped one. . . .

MRS. ST. MAUGHAM (*gripping tooth and nail to the behaviour of a hostess as she lets fall the tin clatter of words to the* JUDGE): *What* a precipitation—of melodrama—your visit's fallen on!

(*Glancing at the door—flame beginning to run in her tone.*) Blood is thicker than water I had thought but it appears not!

JUDGE: My dear—my dear old friend. . . .

MRS. ST. MAUGHAM (*at height of passion*): If you were on your *knees* you wouldn't stop me! (*Turning to* MADRIGAL.) *That* was a black patch, Miss Madrigal! If there's a fire to be lit—you've set a match to it! What collusion behind my back! (*To* JUDGE.) You've been a witness to it!

JUDGE (*starts to the door*): You two would be better talking alone, I think. . . .

MRS. ST. MAUGHAM: Stay where you are, Puppy! Men are such cowards! In the name of discretion or a cool head or some such nonsense—they leave one in the lurch. . . .

JUDGE: So much better . . . better not say anything!

MRS. ST. MAUGHAM: There's an undependability in high-minded men! They sit—objective! When they should be *burning* beside one!

But—when things become personal . . . what would you say if your clerk put your wig on!

JUDGE (*unhappily*): I should reflect at length, I expect, and decide on inaction.

MRS. ST. MAUGHAM: So you would! But I've been robbed of my granddaughter!

MADRIGAL (*calmly*): If you face facts, Mrs. St. Maugham, you are tired of her.

MRS. ST. MAUGHAM (*faintly*): Be a man, Puppy! Put her out! Put her out in the street for me!

The JUDGE *makes an unhappy movement of recoil.*

MRS. ST. MAUGHAM (*with mounting passion*): The flaming impudence! The infamy! And I—lavish! Trusting . . . leaning. . . . But I've been leaning on a demon! In your heart—every penny should have scalded you! I've been betrayed! Don't talk to me of wages! You'll see none of them!

JUDGE (*to* MADRIGAL): Perhaps this is where I may be of some use?

MADRIGAL (*smiling gently*): No, Judge. Not now. Fifteen years ago you might have been.

MRS. ST. MAUGHAM: Do you dare to speak! What are these innuendos?

JUDGE (*low*): Least said, soonest mended.

MRS. ST. MAUGHAM: Hints—since lunch—have been flying like gnats from side to side of the room. Nobody tells me—in plain English—anything! Have you two met before then?

The JUDGE *and* MADRIGAL *look first at each other then at* MRS. ST. MAUGHAM.

MADRIGAL (*matter of fact*): I was once sentenced to death by the Judge here.

MRS. ST. MAUGHAM: Ah. (*Sinking into chair.*)

JUDGE (*simultaneously*): Ill-advised. Ill-advised.

MRS. ST. MAUGHAM (*flying robustly up again*): Oh!—If I were not seventy—this would revive me! To *death.* . . . But *there you are!*

MADRIGAL: Those who still live—have to be somewhere.

MRS. ST. MAUGHAM: If it were true . . . it's outrageous! And if I start putting two and three together—*Good heavens—how can you be living at all!*

JUDGE: There was a doubt.

MRS. ST. MAUGHAM: What I doubt is my senses! The thing's impossible! Either I don't believe it—or it's quite private! Besides, if it were true it would be—most inconvenient! Oh . . . I would like the situation annulled! And the conversation put back. . . .

JUDGE: To where?

MRS. ST. MAUGHAM: To where it hadn't happened! And at the interview—how dared you—I let pass—so many excellent applicants in favour of you!

MADRIGAL (*mildly*): No—really—it was not so.

MRS. ST. MAUGHAM (*struck by another thought*): . . . and the references! The references I had . . . I am amazed! You must have forged them!

MADRIGAL: I gave you none.

MRS. ST. MAUGHAM: Why?

MADRIGAL (*simply*): I had none.

JUDGE (*moves R. Explaining mildly*): This lady came to you out of prison.

MRS. ST. MAUGHAM: Prison! I would have thought a University! Oh, you have been most satisfactory—I *thought* —but now a light is thrown—I'm growing more and more thunderstruck! ...

MADRIGAL: But—

MRS. ST. MAUGHAM: Don't speak to me, if you please! You who come out of God-knows-what ancient Publicity! Blazing—from heaven knows what lurid newspapers! A headline! A felon! And how can you lunch with me, Puppy, and know such things! Oh I'm dumbfounded! What's more, I've been defrauded! (*Sits exhausted.*) Go! Pack your bags! Pack your bags! Out of the house with you!

Enter MAITLAND, *on a light wind of impatience.*

MAITLAND: I can't wait ... I can't wait forever! (*To* MRS. ST. MAUGHAM, *who has practically collapsed.*) Is she ... who we think she is!

MRS. ST. MAUGHAM (*in a faint groan*): She is.

MAITLAND (*turning radiantly to* MADRIGAL): Oh ... Miss ... Oh ... Madam.

MADRIGAL *gives a tiny bow.*

MAITLAND *returns it.*

MRS. ST. MAUGHAM: Heavens! What an anti-climax! What veneration! One would think the woman was an actress!

MAITLAND: When one is a humble man one can't express it. I think it is—to *think*—that after such a gale she is with us!

MRS. ST. MAUGHAM (*feebly*): That's enough, Maitland.

MAITLAND: To have stood one's life before the Judge here if you'll pardon me, m'lord, even though you eat your lunch like other men—making the same light talk— (*Turning sharply as the door opens.*) Here's the Nurse ... all of a dither!

NURSE (*rushing in. Stopping short at sight of guests*): Mrs. St. Maugham. ...

MRS. ST. MAUGHAM (*in a daze*): We have friends now. It can wait, Nurse.

NURSE: Mr. Pinkbell is dead.

MRS. ST. MAUGHAM: You can go, Nurse. I'll attend to it later.

 NURSE, *aghast, backs to the door.*

I say we *have friends*, Nurse!

 NURSE *exits, horrified.*

JUDGE: But ... good heavens ... Pinkbell!

MRS. ST. MAUGHAM (*dazed*): He is in expert hands.

MAITLAND: But the poor old bastard. . . . He has passed over!

MRS. ST. MAUGHAM (*coming to*): Is *that* what she said?

MAITLAND: They've downed him—stiff as a rod. He hasn't tomorrow. . . . (*Struck by a worse thought.*) He *hasn't the rest of today*!

MRS. ST. MAUGHAM: Dead ... and my Past goes with him. . . .

JUDGE: Dear me, dear me. I am shocked. First to know he is alive. Then to learn that he isn't.

MRS. ST. MAUGHAM (*musing*): When I was a young woman he educated me . . . my manner with distinguished foreigners. . . . He saw to my Ascots. He bought my wine in France for me. Is there an afterlife, Puppy?

JUDGE: I don't give judgements easily. But in this life you will miss him.

MRS. ST. MAUGHAM: Alas, no. (*Rises, robustly disposing of Pinkbell.*) Shall you come again, Puppy? When the excitement of your week is over?

JUDGE: Too much happens in this house—for an old man.

MRS. ST. MAUGHAM: I am coming with you to your car. Everyone—accusing everyone—has been tiring. (*Full return to her old manner.*) Stay with her, Maitland, I shan't be long. Keep an eye on her. (*Exits past* JUDGE.)

JUDGE (*turning back and motioning to* MAITLAND *to leave them; to* MADRIGAL): After all—have you liked the life here?

MADRIGAL (*with an ironic smile*): It has a hollow quality—which soothes me.

JUDGE: What shall you do?

MADRIGAL: I shall continue to explore—the *astonishment* of living!

JUDGE (*taking her hand*): Goodbye, Miss Madrigal. No man's infallible. (*Exit.*)

MAITLAND (*re-entering in eager excitement*): Can I come where you're going? I will serve you. We could throw our five and fifteen years away from us! In the dustbin!

MADRIGAL (*smiling*): Not mine! Not *my* fifteen years! I value them! They made me.

MAITLAND (*ecstatic*): Ah—that's the strength I hanker after! That's what I've been missing! I was born to worship the stars! But I've never known *which* stars ... (*spreads his arms wide*) ... when the whole heaven's full of them!

MRS. ST. MAUGHAM *returns.* (*On the same note*): I wish to give my notice!

MRS. ST. MAUGHAM: Again! You choose such odd moments!

MAITLAND: I wish to accompany Miss Madrigal!

MRS. ST. MAUGHAM: Where to?

MAITLAND: Where she's going.

MRS. ST. MAUGHAM (*chooses a rose from vase on table, with irony*): Yet now you have it all your own way, Maitland.

MAITLAND (*wincing, glancing up at the ceiling*): Don't say that!

MRS. ST. MAUGHAM: I'll talk to you later ... I must go up ... (*as she exits, to herself*) ... stiff as a rod ... the poor old bastard. ...

MADRIGAL *instantly turning to* MAITLAND, *refers to notebook and talks in clear articulated haste like someone leaving important messages they have hardly time to deliver.*

MADRIGAL: Thin out the wallflowers—as I showed you ... the cherries want pruning. ...

MAITLAND (*trying desperately to interrupt*): But. ...

MADRIGAL (*rapidly, in case* MRS. ST. MAUGHAM *should return before she has finished*): . . . tie in the black grape! Cut the heads off the moss rose. . . .

MAITLAND: But. . . .

MADRIGAL (*taking no notice*): . . . divide the Bearded Iris . . . watch out for mildew. . . .

MAITLAND: But what's to become of *my* decision!

MADRIGAL (*in irritated despair that he doesn't listen*): Oh—don't give notice so often! It's a fidgety habit!

OLIVIA *and* LAUREL *enter from main house door Left, putting down a light suitcase and* LAUREL'*s hat and coat.*

MAITLAND: You look a proper daughter!

LAUREL (*going to him*): You may kiss me, Maitland.

MAITLAND *kisses her brow.*

(*To* OLIVIA.) Maitland loves me.

OLIVIA: Loves you?

MAITLAND *gets her hat and coat.*

LAUREL: I had to have someone—*someone* who thought the world of me.

OLIVIA: As I did?

LAUREL: As you *do.*

MRS. ST. MAUGHAM *returns.*

MRS. ST. MAUGHAM: Leave us, Maitland!

MAITLAND *exits.*

MRS. ST. MAUGHAM *playing this scene magnificent, relentless, and, towards* LAUREL, *dry and gruff*:

You were right, Olivia, when you said he and I had the same standards—(*with slight glance at Pinkbell's door*).

Well, Laurel . . . now you have a mother! It's not so rare! Every kitten has one!

LAUREL: Have you often seen death before, Grandloo. . . .

MRS. ST. MAUGHAM: Up till now I have managed to avoid it. Don't begin badly! Where are your gloves?

LAUREL (*shows her gloves, one step forward*): Grandloo. . . .

MRS. ST. MAUGHAM (*her hand up to ward her off*): No goodbyes! I'm too old for them. . . .

OLIVIA: Go to the car, darling. (*Pause.*) Begin by obeying.
LAUREL *exits.*

MRS. ST. MAUGHAM: Well, Olivia? What are you going to
do with her? Teach her the right things? After I've taught
her the wrong ones?

OLIVIA: You're like an old Freethinker—who finds he has
a son a clergyman!

MRS. ST. MAUGHAM: Is that so dreadful?

OLIVIA: No. . . . But to you inscrutable. (*Moves towards door,
then turns.*) *Why* did you want her?

MRS. ST. MAUGHAM: Is it a crime to want to be remembered?
(OLIVIA *moves to the door.*)
The Pharaohs built the Pyramids for that reason. (OLIVIA
turns, stung.)

OLIVIA (*low*): Are the thoughts of a daughter . . . no sort of
memorial?

MRS. ST. MAUGHAM (*unconquered*): Is that an obituary?
OLIVIA *with a little defeated shake of her head goes out.*
Left alone MRS. ST. MAUGHAM *runs to the window, Left,
leans out, waiting for them to appear outside the front door.*
(*Calling through window robustly, the old Adam in her still in
full sway*): Leave her hair long!
It gives her the choice later! (*Pause.*)
(*Louder.*) Keep her bust high!
(*She waits a moment. They are gone. She turns, draws herself
to her full height.*)
(*Aridly, stoically.*) What do women do—in my case?

MADRIGAL (*from the other side of the room*): They garden.

MRS. ST. MAUGHAM: But it seems I am not very good at that
either. Are your things packed? (*Picks up garden catalogue.*)

MADRIGAL (*coldly*): I am a light-footed traveller.

MRS. ST. MAUGHAM (*holding out the catalogue*): Before you
go will you point out the white crinum? (*She hands it to her.*
MADRIGAL *takes it and looks at it.*) You, who have an im-
pertinent answer to everything—is there an afterlife? (*Sits
in armchair—centre stage.*)

MADRIGAL: Certainly.

MRS. ST. MAUGHAM (*surprised*): You say—"certainly"?

MADRIGAL: One does not sit alone for fifteen years without coming to conclusions.

MRS. ST. MAUGHAM: Is there ... affection in it?

MADRIGAL: But you have been living all this while without affection! Haven't you noticed it? (*She hands her back the catalogue.*)

> To this no answer. MRS. ST. MAUGHAM *reads aloud from catalogue.*

MRS. ST. MAUGHAM: ... "very rare ... from the High Andes of Bolivia. Jasmine-like, tubular flowers." ...

MADRIGAL: Don't waste your time. They are beyond you.

MRS. ST. MAUGHAM (*not raising her head*): It speaks wonderfully of the Uvularia.

MADRIGAL: When will you learn you live on chalk?

MRS. ST. MAUGHAM (*on same tone*): I have made such a muddle of the heart. Will Olivia forgive me?

MADRIGAL: It is pointless to wonder. You have no choice how she will sum up. (*Pause. Quietly.*) She will live longer.

MRS. ST. MAUGHAM (*vexed*): Am I to die unloved?

MADRIGAL: If necessary. *I* was prepared to do it.

MRS. ST. MAUGHAM (*looking at the ceiling and letting the catalogue fall in her lap*): The Unicorn Root. ...

MADRIGAL: ... needs a sheltered spot. You haven't one.

MRS. ST. MAUGHAM (*slowly, to the ceiling*): If you stay here—you can grow windbreaks. ... (*Suddenly, bringing her head down.*) I must know one thing!

MADRIGAL: What?

MRS. ST. MAUGHAM (*her face agleam and smiling with human curiosity, she looks up at* MADRIGAL): Did you do it?

MADRIGAL (*unperturbed and calm*): What learned men at the top of their profession couldn't find out in nine days—why should *you* know?

MRS. ST. MAUGHAM (*looking down at the catalogue after a second's pause*): ... the Dierama ... the Wand Flower. ...

MADRIGAL (*with a strange still certainty which sits like a Nimbus on her*): It won't grow on chalk. But if I stay with you—(*Putting her hand like a blessing on* MRS. ST. MAUGHAM's *shoulder.*) and we work together ... with potash—and a little granular peat. ... WE can *make* it do so.

CURTAIN

The Last Joke

THE LAST JOKE was presented by H. M. Tennent and Irene Mayer Selznick at the Phoenix Theatre, London on 28th September 1960, with the following cast:

ROSE	Anna Massey
BARON SANTA CLARA	Ernest Thesiger
HUGO CAVANATI	Robert Flemyng
PRINCE FERDINAND CAVANATI	John Gielgud
MATTHEW	Paul Curran
MRS. WEBSTER	Hazel Terry
ROBIN	Robin Hawdon
EDWARD PORTAL	Ralph Richardson
A CHAUFFEUR	Robert Tunstall

The Play directed by
GLEN BYAM SHAW
with Setting by
FELIX KELLY

CHARACTERS

PRINCE FERDINAND CAVANATI
His brother HUGO (who does not use his title)
Their manservant MATTHEW an old Scotsman
EDWARD PORTAL a millionaire and art collector
His daughter ROSE
BARON SANTA CLARA, known as OLD TONI
BENZUTO a Turk—born in Egypt—brought
   up in Paris
MRS. CLARA WEBSTER confidential valet
   and body-servant to Edward Portal.
ROBIN a footman

TIME: The present. Summer.

ACT I: A drawing-room in Chiswick Mall,
                overlooking the Thames.
ACT II: Wood Castle—during a ball.
ACT III: The woods of Wood Castle,
                before dawn the same night.

ACT I

The drawing-room in Chiswick Mall.

The drawing-room windows look on to the Thames.
The set of rooms involved (drawing-room and two bedrooms) can either be on the first floor or the ground floor. If on the first floor it would have been originally laid out thus because of the flooding of the river.
If on the first floor then the little "hall" is at the top of stairs leading down to the hall-proper, the front garden, and the road: if on the ground floor the hall and passage lead direct to garden and road. (I have written it as though the rooms were on the ground floor, but for the set the artist may prefer an upper-floor view over the Thames.)
Wall, stage left—a bay window from which the trees on the river's edge can be seen.
Fairly high up on the wall, stage right, hangs a brilliant blue (lapis colour) piece of Persian silk on a roller—like a small blind with a rod to weight it fastened to the bottom. It covers a ventilator or louvre through which Prince Ferdinand in his bedroom can overhear the talk in the drawing-room.
Furniture important to the action are: an armchair (with its back to hall door), a small upright escritoire of mother-of-pearl inlay. This has a narrow drawer and a top shelf. On the shelf stands a photograph, whose frame is also of mother-of-pearl. On either side of the photograph—thus drawing attention to it—is a small vase of white roses. The photograph is of a portrait painted by Edouard Vuillard. It is hazy and leafy and—vaguely—a woman sits amid leaves in a garden dress. The size of the photograph is governed by the drawer—in which it later sticks. There is a

table near the armchair. Another, small one, near hall door. A circular table, whose top is of lapis lazuli, a violent blue, has on it a tray with sherry glasses, decanters, a small French cake, biscuits.

General description of room and pictures:

The colour of the room is in river-tones of faded silver and grey (probably Japanese wallpaper). Much of the furniture is from a collection of mother-of-pearl.

These river-tones (curtains, wallpaper) set off a brilliant collection of pictures in a special period of French painting:

Renoirs, Gauguins, Chagalls, a Seurat "Self Portrait", Picasso, the Dounaier Rousseau. As pictures on a Set cannot hope to look like great painting it should be possible to get a "tapestry effect" by covering them with nylon or silk net, and by a deceit-treatment to indicate the quality of the painting. Except in the case of the Seurat "Self Portrait" (which could be hung so that it is only seen at an angle), it would be wiser to use solely the paintings of outdoor subjects—foliage—forests—leaves.

The high notes of the room should depend on the bay window with trees, the brilliance of the paintings—the intense blue of the lapis tables.

   The moment when the Curtain Rises is the end of a small sherry party. The door to the hall stands partly open.

   HUGO—*unseen*—*is saying goodbye to his guests.*

   MATTHEW *passes the opening holding a hat or a light summer coat.*

   The word "goodbye" flits in and out of a subsiding murmur. Inside the room two guests remain.

   ROSE PORTAL *sits waiting for Hugo. She is dressed to the point of sophistication that only money and Paris can give her.*

   OLD TONI—*Baron Santa Clara—stands looking with a dry ecstasy at a picture on the wall. He has once been a diplomat: one does not know for what nation. He has the powdery elegance of an old dried fern. His English is perfect (that is his pride); but artificial, mannered, finnicking. He might be anything from seventy to ninety, but will live for ever.*

HUGO (*coming just inside the room and collapsing on to the nearest chair inside the door; with a comic gesture of mock-fatigue*): Aren't you going aren't you going aren't you going?

ROSE (*amused*): No. *Toni* is going.

OLD TONI (*gazing at a picture; rapt*): Leave me a moment! A charming party—but with so many bodies one couldn't see the pictures! (*With veneration.*) Surely. . . . Seurat?

HUGO: Self-portrait. (*Yawns.*)

OLD TONI (*moving to another picture*): Picasso!

HUGO: Blue period. (*Jumping up, as though disposing of the subject.*) My brother's pictures. He leaves them with me. (*Crossing to* ROSE, *picking up one of her hands, then the other, kissing them. Comically, without offence.*) I suddenly get tired of guests!

OLD TONI (*walking to the window, standing looking out; rapturously*): And what a view ... what a view over the Thames! (*As though struck by a thought he turns, and pointing with a smile across the room.*) *Two!* Under that blind—I'll swear there's a mirror—to reflect the water!

HUGO (*uneasy, smiling*): What makes you think so?

OLD TONI: That Persian silk! You had it in Constantinople. Your brother hung it over a mirror he had fixed so that he could see the Bosphorus! He insisted one could be hypnotized by moving water!

ROSE: Is there a mirror there? Why cover it then?

HUGO (*lightly*): It makes me giddy at high tide!

OLD TONI: Did we meet—in those days?

HUGO: In Constantinople?—I was a child then. He's years older!

OLD TONI (*mannered—to* ROSE): Hugo has a brother who is little short of a god! (*Clasping his hands sentimentally.*) At least to me, when I knew him.

HUGO (*an obvious and insolent non-sequitur*): How is your wife?

OLD TONI (*for a moment taken aback*): What? ... She is well.

(*Amused by the "check", but not deflected by it. To* ROSE.) He
was in the Diplomatic Service when I knew him.

HUGO (*off-hand*):—His *public* setting!

ROSE: What was his private one?

HUGO (*short*): He is a mathematician.

ROSE: Why don't we see him?

HUGO (*as short*): He travels.

OLD TONI: Ah, what a brilliant and delicious man!...

HUGO: Let's leave the subject of my brother.

OLD TONI (*not to be stopped*): Cruel and miraculous.—Unique
and mocking!

ROSE: Cruel?

OLD TONI: He had a tenderness so extreme—it had to be
hidden! Women were mad about him, Rosie! You would
fall in love—but it would be hopeless!

ROSE: Why?

OLD TONI: He loved his calculations—better than women!
"I don't love women!" he said. "I fill their imaginations!"

ROSE: And didn't he love them?

OLD TONI (*comically rueful*): Alas yes he did.

HUGO (*irritated*): Poor Baron!... Unlucky in love!

OLD TONI (*peaceably*): I am so old now that nothing is shocking! (*Finishing.*)—And a rage for life, Rosie! A divine
appetite!... And the prince of hoaxers!...

HUGO (*same deflecting intention*): Shall I see you at Ascot?

OLD TONI (*amused*): Ascot—alas—was last month! (*To* ROSE.)
He preached in the streets of Paris as a Revivalist! And took
the crowd out to supper!... His jokes had a quality of
clairvoyance. A violent, comic genius! (*Moving at last towards
the door.*) A Prince-Buffoon! Who used his buffoonery to
keep himself secret! (*Suddenly pausing at the photograph.*) The
Master's hand! Vuillard. You have the original. (*To* HUGO.)
I remember it when I stayed with you in Roumania.

HUGO: You stayed with *us*!—But was I in the nursery?

OLD TONI (*by-passing*): To me—as yesterday. (*Turning to*
ROSE.) A palace, Rosie. A private house that was a palace!

Such things don't exist any more. A magnificence—like the
gold crust of a picture's frame . . .

HUGO: Gone, gone—all that!

OLD TONI (*with his old leech-like mind, continuing*): Mountains.
Endless marshes. Ducks rising. —And your peasants—
liveried and undisciplined! Secure and joking! Wit—and
snow! Talk—and ortolans . . .

HUGO: —netted in great numbers! Kept in darkened rooms—
served on gold plates!—Who knows an ortolan now!

OLD TONI: The picture is still there?

HUGO: No. It was stolen. Years ago.

OLD TONI: . . . *Stolen!* Pictures can't hide! (ROSE *gets up.*)
What brushwork . . . even in a photograph! What grace—
in the sitter!

HUGO: It was painted for my brother. (*To* ROSE.) What
Vuillards has your father?

ROSE (*coming near them*): None.

HUGO: No Vuillard! In that great collection!

ROSE (*staring at the photograph*): I don't think . . . No, I'm sure
he hasn't . . . Who is this?

HUGO: What . . .

ROSE (*looking up into his face*): *Who is it?*

HUGO: My mother.

ROSE: It can't be your mother!

HUGO (*misunderstanding her*): She looks a girl there. She died
when I was two.

OLD TONI: She looks like you, Rosie.

ROSE: Oh no! Oh no . . . Not like me!

OLD TONI (*to* HUGO): Do you mean you've never traced it?
It's never come on the market?—But it will! It will! Pictures
of that magnificence don't disappear for good! Some rascally
rich man dies. . . . They always turn up in the end. . . .

ROSE (*cutting right across the picture-conversation, and reaching for
a card that stands on the bureau*): Oh there's my card—to ask
you to my ball! (*To* HUGO.) You're coming, aren't you?

HUGO: I don't go to balls.

FP—D

ROSE: Not to mine? ... (*Sharply disappointed.*) ... Why not to mine?

HUGO (*light, evading*): I might fall in love with you!

OLD TONI: Better than diamonds—for a girl at her first ball!

ROSE (*passing this off*): Toni—I forgot! Father rang from Paris this morning ...

HUGO: Isn't he coming for your ball?

ROSE: Coming! Of course he's coming! He took Wood Castle —to bring me out—this year.

OLD TONI (*rueful*): He took me too. But me he interviewed in Paris!

ROSE: Toni arranges everything. —He says all London's coming!

HUGO: Don't you know yourself?

ROSE: Oh—*we* don't know anybody! *We* can't ask anybody. We've only just set up shop as Pretenders! If you're rich, Toni says, you can always buy your way in! The foie gras's direct from Strasbourg and the pink champagne's from Rheims. The pictures are in the galleries, and the treasures are lit in the show cases ... (*She takes a deep breath and goes into fast "catalogue-language".*) Baccarat Bouquet Weights Musical boxes in agate the crystal pelicans the Fabergé parrots ... (*Pants.*) hippopotamuses in obsidian ... the Chinese ducks Ch'ien Lung ... (*Exhausted.*) ... and two superb Bactrian camels ... complete with grooms ...

HUGO: What a language!

ROSE: It's my cultural language. It does instead of Latin. There's to be a searchlight to light up the woods for thieves and an army of detectives. Come and see what we've made of Wood Castle! It's hideous.

OLD TONI (*reproachful*): Rosie ...

ROSE: People who collect things never have any taste! (*To* OLD TONI.) Father says he wants a third band ...

OLD TONI:—at *this* hour! But the ball's *tomorrow*!

ROSE:—to play in the water garden. And Mrs. Webster ... (*makes a face*) ... wants a list of the guests—in triplicate?

OLD TONI: I was once a diplomat. Now I earn my living catering to the wishes of her father's body-servant.

ROSE (*to* HUGO): Mrs. Webster attends to his body. But anything further would be a grizzly joke. She runs his bath for him and sees that the hotel beds face east and west. My father says men are too full-blooded for indoor work. Don't wait for me, Toni. Go without me.

OLD TONI (*going through door*): At least—whatever else I am—I'm not your chaperon! (*The door shuts on him.*)

ROSE (*instantly, with anxiety, to* HUGO): What's wrong with me—that you won't come to my ball?

HUGO (*soft*): I said . . . the reason!

ROSE: I wish you weren't joking.

HUGO: So do I.

ROSE: Last time we met you kissed me.

HUGO (*tender*): You dreamt it!

ROSE (*low*): I adore you.

HUGO (*teasing*): Why?

ROSE (*trying to make a joke of it*): Because you're a gentleman!—

HUGO (*something has caught his ear. He turns slightly towards bedroom door. As lightly*): Don't you know any gentlemen?

ROSE (*same*): No. Only collectors! (*Pause. He comes near her.*) —and because I feel at home where you are. . . . (*He takes her face in his two hands, without a word. Low.*) You don't say . . . much!

HUGO (*smiling*): When I was a boy my brother did all the talking! I'm unused to it!

ROSE (*softly, as though she spoke of love*): The one—much older?

HUGO: He brought me up . . . (*Breaks off. Listens.*)

ROSE: Are you listening for something? (*He doesn't appear to hear her, her hand on his sleeve.*) For what? (*Teasing.*) For her foot in the hall? . . . (*As he turns and looks at her.*) The next girl—after this one!

HUGO (*light*): Is that how I strike you?

ROSE (*stepping back—to look at him*): I don't know how you strike me! Since I met you I'm nervous—nervous about my life! I'm a ship, painted, and my sails flying! I'm about to be launched and the bottle broken over me. But I've never tasted the sea and tomorrow I must trust myself on it! (*Walking up and down restlessly.*) I shall have to look—as though I knew everyone! ... Amused, easy yet difficult! I shall have to live surrounded by men and be mysterious yet confidential! I shall have to invent secrets and call out intimate things ... (*Halting at a distance from him.*)

HUGO: Who tells you to?

ROSE (*pointing to the door*): My Confidante! He says I must whistle up success—like a dog out of a wood!

HUGO: And can't you?

ROSE: A man has all his life to make himself. A girl has to do it on a knife-edge!

HUGO: What does your father want for you?

ROSE: Something obscure ... but dressed in white!

HUGO: Doesn't he tell you?

ROSE: Sometimes a word is rung from him.

HUGO: By what?

ROSE: By a long silence.

HUGO (*moving close to her*): How old are you?

ROSE: Nineteen. (*With a kind of anxiety.*) But not young!

HUGO: Have you had other love ... affairs?

ROSE: Some.

HUGO (*something again catches his ear*): Then you know that, if necessary ... one can forget everything. (*Gravely.*) Especially love.

ROSE (*steadily, looking back into his face*): No.

HUGO: Yes. (*But his face stoops to hers. In an altered voice, loud.*) Rose ... Little Rose ... (*His arms round her.*)

ROSE (*her face turned up to his*): If I had you ... (*He draws her close.*) If you loved me ...

HUGO (*his face very near hers*): What day is it?

ROSE (*in a whisper*): Tuesday.

HUGO: I must only love you—(*Stops, then whispers.*)—on a Wednesday (*Begins to draw her head down on to his breast.*)

ROSE (*now hearing a noise herself, startled, turning*): What's that! *They turn. A hand has come through the bedroom door, Right. It holds a crumpled bunch of flowers, evidently taken from a vase.*

HUGO (*change of manner, nervous, imperative*): Take it! Take them! (*Pushes her. Low.*) Take the flowers!

ROSE (*reluctant*): Who is it?

HUGO (*urgent*): For you! Take hold of them! *She moves to the door and takes the bunch. Immediately the hand is withdrawn. The door is left just ajar.*

ROSE: Oh! . . . (*Brushing water from skirt.*) They're dripping!

HUGO: I'll wipe them. (*Takes bunch from her, wipes stems, brushes her skirt with his handkerchief; then moves towards the Exit door.*)

ROSE: But who was it?

HUGO (*nervous, overloud*): My lodger. (*Closing the bedroom door completely as he passes it.* ROSE *stops a moment and looks back at the door.*) Have you got your car?

ROSE: No. I'm walking. (*As he presses her towards the door.*) Must I go? Now?

HUGO: Take the flowers . . . Carry them! I'll come to the gate with you. (*She takes the bunch.*) If I ring . . . will you be in?

ROSE (*glancing over his shoulder at the bedroom door*): I sit all day by the telephone, so as not to miss anyone! I have to collect friends!

They pass through, leaving door open.

For a moment the room is empty. Then a tall figure in a dressing gown comes through the bedroom door, Right. PRINCE FERDINAND CAVANATI *has ceased to take any care of his appearance. His hair is unbrushed as though he had been lying down. The collar of his dressing gown stands up, and is kept up by a white silk scarf which is round his neck—to hide a certain slight crookedness on one side of his face. He has had a stroke: though now it hardly shows. He is a passionate, impatient, tyrannical, and charming man; shaken with the gaiety of inscrutable jokes—or with unheralded furies. When he speaks it is with a gusty energy, vigorous, imperious. His gestures are clumsy and violent and objects break that do not obey his will.*

HUGO (*re-entering; vexed*): Why the flowers?

FERDI: My blessing!

HUGO: On what?

FERDI (*airily*): Your love. Your marriage. And your begetting.

HUGO: You see a long way! Did you listen?

FERDI: Even the noblest Roumanian will listen if he can! (*He snaps up the silk blind which conceals what now turns out to be a ventilator. No mirror there.*) How long have you known her?

HUGO (*grudging*): A week.

FERDI: So it was a stroke of lightning and a thunder clash?

HUGO: Leave it.

FERDI: But I'm passionately interested! . . . Are you in love?

HUGO: Shall we say—in the first stages.

FERDI: What's her name?

HUGO: Rose. (*Adds.*) Portal.

FERDI: *Edward Portal*'s daughter! The man with the pictures!

HUGO (*returning good humour*): You know everything!

FERDI: I know where his money comes from. Arabs—and oil —and vision! With what speed these oil emperors put on magnificence! He bought a Braque last Wednesday—by cable. Simply instructing Sothebys to outbid everyone. I read it in *The Times*.—And that he's taken Wood Castle. And flown over his marvellous collection! . . . Except that I shall be dead this year I'd go down and see it.

HUGO (*passing this over*): No Vuillard—apparently.

FERDI: Of course he must have!

HUGO: She said not.

FERDI: Girls will say anything! How could he own that period —and have no Vuillard?—And how can she know! . . . Is she pretty?

HUGO: Yes.

FERDI: Young? (*Picking up the card, looking at it. Furiously.*) "*Mister*" Hugo Cavanati! . . . She gives a formal ball! (*Turning on him.*) Why always your title in your pocket?

HUGO: We have been over the arguments.

FERDI: Six hundred years a prince! . . . It isn't a trinket you inherit from our family!

HUGO: Since I live here . . . and know how the English react to Balkan princes. . . .

FERDI (*sarcastic*): . . . one has to be *so* careful?

HUGO: Of what?

FERDI: Of being too foreign! (*Abandoning sarcasm: stern.*) We who run like a steel cord through history—is that nothing? We who ruled—in that jungle which is the middle of Europe!—Tell me a tight moment where *we* didn't make a difference!—Tell me a battle! *We* were there! (HUGO *is silent. Change of tone.*) Are you going to this ball?

HUGO: No.

FERDI (*irritably*): Why not?

HUGO: A few reasons.

FERDI: *And I'm all of them!* —How you irritate me! And because it's the irritation of love—it's no better! Must you stick in my responsibility like a fishbone! (*Suddenly struck by a thought.*) . . . Would she marry you?

HUGO: She might.

FERDI (*with a sick man's sudden anger*): Go to her ball! Make love to her! Live a life of your own—and leave me to live mine!

HUGO: If it were that . . .

FERDI: To die my death then . . . (*Moves restlessly round the room, picks up a sherry glass, sniffs it, puts it down.*) Why must people who meet each other . . . *drink*? A boring party!

HUGO: I scrape up London to amuse you—through the wall!

FERDI: And get the Baron Santa Clara.

HUGO: I don't move any more—as they say—in the swim!

FERDI: Let me remind you that idioms get dated!—That old pansy who leaves a bearded wife at home! —He thought he "adored me"—in Constantinople! (*Stopping near photographs.*) I heard him speak of—the "grace of the sitter".

HUGO: He's seen the original. He says he stayed with us in

Roumania.

FERDI: He's boasting! (*Picking up the photograph and looking at it. Pauses.*)—Our guests! ... (*Remembering.*)—Rooms full of men and women talking—of remarkable things! Of a note of music—of a light seen—of a word said! (*Pause.*) There was applause for words! (*With a sudden flash of anger against the Present.*) Let us forget everything! *This* should be put away ... when you have guests!

HUGO: Put it away then. Anything you like.

FERDI (*with his clumsy violent movements trying to stuff the photograph into the narrow drawer of the escritoire; imperiously*): I like an end to it! I like the Dead to be dead! ... My mother's house was a university—where a young man blossomed like an apple tree! This picture doesn't exist any more! It's gone with a way of life! (*Vexed.*) ... And now the glass has broken! (*He abandons the drawer, leaving the photograph half in, half out of it. Rings the bell.*)

HUGO: Did you sleep badly?

FERDI: No. But I've given up the world—as one gives up smoking. And all the same, from time to time it makes one irritable! (*Remorsefully.*) I am bad tempered.

HUGO (*with humour*): I am used to living with a bad-tempered man!

FERDI: "A rage for life!"—I heard him say of me. (*As MATTHEW opens the door in answer to the bell, changes to gaiety, teasing him.*) A rage for *death*—haven't I, Matthew!

MATTHEW (*automatically, like an old nurse*): Now, now Highness ...

FERDI: Matthew drives out the Devil with my morning tea! But by eleven he's back again!

MATTHEW (*reprovingly*): Those who hate the world ...

FERDI: I don't hate the world. I've adored it. But I've been through it at top speed! (*Leaning forward to pick up something from a plant.*) A ladybird!—Look! (*Hand, palm upwards, holding ladybird. Then watching it, he turns the thumb upwards.*) She walks on my thumb!—On my complications of blood and skin! On my sensory tangles! (*Suddenly holding his thumb right under* MATTHEW'*s nose, making him jump.*) *On my thumb!*

MATTHEW: Yes, Highness.

FERDI: She feels me with her divine fear. She has no idea who I am! (*Leans forward to put ladybird back on plant. Turning suddenly.*) But if she were a ladybird of genius—if she knew in a flash—of all ladybirds—that I am Man! Then everything would drop into place! She'd have no need to go ladybirding! (*to* MATTHEW) Get me my orange juice. *And my Will.*

MATTHEW (*who has picked up the tray of glasses to take away; sourly*): Where is it?

FERDI: It was under my pillow when you made my bed! How should I know! (*As* MATTHEW *crosses to bedroom door.*) You saw the young lady?

MATTHEW: Aye.

FERDI: Was she pretty? (*He gets no answer to this. Using the title as a reproof.*) Should the *prince* marry her?

MATTHEW (*stolid*): I haven't thought.

FERDI: Then think.

MATTHEW (*hand on bedroom doorhandle*): My father was a Meenister. Unfrocked—as the Romans say. He became a Freethinker. He warned me against thought.

FERDI: The devil he did!

  MATTHEW *disappears into room*

(*He sits down at table. To* HUGO.) I must arrange a present for her in my Will—if she is to be a candidate! Would she like diamonds? (*Looks at* HUGO *who doesn't answer.*) Or could she appreciate the Chagall?

HUGO: *I* haven't thought!

FERDI: Then think. Otherwise I shall leave it to Father Gentilotti. Or might he think it a sin to accept a present from a suicide? These Catholics have such odd rules!

As MATTHEW *returns with some long parchment foolscap sheets. (Taking them from him and spreading them before him on table. Looking up at him.)* What shall I leave you? You'll want a keepsake. —the sculpture of my head?

MATTHEW (*sourly*): I hate it.

FERDI (*as he goes to door*): Have you made your Will, Matthew?

MATTHEW: Why should I?

FERDI: You are old. God will get you!

MATTHEW (*grim*): God will forgive me for never casting a thought towards Him. (*Exits.*)

HUGO (*as* FERDI *draws up the sheets of his Will*): Must we discuss it?

    They are both sitting.

FERDI: A Roumanian loves his Will! I like to be occupied by *in*essentials! —And people must be suddenly enriched! That's so amusing!

HUGO: What are you leaving to old Matthew?

FERDI: It's boring to leave things to the Old! Everything has to take a second journey! I've left him money. . . .

HUGO (*wryly*): This amuses you?

FERDI: Tremendously.

HUGO: Go ahead then.

FERDI (*getting up*): Am I a sadist? (*Walks towards a mirror on the wall.*)

HUGO (*shrugging*): You crack your death like a whip over my head!

FERDI (*over his shoulder*): Can't you take it?

HUGO (*lightly—because it is the only way it can be said*): One can't write a man's obituary—and the next moment quarrel with him! Say goodbye—and *not* say it! —It's like standing on a pin! (*Watching him look at himself in the mirror.*) Is it your face you're looking at?

FERDI: I am looking at my face. (*Tracing his features comically.*) —The spiral ears—the hole for feeding—the hole for breathing—like all mammals—(*Softly, to himself.*)—But is there memory. . . . (*Turning round towards* HUGO.) Why don't you get tired of it and let go? And let *me* go?

HUGO (*smiling*): I was always a dogged little boy.

FERDI: I have a rage for death! An explorer's rage! If a man

wants to travel—must he trip over the reproaches of his
stupid brother?

HUGO: I don't know. I only know how to be stubborn.

FERDI: What an ass you are! And I who genuinely prefer
dying! . . . (*Walks over to the window.*)

HUGO: Where does this lead to?

FERDI (*whipping round; a finger on his damaged cheek*): The night
this happened!

HUGO: When you hung over your eternal sums—and talked
me to sleep—murmuring with a pencil. . . .

FERDI (*returning across the room*): I asked you the time.

HUGO: It was four in the morning.

FERDI (*flippantly*): I got God that night!

HUGO: With your sums?

FERDI: I got a possibility—by calculation.

HUGO (*irritated; taking his cigarette case from his pocket*): You
were lucky!

FERDI: Unique! . . . Must you smoke? . . .—God's Feet—
moving in numerals!—(*Laughing sourly.*) He struck back. He
wasn't having it! He struck the gong for my disintegration!

HUGO (*slipping the case back in his pocket*): It doesn't show any
more.

FERDI: I am indifferent.

I use the symbol of God because it's a good one. It's
easier than X plus Z. It's Man's name for the Mystery.
(*Shrugging.*) You always hated mathematics! Besides—

HUGO: Not "hate". I can't perform!

FERDI: But piled on their alabaster steps—there's a territory of
unimaginable guesses! Do you suppose that when Einstein
predicted that the ray would be found to bend as it passed the
pull of the sun—and waited through four years of war for
the eclipse that would confirm it—that his was a *factual*
arrival of the mind?

HUGO: I should have thought it was.

FERDI: No. It was the lassoo of a genius—by which what was
outside human experience—was caught and drawn within it.

And during the last twenty-five years of his life in Prince-town he tried to get beyond it. And he couldn't. He knew that when it all adds up—all that he had guessed, all that he had proved—it still doesn't explain existence. (*Thoughtfully*.) I too. . . .

HUGO: What?

FERDI: Would you listen?

HUGO: Why not?

FERDI (*lightly*): Because, though you don't want to, you think me mad. (*Smiling indulgently*.) But is all China mad, all India mad, who treat life as a waiting room? —Am I to tell you?

HUGO: You owe it to me.

FERDI: Perhaps I do. (*Sits down opposite* HUGO *at the table*.) What's beyond experience? We can make guesses.

HUGO: And if the guesses are wrong?

FERDI: They always have been. It's immediately obvious—because of the enormous misfits. By mathematics we can conceive the unimaginable. Provided there's a clue. But there have been no clues. So we are driven back to picture, by analogy, from within our human experience. (*Pause*.) Imagine a tea party in a garden. The sun is low. The human shadows are thrown upon a wall. Who do they think they are?

HUGO: The shadows!

FERDI: Yes the shadows. Do they deduce who put them there? Who causes them to move, melt, vanish, reappear? They can't. They're flat, poor things! They're two-dimensional. —Pretend for a moment they are a group of scientists. . . .

HUGO: Come!

FERDI: No I am serious. Stick to it! —They work on the explanation of existence. As we do. One of them is so good at it that he guesses a third dimension, by analogy—though he has but two. Inventing an imaginary geometry he deduces the tea party. That was a pretty good achievement! But further he couldn't go. He couldn't imagine weight, or resistant edges causing collision, bumping, pain. Being a shadow—he had no clue.

HUGO (*fascinated*): And you?

FERDI: I'm the chap who was good at it. I found a clue. (*Pause.*) I have deduced—but not understood—the Reality of which I am the silhouette.

HUGO: And . . .?

FERDI (*levelly*): I am going to cross the garden to join the party.

HUGO: Suppose—when you cross—it cuts out the memory of the wall?

FERDI (*touching his cheek*): I crossed. That night. And there *was* memory. It's my return that cut it. (*Pause.*) Do I convince you?

HUGO: No.

FERDI (*hard*): I speak in parables—but I mean business. —I *don't* convince you?

HUGO: You see things clearly but I think you distort the deduction.

FERDI (*immediately in a rage*): You think I am some sort of paranoic! That's an insult to a mathematician! What can you do if I take a decision! *Fifty* means of escape!— You can't watch me for ever! (*Taking revolver from pocket and throwing it on the table.*) This one! Forty-nine others!

HUGO: I had supposed so.

FERDI: Then how prevent me?

HUGO (*bringing out his own small revolver and balancing it quietly between his fingers; softly*): By going with you.

FERDI (*aghast*): What! (*Then furious.*) Play-acting goose! Obstinate goose!

HUGO: Bien.

FERDI: *You won't use it!* (*No answer.*) . . . You don't *want* to die?

HUGO: I may have to.

FERDI (*beside himself*): I am a dead man! You are not a dead man! There's the difference! Why should you do what I do! . . . We are not twins—to wear the same tie! . . . (*Striding to his bedroom door, leaving the revolver forgotten, on the table.*) I am going to my room! (*He pulls roughly at the door handle.*)

HUGO: Ferdi ...

FERDI: With your "Ferdi" ... (*Drags the handle towards him; the door seems to stick. Turns and speaks with violence.*) When it's reasonable to die—men *don't* die! When they are in pain, in disreputable disease, in prison—they don't die! There's a small fear placed in men that keeps them alive! (*Shouting.*) But I no longer have it! (*Dragging at the door—the handle comes off in his hand.*) I told you yesterday it was loose! (*Pushing the handle back on to the shank but the shank falls back into the inside room. Turning and holding up the handle.*) The smallest of screws would have allowed me to get away from you! (*Shouting louder.*) It's fallen inside! Go round and put it back! (*Sinks panting into an armchair and hammers with his fists on the arm of it.*)

MATTHEW (*coming in with a glass of orange juice on a small tray*): You are driving the little one crazy! I could hear you in the pantry!

FERDI: Did no one come to mend that handle?

MATTHEW: I mended it myself, but you are so rough. (*He signs to HUGO to go round. HUGO goes through hall door.*) You are all he has, Highness. He suffers.

FERDI: Don't *I* suffer!

MATTHEW: And you drive him into a corner! You know what he is! He gets obstinate!

FERDI: He won't let me alone! He won't let me *die* alone!

MATTHEW (*kneeling with an old man's difficulty in front of him as he sits and putting on a velvet slipper that has come off*): It needs your mother here to think that important.

FERDI (*kicking off slipper again*): I forbid you!

MATTHEW (*reaching for the slipper*): Forbid me? I'm a man like another.

FERDI (*like a naughty child*): I am a gentleman and you are my servant.

MATTHEW (*smiling grimly; getting the shoe on*): Aye. That's long over.

FERDI (*getting to his feet; with a sudden sweet smile of affection*):
It never began, did it? . . . Come and put me to bed.

MATTHEW: Are you ill?

FERDI: Perhaps.

MATTHEW (*as* HUGO *opens the door and stands in it*): What do
you feel?

FERDI (*as he goes through; histrionic to annoy* HUGO): The bowels
of the earth—pulling me. (*He goes into his bedroom, drawing
the door shut after him.*)

HUGO (*looking at the shut door*): For God's sake . . . what's he
after?

MATTHEW (*picking up the handle, setting it on the shank*): His old
friend Death. . . . Let him alone, Mr. Hugo.

HUGO: If I let him alone—what's to become of him?

MATTHEW (*shrug*): What becomes of all of us. (*The door opens
and* FERDI *stands again in it.*) Changed your mind, Highness?

FERDI (*re-entering room*): People who suffer—suffer most in bed.

HUGO (*touching the revolver lying on the table*): That's my
brother's. Give it to him. . . . I'm going for a walk.

MATTHEW (*fetching the revolver, grumbling*): Guns and pills and
poisons . . . what a house! (*Gives the gun to* FERDI.) You
ought to sleep in a coffin!

FERDI (*pocketing the gun*): I shall.

HUGO (*as he crosses to the hall door; holding up two fingers,
mocking*): Two!

FERDI: What?

HUGO (*going out of the door. Smiling*): Two coffins! (*Goes out.*)

FERDI (*after him in a second, crosses the room to the door, which
he drags violently open; calling after* HUGO): Look out then
. . . if you don't believe me—look out for my *good* days!
Look out for my jokes! *A suicide always kills himself—when
he's at the top of his form!* (*He slams the hall door shut, and
returns, pleased with himself.*)

MATTHEW (*taking his knife from his pocket and using the blade
as a screw driver to fix the set-screw on the handle*): You used

to be so gay.

FERDI (*seating himself in armchair, back to hall door*): That's the measure by which I'm sad!

MATTHEW: You could keep it to yourself.

FERDI (*complacent*): I rub his nose in death!

MATTHEW: What would your mother say?

FERDI: She would not recognize me.

MATTHEW (*straightening himself; direct*): And you do it with torture, Highness. You make him die every day without stopping. (*Squarely.*) He'll be better when you've done it.

FERDI (*laughing*): I never heard it put so straight! You take the fun out of dying!

MATTHEW (*exasperated*): You have your own way too much!

FERDI (*amused*): I shall meet God soon. He'll put me in my place!

MATTHEW (*placing a small stool in front of* FERDI's *armchair*): Put your feet up, Highness. Have some sleep.

FERDI: Sleep! —Have you put something in my orange juice?

MATTHEW: Why not?

FERDI: Bring me the photograph. There ...! Stuck in the drawer.

MATTHEW (*fetching it*): It's broken.

FERDI: Leave it beside me. Here on the table. You can measure it for a new glass later. If I'm to sleep—(*Smiling up at him.*)—tell me your bedtime story!

MATTHEW (*cross*): Laugh at that now!

FERDI (*tender*): I don't laugh—old nurse.

MATTHEW: You could tell it to yourself!

FERDI: "There was once a palace ... in the middle of Europe ..." ... go on ... (*Smiling up at him.*) "where a princess had a baby ..." It's not the same—if *I* tell it!

MATTHEW: I was brushing the lawn—after a summer storm. Ye know well! And Her Highness came out ...

FERDI (*leaning back and closing his eyes*): In what dress?

MATTHEW: One of those she wore in the garden—like a yellow plum. She came down over the steps from the terrace, carrying the baby ...

FERDI (*eyes shut, murmuring*): ... better than books ...

MATTHEW: "You are an English gardener," she said. (I was Scottish but she didn't know the difference.) "Make me an English garden for the baby. Hold him while I draw a plan." And I held you, Highness, —grimed with the summer leaves. —And she sat down on the steps and drew in a little book she had.

FERDI (*murmuring like a child who knows well what should come next*):—And the garden?

MATTHEW: "A square of rosemary,"—she said. "And inside a square of lavender. And inside again a little lawn with daisies."—I carried your Highness up the steps for her. And she took you—and went in.

FERDI: The most beautiful woman in the world.

MATTHEW: Yes Highness.

FERDI: And dead.

MATTHEW: Yes Highness. It's natural.

FERDI: Not to me.

MATTHEW (*turning towards door; stopping*): When your father died you had too much power—and too early! You were too clever, you were too much loved! *That* is what is not natural!

FERDI (*smiling—looking in front of him*): And when I grew older—*still* no one could resist me! (*Turning round to* MATTHEW.) Too many women—you seem to think— Matthew? (*Looking round the arm of his chair. As there is no answer he continues gravely, looking in front of him.*) And yet— au fond—I have had only two loves! My mother—and my brother. The dead and the living are mingled in pain. ...

    MATTHEW *goes into the bedroom and closes the door.* (*Sleepily, putting his arm out so that the hand lies palm upwards on the pieces of glass that cover the picture.*) ... the dead ... and the living ... are mingled ... (*Softly.*) in pain. (*His head drops a little forwards.*)

The hall door opens noiselessly behind him. ROSE *looks in. Then slips in, Gently she shuts the door.*

FERDI (*raising his head without looking round*): What's that!...
Who's there?

ROSE: God knows!... (*Moving quickly to the bedroom door
Right to cut off his retreat.*) I wish I knew!

FERDI (*springing to his feet and withdrawing his hand so quickly
from the broken glass that the hand is lightly cut. He stands with
his back to her, his hands fly to the back of his neck trying to
pull up and adjust the white silk scarf so that it again covers the
lower half of his face*): Go away!... Excuse me!... I don't
see people. ...

ROSE: There's blood!

FERDI (*without turning round*): What blood?

ROSE: On your scarf. On your hand. You've cut yourself.
(*Looking up at ventilator.*) As I thought ... There's a hole
through! You were listening!

FERDI (*aware by a side glance that he cannot get to his bedroom, he
moves quickly to the window, wrapping up his hand as he goes
in one end of the scarf. He speaks to her, his back turned, as he
looks out of the window*): Go away! Why did you come back?
... Shall I call Hugo?

ROSE (*from in front of his bedroom door*): You can't! I watched
him go out. ... Won't you turn round?

FERDI: I am ill.

ROSE: Why did you give me the flowers?

FERDI: What did you do with them?

ROSE: I threw them away. They were only out of a vase. He
said you were the lodger.

FERDI: He is too kind. I am a poor relation. Why did you
come back?

ROSE: I reasoned with myself you might be Hugo's brother.
... *Please turn round.*

FERDI: One side of my face is not the same as the other.
(*Slowly he turns. She looks at him.*)

ROSE: But all the same you are a handsome man.

FERDI: Thank you.

ROSE: Don't you believe me?

FERDI: I have outgrown young women. But thank you.

ROSE: You must have had lots of love affairs.

FERDI: The latest is with God.

ROSE: Are you a religious man?

FERDI: I am a mathematician.

ROSE: Is that why your hair's not brushed and you don't put on your clothes?

FERDI: I am going on a journey and it's not yet time to dress.

ROSE: People who are leaving (*Hesitates.*) make the best kind of confessors. . . . I'm in love with your brother.

FERDI: Why do you tell me that?

ROSE: Because I have taken a sort of pill for truth. When one means to come into someone's family—one should warn them.

FERDI: Of what?

ROSE: Of who you are.

FERDI (*rudely*): Who are you?

ROSE (*with an arrogance to match his rudeness*): I'm to be this season's top production. (*Pause. Same arrogance.*) And rich.

FERDI (*mocking*): We are rich too.

ROSE: And pretty.

FERDI: I am indifferent.

ROSE: I'm not flirting. I'm cataloguing. What do you want to know—that would make me suitable?

FERDI: The depths of your heart—and the length of your constancy. What do you want—in a man?

ROSE: That he should know his way round—at the top of my mind.

FERDI: And the bottom of your heart?

ROSE: That's not so important.

FERDI: Are you a virgin?

ROSE: Why?

FERDI: Virgins have a driving force—without stopping to consider! And a conception of men—got by whispering together! They have little to recommend them.

ROSE: Are all the rules wrong then?

FERDI: Some other man will have more time to tell you.

ROSE (*hotly*): No! No one tells me—anything! Even my dog can't tell—what he sees when he sees me! Even my father . . .

FERDI: Do you and he get on together?

ROSE: We share a sort of silence.

FERDI: That is family life!

ROSE: He has his private dream about me—in which everything is mistaken. He hunts in silence—for a likeness . . .

FERDI: To your mother?

ROSE (*lightly*): To some woman—some ideal! We are shy of each other. I am shy of a man who doesn't know who I am! When he sees me in the morning he says "Have you slept well?" Sometimes I have slept with the gardener's boy.

FERDI: My ears, which are sharp, detect the accents of untruth!

ROSE (*annoyed*): That's as well! It was only a play on words!

FERDI: You are like somebody drunk—who has lost the exact meaning of words! You should be alone till it passes.

ROSE: It s a marvel you can be so rude!

FERDI: I am now a man of frightful purity! But if I had been as I once was I would have slept with you.

ROSE (*opening her little bag and drawing out a small jewelled revolver*): I take precautions.

FERDI (*a roar of laughter*): Good God—what a house for guns! . . . Is it loaded?

ROSE: Unless my maid forgot it.

FERDI: Who gave it to you?

ROSE: My father. We travel together. I get left about in odd places . . . (*Pause.*) . . . like a cat in the garden of Europe overnight.

FERDI (*mocking*): You read too much!

ROSE (*defiant*): Yes! In hotel bedrooms.

FERDI: So it's all invented?

ROSE: But there's the revolver!

(*Enter* MATTHEW *suddenly, and stops short at sight of the little gun. He carries a square of glass.*)

FERDI (*coldly, to* MATTHEW): What astonishes you?

MATTHEW (*embarrassed, mumbling*): I found a bit of glass downstairs . . .

FERDI: It might do. Give it to me. I am entertaining a visitor.

MATTHEW (*backing to door*): Pardon . . . Highness . . . (*He exits.*)

ROSE: "Highness"?

FERDI (*carrying the glass to the table; over his shoulder*): I am a prince. (ROSE *follows him; mocking.*) The first time you meet love in the fairy stories—it's a prince! (*He stands at the table picking the broken bits of glass away from the photograph.*)

ROSE (*taking up her own card of invitation and scrutinizing it*): Is Hugo too a prince?

FERDI (*mocking*): Do you want a prince at your ball? (*She looks up at him.*) Has he made love to you?

ROSE: Doesn't it show on my face?

FERDI: Nothing. You could pass in the street! What did he say to you? (*She is silent.*) But there's one thing one never knows—what one's brother whispers to a woman!

ROSE: You're jealous!

FERDI: As a mother.

 What sort of girl are you?

ROSE (*with a shrug*): It seems no use answering.

FERDI: When one buys a horse one says— "Has it heart?"

ROSE (*inimical*): But the horse doesn't answer. You don't think I'm good enough. It's because you stopped him that he won't come to my ball!

FERDI: I . . . !

ROSE: Did you quarrel?

FERDI: What about?

ROSE: About me. (*Putting her finger on the photograph.*) That wasn't broken when I left!

FERDI (*cold*): But now it's broken.

ROSE (*picking it up*): It's Hugo's mother, isn't it?

FERDI: Leave his mother out of it!

ROSE: Ah but I can't! She's my trump card! Or her photograph is ... (*He looks at her.*) If I told you I'd seen this picture. ...

FERDI: You haven't.

ROSE (*watching him*): If it came back to me ... (*Tantalizing.*) If I could remember ... (*Waits.*) I don't ask much! Just Hugo at my ball!

FERDI: And if he came you'd say that in some gallery or other. ...

ROSE (*moving away to the mirror*): Do I look like her?

FERDI (*exasperated*): Only as one chair looks like another! Two arms. A back. The seat!

ROSE (*goaded by his manner—turning round*): This isn't all the picture! It's the central figure—enlarged!

FERDI: How do you know?

ROSE: I've seen it.

FERDI: Do you know one picture from another?

ROSE: I ought to! I ... (*Stops.*)

FERDI: What?

ROSE: Do I get Hugo?

FERDI: You've told me nothing! Describe the picture.

ROSE (*hesitating; her eyes closed, remembering*): ... all sorts of yellows ... It's a garden. —Painted like amber. It's the light. Down at the bottom—leaves, with veins, like fish-bones. And on the left—stripes. ...

FERDI: Stripes?

ROSE: Rods. Like bamboos. Yellow. ... (*As though suddenly and clearly remembering.*)* They're the slats—of a shutter— outside a window.

FERDI (*breathless*): And the *dress*? *What colour?*

ROSE: Do I get Hugo?

FERDI (*shouting at her*): *Yes, you get Hugo!*

ROSE: It's an apricot dress.

FERDI: *He* has it! Your *father*!

ROSE (*alarmed*): No!

(*Note: This has to be recollected in Act Two.)

FERDI: Nonsense! With that description! You've seen it lately. —The *one* private collection! For years my lawyer's watched them. . . .

ROSE: It's not in his collection!

FERDI (*contemptuous*): No! Because it's in his safe! My God— the rascal . . .

ROSE (*in angry defence*): My father bought it!

FERDI: Yes and from whom? And knowing it was stolen! The whole art world has known it! Yes, yes you get my brother! I'll send him down to see it.

ROSE (*desperate*): You can't! He can't. . . . It's in his bedroom . . .

FERDI (*incredulous*): Openly? On his wall?

ROSE (*defeated*): It's hidden. Behind another picture. Over his bed.

FERDI: Behind—a *picture*!

ROSE: A painting by Sargent. A man with a dog. I saw the Sargent—hinged and swinging open . . .

FERDI: Over his bed! And mad enough to hide it! (*Crosses room to bell.*) And what did you think—when you saw it hidden? (*Keeps his finger on the bell.*)

ROSE (*reluctantly*): I thought perhaps—he might have loved her.

FERDI: You *did*!—My *mother*!—(*As* MATTHEW *opens the door, dishevelled from sleep, waistcoat buttons undone.*) You shall hear what *I* think! (*To* MATTHEW, *violently.*) When my mother's portrait was stolen . . .

MATTHEW (*bemused*): Stolen . . . Highness . . .

FERDI: Wake up! More than twenty years ago! When the picture was taken . . . whom did we suspect?

MATTHEW: The . . . valuer. When your father died—the one who came to value the gold snuff boxes.

FERDI: Did they look for him!

MATTHEW: The police did.

FERDI: Was he found?

MATTHEW: They found his body.

FERDI (*lightly*): Too dead!

MATTHEW: Too dead for what?

FERDI: To be this young lady's father!

MATTHEW (*deprecating—to* ROSE): His Highness makes jokes, Miss.

ROSE: I don't like his jokes.

FERDI: When's your ball?

ROSE: ... Tomorrow.

FERDI: Put me on your list.

ROSE: To come to Wood Castle!

FERDI: To come to your ball and see the picture.

MATTHEW (*horrified: Ferdi hasn't been out for years*): Highness....

ROSE: I can't take a guest into my father's bedroom!

FERDI: I'll come as a waiter.

ROSE: The detectives know all the waiters.

FERDI: I'll come as a clown.

ROSE: And what do I get out of that?

FERDI: A joke.

ROSE: I don't care for jokes. I'm too young for them.

MATTHEW: His Highness doesn't mean it.

FERDI (*gay*): His Highness *means* it! I'll come as an art dealer! I'll offer to sell him his picture! —"from unknown sources —a Vuillard of importance—lost for twenty years" ...

ROSE: My father would see through you!

FERDI: Not he! I was the *friend*—of the men your father only buys! (*Catching at the corner of the frame of the Self-Portrait by Seurat.*) Has he *met* Monsieur Seurat?

MATTHEW (*hurrying forward as the picture, dragged by its frame, appears about to fall*): Highness. ...

FERDI (*letting go of picture; delighted with himself*): I'll twist his tail for him! (*To* MATTHEW.) It's a long time since we had a joke Matthew. We'll have a last one! By God, we'll have a last one! (*To* ROSE.) Has your father a private number? I'll ring him.

ROSE: He's in Paris. ... Are you mad?

FERDI (*mocking*): I have my channels of unreason. But they're private! (*To* MATTHEW.) *Get a taxi—for the lady!*

ROSE: Oh. ...

MATTHEW: Shall I stay, Miss?

FERDI (*waving him away*): Unnecessary! She's armed to the teeth!

ROSE (*to* MATTHEW, *as he goes to door*): *Is* he mad?

MATTHEW (*in doorway*): No, Miss. But so wilful it comes to the same thing. (*Exits.*)

FERDI (*airily*): So you get a prince at your ball!

ROSE (*angry*): I want the other one!

FERDI: Contrive I see that picture . . .

ROSE: What can I do?

FERDI: A girl in love can do anything!

ROSE: You're a devil!

FERDI (*laughing*): Well, make a bargain with the Devil! What time's the ball?

ROSE: At ten.

FERDI: Get dressed at eight. This is good measure! I'll send him down at nine. I'll come at midnight . . .

ROSE: How shall I know you?

FERDI (*histrionic*): By my dark glitter. . . . (*Turning as he hears* HUGO *come into the open doorway.*) *I've news for you!*

ROSE (*nervous*): Oh! . . .

FERDI (*mocking*): *Such* a little word!

ROSE: . . . what are you going to say—in front of him . . .

FERDI (*to* HUGO): She wants to marry you! . . . We get on badly—I said I'd turn it over in my mind!

MATTHEW (*reappearing*): The taxi's waiting.

ROSE (*rushing over to doorway, pushing past* HUGO; *turning, furious, to* FERDI): *I came to make friends.* . . .

FERDI (*laughing*): I don't make friends!

ROSE: *I hate you!*

FERDI: I forgive you.

She dashes out. HUGO, *after a look at his brother, goes after her.* MATTHEW *remains standing in the doorway, looking down the passage after them.*

(*In high good humour, to* MATTHEW.) Order a car for tomorrow!

MATTHEW (*grumbling, coming into room*): Tomorrow's my silver day.

FERDI (*sitting down at the table where the parchment sheets of the Will are lying*): Silver? ... We have only jade, malachite, onyx, shagreen ... (*Making a mark with his pen against something on the Will; looking up*): Have I a coat still? Or have you let the moth get into everything?

MATTHEW: Why should I?

FERDI: Because you counted on it I should never go out again! (HUGO *is again in doorway. Shaking the parchment sheets at him.*) *The Czarina's Gold Vanity Set—to Old Toni!* I've just thought of it!

HUGO: Why did she come back?

FERDI (*joyous—further thought*): *The gold razors—to his bearded wife!*

HUGO (*steadily*): Why did she come back?

FERDI: To ask us to her ball! —One last joke dearest! The very last one! She loves you! ... Don't you want love?

HUGO: Everything I want is in abeyance.

FERDI: *Cancel the coffins!*

HUGO: What's in the wind, Matthew?

MATTHEW: His Highness is over-excited. It will all end in tears.

CURTAIN

ACT II

Time: The ball has started.

The Scene: Wood Castle: in Edward Portal's "library" in his private wing which is on garden-level.

Description of the "library".

Stage Left are two doors—next to each other—of Portal's bedroom and bathroom. The bathroom door must be taken as connecting with the bedroom by another unseen door within.

The main ballroom and castle-proper lie on Stage Right, reached through double doors.

Upstage Centre: a long, low casement window, the garden not much below it.

Upstage Left is a small service door, flush with panelling, and not very noticeable.

This library is a room of horror. The ceiling: embossed gold lincrusta, heavily strapped with beams. The walls: panelled dark oak, and here and there lightened by sets of shelves with imitation books of gilt and leather. One such set hides a wall cupboard (for drinks) and can be opened. Heads of Romans stand on columns. There are altogether seven Roman heads. Four are on short plinths of marble—and stand on bookcase or side-table. Two are on floor-columns—either side of the double doors. The seventh has a gilt base and surmounts the pediment of the door to Portal's bedroom. The fireplace (mock Tudor) is of carved stone. A pyramid of griffons reaches to a shield with a crest of cartwheels. The flagged hearth has "Gothic" dogs. The hearth's base is piled with three-foot logs electrically lit.

"Jacobean" velvet curtains, heavily embossed in raised red and white "cut" patterns, blot out the over-leaded windows. Side *tables and chairs are of the extreme "meubles français" type (priceless pieces, but ill-suited to the room). A large Buhl writing table stands centre, inlaid with tortoise-shell and brass. Papers are laid in order on this table, weighted down with glass paper weights. There is an airmail package lying on the table.*

Somewhere in the room is a complicated house-switchboard so that Portal may speak to any department in the castle. Over a chair are laid ready two dressing-gowns. One is of dark royal blue silk, with peacocks and palm fronds heavily embroidered in gold and silver threads—Indian or Chinese; the other a simple short black silk kimono. A gold skull on a stand (possibly for cigarettes) is on a side table.

★　　★　　★

Description of Edward Portal: Powerfully built, over-dressed; jewels on his fingers, astrakhan on his collar (his errors in taste are his own affair); silent, controlled, sardonic (he can smile, but he does not share the smile). An alarming man.

When ROSE *comes on she wears a white ball dress, the most beautiful dress that Paris can devise. Perhaps a dead-white organza, so that she has the frilled whiteness of a daisy—but a daisy of the world.*

Mrs. Webster wears the dark dress of a housekeeper. No apron, soft white cuffs.

Hugo wears tails, white waistcoat.

Old Toni, the same, but with a buttonhole.

Benzuto is a Mohammedan. He wears a fez. Otherwise he wears well-cut English clothes (black). He must wear glasses of some kind, or use them occasionally, because in the Act it will be necessary for him to polish them with his handkerchief, which he shakes out of the window. It is possible that, in order to disguise the effect of his stroke, he wears sideburns. He has no accent at all; or, if anything, a slight French accent. He has dignity, is suave and polished. He is a Turk, born in Egypt, brought up in Paris. He may have had a year at Eton.

When the CURTAIN *goes up,* MRS. WEBSTER *and a young footman—*ROBIN—*are momentarily expecting* PORTAL'*s return from Paris. He is very late. They both stand near the double doors, ready to draw them open when* PORTAL'*s step is heard.*

ROBIN *is of fresh and boyish appearance. He wears the yellow and black striped waistcoat of a footman. Talk is subdued while they listen.*

ROBIN: The caterer's men smashed a case of champagne glasses.

MRS. WEBSTER: That's their affair. (*Silence. She draws up a soft white cuff and looks at her wrist-watch.*)

ROBIN: He's late.

MRS. WEBSTER (*dry*): He's his own master. (*Silence.*) When he comes—wait by the door for orders.

ROBIN (*hearing something, puts his hand on the large black door handle; tonelessly—listening*): The second lorry with the ice is just unloading. (*No answer.*) There's a waiter drunk.

MRS. WEBSTER: Send him back in the ice lorry. (*A sharp movement: Arrival. They draw the doors open.*)

PORTAL *enters, barely nods.*

A chauffeur follows carrying a light overcoat and an air-travel suitcase.

PORTAL *carries a "serviette" of black leather.*

ROBIN *takes the suitcase and overcoat from the chauffeur (who exits) and is about to carry both into the bedroom.*

PORTAL: Leave my coat. I've things in the pockets.

ROBIN *puts the overcoat carefully on a chair and carries the suitcase into the bedroom. He then remains waiting for orders at main doors.*

PORTAL *goes to centre table, takes off his gloves. Glances at papers arranged for him.*

MRS. WEBSTER *picks up the black silk kimono and holds it ready.*

PORTAL (*as he takes off the coat of his suit*): The other one.

She puts down the black one and helps him into the Eastern one. Now, glittering from head to foot, he feels at home.

PORTAL: Any messages? —Don't tell me more than you have to.

MRS. WEBSTER: Your number was wanted in Paris. The name's there.

PORTAL (*moving to another table, to empty contents of serviette*): He rang me. An art dealer. He'll be here in half an hour.

MRS. WEBSTER: *Tonight?* You've hardly time to dress!

PORTAL: The ball goes on till morning.

MRS. WEBSTER: You'll be late.

PORTAL: I shan't be missed. (*Taking small parcels, spectacles, a book, etc., from serviette.*) Robin.

ROBIN: Sir.

PORTAL: Two brandy glasses. And sandwiches. (*As* ROBIN *goes.*)—And Robin. (ROBIN *turns.*) Ring the two lodges. There's a gentleman—*not* on the guest list—expected. He's to be brought here—to me.

The name's—(*Hesitates.*)

MRS. WEBSTER: Benzuto.

PORTAL (*as* ROBIN *is half through the door; louder*): Instead of sandwiches—bring lobster.

MRS. WEBSTER: With brandy it'll kill you.

ROBIN *waits.*

PORTAL: It'll kill the visitor. I've eaten. (*To* ROBIN.) Bring cold tongue then.

ROBIN *exits.*

PORTAL *goes to the concealed bottle-cupboard, behind some books and a grille of wire; opens it, takes out an old brandy liqueur bottle.*

MRS. WEBSTER (*indicating list on centre table*): The list of the guests.

PORTAL: I don't want it.

MRS. WEBSTER (*under her breath*): The *list* won't bite you!

PORTAL (*as he looks at the label on the bottle*): Did the dress come in time?

MRS. WEBSTER: Yes.

PORTAL (*returning with bottle—to table*): How does she look in it?

MRS. WEBSTER: Overdressed. (*It is apparent by now that she allows herself, and he allows her, a certain dry intimacy.*)

PORTAL: God help her.

MRS. WEBSTER: She won't need it.

PORTAL (*by-passing this*): Are the gloves here? I sent three pairs.

MRS. WEBSTER: She left them here—in the parcel.

PORTAL (*a glance: no comment. Opening another parcel*): New bath salts. (*Fumbling with key chain.*) And a new sponge. Run my bath. (*Detaches key.*) If he comes while I'm in the bath— *lock my bedroom door.* (*Quietly.*) I may want cash from the safe tonight.

MRS. WEBSTER: Much?

PORTAL: How much is there?

MRS. WEBSTER: Four thousand. In tens.

PORTAL (*giving her the safe key*): That will do for a deposit. (*She goes into the bathroom, picking up the bath salts on the way, leaving door ajar.*)

OLD TONI (*opening main door and coming in; flutingly*): Home again!

PORTAL (*with distaste*): Ah. (*Pause. Using paper-knife from table, he slits the airmail parcel, shakes out one pair of long white gloves.*) People seem still arriving.

OLD TONI (*a touch of explaining*): That goes on all night.

PORTAL (*sarcasm*): Really? (*Putting him back in his place.*) Have the gold bowls and the centre pieces for the supper tables come down from the bank?

OLD TONI (*in his artificial voice*): I believe so.

PORTAL: And breakfast—now it's so fine—in the woods?

OLD TONI (*poetical*): Trestle tables under the trees at dawn.

PORTAL: Very uncomfortable. (*Laying the gloves on the table.*) Did they in the end wire the pictures to the main house-alarm?

OLD TONI (*off-hand*): I think men came down to see about it this morning.

PORTAL (*slipping off his dressing-gown; displeased*): Did they—in the Diplomatic Service—take a loose view of tight orders? (*Puts on his coat.*)

OLD TONI: I can assure you—everything has been seen to!

PORTAL: When people work for me (*Grim.*)—I like everything seen to—*twice*. (*Exits by small personal door leading to iron staircase and picture gallery.*)

MRS. WEBSTER (*from bathroom doorway; steam comes out*): And you a baron.

OLD TONI: As you say. No doubt it puts an edge on it.

MRS. WEBSTER: As you say.

Enter ROBIN, *tray, glasses, tongue on small oval silver dish, etc. When he puts the tray down on the centre table it can be seen that the dish of cold tongue is on top of the plate, to save room.*

ROBIN (*to* OLD TONI): Mr. Portal, sir, asking for you.

OLD TONI (*wry—to* MRS. WEBSTER): Whose dog am I?

MRS. WEBSTER: His. (*Disappears into bedroom.*)

OLD TONI: I've wagged my tail too long! (*Moving towards door, pauses by* ROBIN. *Mock-tender.*) Pink as a peach—and brown as an apple. (*Moving to door—flicking* ROBIN'*s face as he passes.*) Edible! (*He exits.* ROBIN *stares after him.* MRS. WEBSTER *comes in from bedroom.*)

ROBIN: What's that then?

MRS. WEBSTER: He's had his face tidied. (*Inspecting tray.*) Take the dish *off* the plate, heavens! It should never have been carried in *on* it!

ROBIN (*solemnly*): I've been upset, Mrs Webster. (*She looks at him.*) Miss Rose kissed me.

MRS. WEBSTER (*laconic*): When did she have time to do that?

ROBIN: She sent for champagne in her bedroom. She said she needed it.

MRS. WEBSTER: You're a footman, aren't you? . . . Take the rough with the smooth and the kicks with the kisses. (*To bedroom door.*) And if you want to grow up—go and listen to the hired waiters talking. (*Exits into bedroom.*)

ROSE(*from garden;* HUGO *behind her but out of sight*): Robin! ... (*Puts her head in.*) Robin. ... Has my father come?

ROBIN: Yes, Miss Rose.

ROSE: Where's he gone? (ROBIN *makes no reply because he is a bit scared—having been so recently kissed. Half scrambling on to sill.*) Give me a hand, Robin ...

HUGO (*from garden*): Oughtn't we to go back?

ROSE (*kneeling on sill, turning to speak to him*): As nobody knows whose ball it is—what does it matter? (*Putting her hand out to* ROBIN.) Pull! *Pull!* (*Laughs.*) Are you afraid of me? (*She scrambles in, jumps down. To* HUGO *behind her.*) Come on in! ... (*Noticing that* ROBIN *is exiting through Main Door.*) He's in a panic! (*Smiling after him.*) ... I kissed him! (*Dropping her head on* HUGO'*s shoulder, uninvited. Laughing—looking into his face.*) I was so starved for love! (*Pivoting her head on his shoulder she catches sight of* MRS. WEBSTER *in* PORTAL'*s bedroom doorway. Not moving.*) ... I am drunk, Mrs. Webster.

MRS. WEBSTER: What am I to say to that?

ROSE (*head still on shoulder*): I want this young man for a husband. I want to worship and obey him. (*She leaves* HUGO'*s side. He takes a step back near window ready for exit into garden.*) What good word can you put in for me?

MRS. WEBSTER: You should be with your guests.

ROSE: I've shaken hands for half an hour. Half of them hustled by me. (*Going a step towards* MRS. WEBSTER.) Have you heard about love? (*Beginning in irony but growing in feeling.*) Do you know the blazing anticipation? As though one was heading for heaven? (*Pause.*) We met last week. (*Catch in her voice.*) I seemed to walk towards an enormous glory—

MRS. WEBSTER (*cutting her short*): As you say—you've had too much to drink.

ROSE: I've been stoking—stoking—stoking ... as the boiler-men keep at the dying fires! But the ship's sinking! I can't

FP–E

blow the embers even with stoking!

As MRS. WEBSTER *turns to go into bedroom again.*

Aren't you ashamed of yourself being a woman and not helping me?

MRS. WEBSTER *disappears into the bedroom.*

You should tell him I have a heart of gold— (*Leaning against door jamb.*) —for I have! But if a man doesn't care for you —does one get over it?

MRS. WEBSTER (*reappearing so suddenly that* ROSE *takes a step back*): Some can. Some can't. Most do.

ROSE (*startled*): You're very brief! —If you can spare me one more sentence . . .

MRS. WEBSTER: What do you want to say?

ROSE: Things that are too hard to ask a woman standing in a doorway! (*Pause. With bravado.*) There comes a time when you want to take things further—

MRS. WEBSTER: How much further?

ROSE: Are there men who—go backwards—the more one goes forwards? (*Waits.*) Should I run after—a man who runs away from me?

MRS. WEBSTER: D'you think I'd know?

ROSE: You're a woman! (*Infuriated—ready to say anything.*) —And now that I need all the wits of the Serpent in Eden— to *trap* a man—can you tell me how to?

MRS. WEBSTER: No.

ROSE (*half following her—as a child does—continuing an argument*): He won't love me as I seem to be!—Shall I tell him— how I am?

MRS. WEBSTER (*ominous*): Count ten then! (*She takes the evening papers from a table near main doors—and puts them on centre table.*)

ROSE: —and while I was waiting about for my father—all over Europe—

MRS. WEBSTER: Are you going to damn yourself?

ROSE (*with despair and violence*):—I slept with seventeen men!

MRS. WEBSTER (*a shrug*): It's told. So what.

ROSE: —Unless I've forgotten someone!

MRS. WEBSTER: It's easy to sleep with a man. Much harder not to.

ROSE (*staring at her*): Why didn't you say so then! *Stop!* Look at me! ... Do you *know* about love?

MRS. WEBSTER: I have work to do.

ROSE (*sharp*): What's that picture—in there—to my father?

MRS. WEBSTER: Ask him.

ROSE: I mean the picture—*behind* the other!

MRS. WEBSTER *suddenly stands straighter.*

How long has he had it?

MRS. WEBSTER: He had it when I met him.

ROSE (*struck by the expression*): "Met" him?

MRS. WEBSTER (*correcting*): When he engaged me.

ROSE: Have *you* ever been jealous. ... (*Insolently.*) —Might you have been his mistress?

MRS. WEBSTER (*icy*): I might have been.

ROSE: You hate me—don't you?

MRS. WEBSTER: You're loose in your ways.

ROSE: You say that in front of the young man?

MRS. WEBSTER: What have you said in front of him?

ROSE: I must be very drunk ... (*Dismissing it all; insulting.*) I hope it's not possible that you're my mother! (*This remark —and* MRS. WEBSTER's *rejoinder—are a couple of insults and contain no hidden meaning.*)

MRS. WEBSTER (*going back into bedroom*): I hope it isn't!

ROSE (*aware that* HUGO *is embarrassed; in the wrong—defiant*): That's how we get on!

HUGO: Where *is* your mother?

ROSE: I never had one! I was manufactured by a convent!— (*Shrug.*)—and a man.

HUGO (*coming up to her; the question he has been waiting to ask*): Was that true?

ROSE: Yes.

HUGO: Did you exaggerate?

ROSE: A little.

HUGO: But all the same?

ROSE (*steadily*): One or two.

HUGO: Out of love?

ROSE: Out of lack of patience.

Out of wanting life to begin.

HUGO: And did it?

ROSE: No. Nothing grows—after the first time. Nothing alters.

HUGO: And so.

ROSE (*gravely*): And so—I am looking for a father. Every girl looks for a father—in the end. (*Pause.*) Are you so stupid—now—as not to love me?

HUGO: I ask myself.

ROSE: Has yourself answered?

HUGO (*with gravity*): It is indifferent to virgins.

ROSE: Yourself? (*She must get this clear.*)

HUGO: Yes. It finds what the body does is the work of a stranger. It looks at the Rose-Quality. Into the Rose-Eyes. At the Rose-Honour.

ROSE (*moving towards him*): Then . . .

HUGO (*checking her by his quietness*): If you want me to say you're lovely—I say it. Honourable and desirable—I say it . . .

ROSE: Damn . . . (*Her ear has caught the faintest noise. She runs across the bedroom, rustling in her dress and pulls the bedroom door angrily fast-shut; with violence.*) I would rather you found me a *monster*—and *loved* me!

HUGO: I'm not a suitor!

ROSE: Why?

HUGO: Because I can't afford you!

ROSE (*aghast*): Afford?

HUGO: The distraction! —My hand might shake! My eye might slide in its socket and miss something! When he comes tonight . . .

ROSE: He?

HUGO: My brother.

ROSE (*with anger*): I'd forgotten him! —*I must be a fool!*

HUGO: Why?

ROSE: Not to see further! —Always your brother! Always your brother! Are you *in love* with him?

HUGO (*angry*): If—to be involved—is love! (*Goes nearer window; turns.*) I'm on the other side of the heart! Among the *unintoxicated* loyalties! My God—you don't ask a soldier —in a battle—to love! He needs his wits, and his breath! He's here or not here—according to his concentration. . . .

ROSE (*bitterly*): You don't do badly!

HUGO: With what?

ROSE: With words! When you're going to hurt—say things simply!

HUGO (*right back against window*): All right! . . . Don't waste your time on me! Don't pester me for love! I'm backing out! —I'm *incapable* of loving!

(*The door bursts open.*)

PORTAL (*coming in fast, speaking irritably over his shoulder to* ROBIN *who stands behind him in the doorway with a silver salver in his hand*): Well—he's before his time!

MRS. WEBSTER *comes out of the bedroom—stands a moment— then goes into the bathroom.* (*To* ROSE): What are you doing here?

ROSE: Taking shelter!

PORTAL: From what?

ROSE: Like you. From the world!

PORTAL (*glancing at* HUGO): And who . . . (*Turns sharply as* FERDI-BENZUTO *moves in quickly past* ROBIN, *taking his own card from* ROBIN'S *salver as he passes him, holding it out to* PORTAL.)

BENZUTO: The *name*!

PORTAL *takes the card automatically but stares at his visitor. The fez surprises him.*

(*Bowing.*) The *body*!

PORTAL (*non-committal*): Ah.

BENZUTO (*gently*): A voice on the telephone—has to have a body! (*He carries a flat bag of black leather.*)

PORTAL (*still a little taken aback*): You find me dressing for my daughter's ball— (*Slight gesture of introduction.*) My daughter, Mr. Zuto.

BENZUTO (*gravely bowing; gravely correcting*): *Ben*zuto. A man's name is like a son to him.

PORTAL (*glancing at the card*): Turkish?

BENZUTO: Born in Egypt. Brought up in Paris. (*Small smile.*) —What they call Levantine.

ROBIN *has not quite shut the door, a burst of music comes through.*

What a night to sell a picture! . . .

OLD TONI *enters and shuts the door:* I passed a savage Jordaens —as I came through!

PORTAL (*surprised*): Not in *my* collection!

BENZUTO (*inscrutably smiling*): Thirty foot long. Wild hares on a dish at a gallop. Boars' heads—tongues lolling. Agony and death—enjoyably conveyed by a knifewound—gushing red jelly. . . .

ROSE: He means—the buffet!

BENZUTO: I didn't know you used it "in the life" still!

PORTAL: I admire your English.

BENZUTO: You must admire my governess.

PORTAL: Fortunes—reversed?

BENZUTO: These are great days—in Europe—for changing pockets. —Why prince— (*to* HUGO)—haven't we met before? (PORTAL *turns at* "prince". *Very slightly bows.*)

HUGO (*smilingly acknowledging the bow*): No, that's my brother! Who's a snob.

BENZUTO: If a man's a prince he should call himself so. (*Polite—to* ROSE.) Is this your home?

ROSE: Since twelve months.

BENZUTO: I had a home—much longer. (*Elegantly reminiscent.*) The front of the house—crested, truculent, like a swan! (*Finishing the sentence to* OLD TONI *who had claimed to have stayed there.*)—The back gentle—like the swan's wake in the water.

PORTAL (*who has a baron up his sleeve*): Have you met? The Baron Santa Clara.

OLD TONI: Ex-First-Secretary ... (*Waiving this away.*) In London—called Old Toni.

BENZUTO (*with pleasant worldliness*): When diplomats get like that—they are no more use to their countries! (*To* PORTAL— *gesture round room.*) A remarkable room!

PORTAL: Of great antiquity.

BENZUTO: Very approximate.

PORTAL (*startled at the odd word*): To what?

BENZUTO: To Tudor. (*Looking round; mock wonder.*) Seven— Roman heads?

PORTAL: Too many of them?

BENZUTO: Not if you like them. *Two*—are genuine.

PORTAL (*taken aback*): They came from—

BENZUTO: —a bad stable. Kranker's. Berlin.

PORTAL (*irritated*): Rose. . . . (*She looks up.*) We have to talk—

ROSE (*who wants to stay*): You *are* talking!

PORTAL: Privately.

BENZUTO (*murmuring; as he moves near a silk banner framed against a screen*): I am better with an audience— (*Touching the banner.*) Geese. On the fringe of a pool.

PORTAL (*with satisfaction; recovering*): Ch'ing Dynasty.

BENZUTO (*low*): Why frame it? It should hang loose. . . .

PORTAL (*who has caught this*): I have always been a man of action. It makes one's ears sharp. (*Cold.*) Perhaps one's taste blunt.

BENZUTO (*putting his fingers tenderly on a paperweight; lifting it with infinite care*): I congratulate you!

PORTAL (*with irony*): Not ... genuine?

BENZUTO (*replacing it with care*): The only one in the world. St. Louis. Purple overlay. *Exquisite.*

PORTAL (*irony*): *Thank* you. (*Looking at his watch.*) Rose. . . .

BENZUTO (*interrupting*): No ... *pictures?*

PORTAL: They are in the galleries.

BENZUTO: But close to your personal life—one would have

thought? (*Moving away from this "edge".*) I myself ring the
changes. I keep *one*. Where I can see it when I wake in the
morning. (*Another "edge".*)

PORTAL (*unable to resist asking*): Which one?

BENZUTO: I change it. Soulage, at the moment. But one comes
to the end—either of one's understanding—or what the
painter meant.

OLD TONI (*suddenly*): You remind me of someone.

BENZUTO (*warning*): But God makes men in dozens. (*He draws
a flat object, an unframed photograph, a little way out of his bag.*)

PORTAL (*impatient*): What have you got there?

BENZUTO: A photograph. Of a painting— My clients—young
men. Painting passably in garrets. Artists caught early on
the wing.

PORTAL (*sardonic*): So you have a hand in both pockets.

BENZUTO: I have to be a double-sided man.

PORTAL (*as BENZUTO puts back the half-shown photograph into
the bag; sharp*): What are you putting back?

BENZUTO: A masterpiece! (*Subtly.*) Don't let us look at it!

PORTAL (*vexed*): You have an odd manner . . .

BENZUTO: Once you start to sell things—you cast a skin. It's
a pitiful thing—to be a go-between! A painter has something
to sell. I pick his trust—before the apple is ripe. (*Touching
the gold skull.*) I engineer the First Fall. . . . (*He picks up the
skull.*)

PORTAL (*delighted he shows interest*): My gold skull!

BENZUTO: Soapstone. Gilded.

PORTAL (*not offended by this; sure of himself*): Tomb Seven!
Mount Alban. Oakaca. Xipe Totec. The Flayed God.

BENZUTO (*turning it*): Devastatingly non-survival. . . . Used
for Black Magic.

PORTAL: Very probably. The Mixtec Death Culture. —A.D.
nine hundred.

BENZUTO (*laying it back on table*): *Nineteen hundred.* It belonged
to Aleister Crowley.

PORTAL (*outraged*): *Prove* it!

BENZUTO (*smooth*): A mark on the base.

PORTAL (*now angry; calling commandingly across the room*): Rose!
I must ask you to leave us! Go to the ballroom! (*Striding
to the door and flinging it open.*)

> She and HUGO *walk through the door in silence*
>
> OLD TONI *remains, hovering, hoping for a word with*
BENZUTO

(*Sharp.*) *I don't need you, Baron!*

OLD TONI (*to* BENZUTO *when level with him*): I make a guess!
... That you once lived ...

BENZUTO (*palm and fingers upwards. Oriental*): I lived in
Paradise. (*Ominous.*) But I don't want it mentioned.

> OLD TONI *exits*

PORTAL (*shutting the door*): Why the charade?

BENZUTO: Of what?

PORTAL: Of knowing everything!

BENZUTO: Self-flattery. Warmth. Before risking ...

PORTAL: What?

BENZUTO: What we spoke of on the telephone.

PORTAL: Wait—we aren't alone ...

> MRS. WEBSTER *appears from bedroom door.*

You can run my bath, Mrs. Webster.

MRS. WEBSTER: It's already run.

PORTAL (*meaning voice*): Then perhaps it has become—cold.
(*As she moves to the bathroom, for her benefit.*) If you'd care to
see the catalogue of my pictures—it's there on the table.

> BENZUTO *sits down at centre table.*

They've been wired against theft—for tonight—and rehung.
If you have time later to see them— But they aren't in that
order ... (*Softly—as* MRS. WEBSTER *has now disappeared into
bathroom.*) Who are you?

BENZUTO: A man in touch—with other men in touch. A
contact-man. My principals—anonymous. (*Holds up the
catalogue.*) But if there's something you haven't got ...

PORTAL: Specify.

> MRS. WEBSTER *comes back in from bedroom door—obviously*

there is a communicating door between bathroom and bedroom—carrying bedroom slippers.

BENZUTO (*smiling at the tray; warning*): I'm hungry.

She puts the slippers down by a chair and goes back to bathroom.

PORTAL: Eat. While I bath. There's brandy ... But—of course ... (*Meaning—Mohammedans don't drink.*)

BENZUTO (*quietly; examining catalogue*): I live on water.

MRS. WEBSTER (*standing again in the bathroom doorway, holding up the bath salts*): Do you know what this smells like?

PORTAL (*irritably*): It's what I *want* it to smell like!

She puts the bath salts down on a table and comes further into the room (much as PORTAL would like to be alone with the "salesman" it is difficult to put a stop to MRS. WEBSTER's normal procedures).

BENZUTO (*turning pages of catalogue*): You have a Neo-Surrealist Picasso of 1930.

MRS. WEBSTER *takes coat from* PORTAL. *Then the black cardigan. He undoes his own tie, gives it to her. Undoes buttons of his shirt.*

PORTAL (*talking as he is valeted*): The Braque you see there—

BENZUTO: —you bought last month. At Sothebys.

PORTAL: You follow everything.

BENZUTO: I read *The Times.*

PORTAL (*now having his shirt pulled over his head*): Chagalls—Ozenfants ... Bombois ... (*Emerging, ruffled hair.*) ... Seurats, Utrillo.

BENZUTO (*watching this operation with interest*): In Paris now—

PORTAL *looks sharply at him, imagining the remarks will have a bearing on a picture.* —they sell them—to unbutton.

Annoyed glance from MRS. WEBSTER—*who has bought him the wrong kind.*

PORTAL (*neutral*): I am out of date. (*Sits down to have his shoes and socks taken off—*MRS. WEBSTER *kneels. Observing that* BENZUTO *has again opened the catalogue.*) You're looking at the wrong end of the catalogue.

BENZUTO: I am. (*Pause.*) No Vuillard.

PORTAL (*getting up—steps out of his trousers, leaving the braces hanging, attached to them, and stands in white, monogrammed underclothes: large, embroidered circles round the monograms; stiffly*): They are all in America. (*As* BENZUTO's *head is down studying the catalogue,* PORTAL *nods to* MRS. WEBSTER *in the direction of his bedroom door—a nod she understands. About to go into bathroom; perfunctorily.*) Have you everything you want?

BENZUTO (*lifting his head and smiling at* PORTAL's *back; softly*): No Vuillard.

PORTAL, *apparently not hearing, goes into bathroom and shuts door.*

MRS. WEBSTER *moves round the room straightening a few things—she picks up the discarded clothes and goes into the bedroom with them—evidently putting them on a chair just inside the doorway, for she comes out at once, locks the door and puts the key in her pocket.*

BENZUTO (*who has watched her; with amusement*): A feudal habit?

Without deigning to answer—she crosses to the window to draw the curtains. BENZUTO *rises, catalogue in hand, and moves towards* PORTAL's *bathroom door.*

MRS. WEBSTER (*near centre table now, indicates the untouched tray; sniff*): Is there anything else—you would prefer to this?

BENZUTO: I don't eat meat. Have you an apple?

Without a word she picks up the tray and proceeds with it to Main Door. (Standing quite close to bathroom door.) Mr. Portal . . . (*Holding catalogue; louder.*) Mr. Portal . . .

MRS. WEBSTER (*about to go through Main Door*): Mr. Portal lies with his ears below the water.

BENZUTO (*returning to the table; comically*): It puzzles me how you know.

MRS. WEBSTER *flounces out of the room with tray, and shuts the door rather hard; at the sound the bathroom door opens.*

BENZUTO *is already seated, with the catalogue in his hands.*

PORTAL, *naked, steaming, bare-footed—a towel thrown round*

his waist—leans out of the bathroom door. He has heard the noise of the door. He glances round the room; then moves softly to his own bedroom door, and lays his hand on the handle.

BENZUTO (*ironic*): That's right! She locked it.

PORTAL (*thrown*): She ... forgot my sponge. (*It is true, the sponge from Paris is lying on a nearby table; in self-defence.*) The place is full of hired waiters. ... (*He doesn't bother to pick up the sponge. Moving to* BENZUTO; *recovered, indifferent; the truth.*) I always lock doors. (*Arrived near the table.*) On the telephone there was a hint dropped. (BENZUTO *looks up.*) You mentioned a name. (*Pause.*) The major works of this painter—are closely held. I don't know one—that would be—

BENZUTO: Available.

PORTAL: That was the word.

BENZUTO: Meaning—money can buy it.

PORTAL: I understood.

   Which painting is it?

BENZUTO (*brief pause*): Then I burn my boats.

PORTAL: We are alone. We can deny this conversation.

BENZUTO (*standing*): If I offered you a Vuillard—*since you haven't one*—

   PORTAL *waits in silence*

—of yellow canaries in a cage, against a forest background? Totally unknown. ...

PORTAL: Not totally unknown. In the possession of the Cavanati family in Roumania.

BENZUTO: You are well infomed. There is another one. (*Slight pause.*) Have they offered you stolen pictures, Mr. Portal?

PORTAL (*toneless*): You shock me.

BENZUTO: I scandalize. But I too—(*Subtly.*)—am easily shocked. (*Silence.*) Fascinating—the subject ...

PORTAL: Of what?

BENZUTO: ... of pictures that get stolen. A man must be mad with love ... But I am keeping you.

PORTAL: Finish what you were going to say.

BENZUTO: The real art-lovers are the millionaire receivers!
A man must be mad with love—I was going to say—who'll
buy a painting—to keep it hidden for a lifetime!

PORTAL: Are you asking whether I am one of them?

BENZUTO: Yes.

PORTAL: Who suggested you should get in touch with me?
(*No answer. He goes to bathroom door as though the talk was
over; turning.*) Describe the picture that your principals might
offer me.

BENZUTO: ... Painted on grey-ochre board. In colle. Light-
hued. A fine use of chiaroscuro ...

PORTAL: Spare me the jargon.

BENZUTO (*leaning back against table; crossing his arms*): ... in
the heart of a fine season—and a fine day ... (*He smiles.*)
... the atmosphere bathed in.

PORTAL (*patiently*): Facts. Please.

Note: BENZUTO *tries three methods with his adversary.*
One: *picture-jargon.* Two: *a simple if trite, statement.* Three:
*he is suddenly carried away in spite of himself, into the subtleties
of a subject he knows profoundly.*

Involuntary PORTAL *and he near the same ground.*

BENZUTO (*almost Ferdi; abandoning his Oriental stillness, moving
as he talks*): There are no facts in a pattern ... of marvellous
hidden geometry. A cloud is puffed like a dress. But the
dress too is puffed like a cloud. The hues hover on the soil,
the path is the colour of flesh. And the flesh of the sitter's
cheek ...

PORTAL (*below his breath*): A woman.

BENZUTO (*same; grave and moved*): She sits—subdued and
glittering—of substance like the garden ...

PORTAL (*following his every word*): Garden ...

BENZUTO: The Nearby and the Far are superimposed—
(*Slowly.*) ... the moss and the jade—and the veins on the
leaves ... (PORTAL *is riveted*) ... *the shutter slats* ...
(*Slight* vertical *movement of hand.*) ... the shutter slats ...

PORTAL: *What* picture?

BENZUTO (*withdrawing the pressure; watching* PORTAL—*slight* horizontal *movement of hand*): I should have said ... the slats —on the back of a garden seat.

PORTAL (*snatching at this hope*): *That* one—the decorative use of the parallel lines in a garden seat—*is in Boston*!

BENZUTO: You're shivering.

PORTAL (*between set teeth*): I was wet. (*He goes back to the doors, but it is on the bedroom door handle that he lays his hand. Pauses, turns.*) You spoke like a painter. "A man must be mad with love"—you said ...?

BENZUTO (*off-hand*): To keep a picture hidden—yes.

PORTAL (*softly*): I was tempted ... (*Moves to bathroom door.*)

BENZUTO: What?

PORTAL (*opening door*): —to do a silly thing (*Goes in and shuts the door.*)

   Directly the door is shut MATTHEW'*s head pushes through the curtains. He is standing below in the garden.*

MATTHEW (*in a hoarse whisper*): That's the lad! ... Highness! ... (FERDI *turns.*) That's the lad! —That's him!

FERDI (*crossing the room to window quickly, oblivious of what Matthew has said and delighted with himself*): Him—I should think so! Did you hear? It's as plain as daylight he's got it! Every brush-stroke known to him!

MATTHEW (*urgent*): Highness! Listen—

FERDI: God knows how he bought it—and from whom! —From finger to finger—what muddy bargainings!

MATTHEW: *Him in the bath, Highness!*
   Listen!
   It's Kutz's boy!
   (*As* FERDI *doesn't understand.*)
   Kutz—he was called. The name's come back—seeing him. (*Impatiently.*) The *valuer*! That time the picture went—he brought his lad with him!

FERDI: This man! ...
   (*Glances round at bathroom door.*)
   Think what you're saying!

MATTHEW: Think! ... I *know*.

FERDI: You're out of your mind! ... Our millionaire! ...
Our ... Englishman!

MATTHEW: Fiddlesticks to the English! Your age—he was.
Sixteen. Did you hear, Highness? The bath salts!
The last time I saw him he had lice! See if he's missing the
tip of a finger. It was new then—not healed over. It used
to turn me. ...

FERDI: Which hand? Which finger?

MATTHEW: I don't know which finger. But the left. Here's
my knife—if you want to cut the canvas. ...

FERDI: He's locked the door, the impudent bastard!
But I'll pull that picture out of his tooth!
We'll ring the bells on him and see what that does! ...

MATTHEW: Bells, Highness?

FERDI: The pictures here are wired to an alarm.
You can get through any door—
      (*Leaning out.*)
—from the garden into the castle. If that finger's missing ...
I'll shake my handkerchief out of this window. ...
      (*Turning to watch bathroom door.*)
When you see it—slip in—and drag a picture down.

MATTHEW: *Which* one?
      (*Hearing a sound.*)

FERDI: The one you fancy!
      (MATTHEW's *head disappears. The bathroom door opens.*
      PORTAL *walks into the room in fresh underclothes, pale blue,*
      same monograms. He picks up his trousers—buttoned ones for
      evening—puts them on—and then the dressing-gown.)
      (*Before either can say a word* MRS. WEBSTER *returns by main*
      door followed by ROBIN *carrying a tray.*)

BENZUTO (*standing by the window; change of manner*): You
have a fine garden.

PORTAL (*as* ROBIN *puts the tray down carefully on the centre*
table under MRS. WEBSTER's *direction*): I never go into it.
      As they talk ROBIN *waits to see if anything further is wanted.*

MRS. WEBSTER *goes into the bathroom for a moment, but is very much present, coming and going in the room.*

PORTAL *watches her with impatience, wishing to be alone with* BENZUTO.

BENZUTO: A man with certain pictures ... doesn't need a garden. He has the essence of the essence ...

PORTAL (*sharp, to* ROBIN): Who's at the door? (*He waits while* ROBIN *opens door.*)

ROBIN (*consulting at door then returning to* PORTAL): The gardener wants to know, sir ... will you wear a red carnation or a white?

PORTAL (*impatient*): Does he think I keep an orchid house— (*Nodding to* MRS. WEBSTER.)—*you* tell him ... to wear a carnation!

MRS. WEBSTER *goes to door.*

(*To* ROBIN.) Are they serving supper yet?

ROBIN: Yes, sir, now.

PORTAL: They'll want you. You needn't wait.

ROBIN *goes out.*

(*To* BENZUTO.) ... You were saying?

BENZUTO (*smiling*): That you need not have a garden.

PORTAL: Nor go into it?

BENZUTO: Not if the Garden of Eden—is painted on your wall.

MRS. WEBSTER *in colloquy at door.*

That's Huxley's theory.

PORTAL (*absently*): Thomas?

BENZUTO: Aldous. His book on Mescalin ... The floor of heaven—he holds—is paved with jewels ... and we remember them. (*Solemn.*) The extra-temporal perception ...

PORTAL (*suddenly*): Are you pulling my leg?

BENZUTO (*softly, as* PORTAL *goes to door*): God is pulling your leg.

PORTAL (*crossly—at door, for gardener's information*): Doesn't he understand? ... The orchid! The *green* one!

MRS. WEBSTER *closes door and goes to tidy the curtains.*

BENZUTO: Is that ... (PORTAL *turns to him.*) ... why *you*

wear emeralds?

PORTAL (*startled*): What? . . . My rings?

BENZUTO (*smiling*): Your memories of the floor of heaven? May I see them?

PORTAL (*looking vexedly at* MRS. WEBSTER; *holding up a hand; off-hand*): The Jasmin Emerald. Of the tenth Shah of Persia. What's the matter?

BENZUTO (*carrying his handkerchief to the window*): I had forgotten I bought a sandwich . . . —at one of your stations. I did not know—(*Shaking it thoroughly out of the window.*)— it had meat in it—

PORTAL (*unable to bear the irritation of* MRS. WEBSTER'S *presence any longer*): Come back in five minutes.

MRS. WEBSTER: But . . . (*A second glance at his face shows her where she gets off—and she goes into the bathroom door—not quite shutting it.*)

PORTAL: Shut that door. (*It is pulled shut from within—with sharp annoyance. To* BENZUTO—*hurriedly—but as though he had rehearsed the words to himself beforehand.*) We toy with guilt. The longing to possess! *But wisdom has returned to me* . . .

BENZUTO (*very smooth, the English idiom pointed with his slight French accent*): No bones broken.

PORTAL (*definite*): I am not a buyer. (*Hesitates.*) It's not of interest now. (*Pause.*) *But—in what general shade* . . .
The alarm bells go, long insistent, stopping and starting like ships' bells for boat drill.

MRS. WEBSTER *comes out of the bathroom. In two strides* PORTAL *is at the house switchboard, presses a switch, listens, there is no answer—his eyes all the time on* BENZUTO: *the two men are frozen in noise. The question he has put to* BENZUTO *is of paramount importance to him. During all the rumpus of the bells he never takes his eyes off his visitor.*
(*During small gaps in bells, uselessly.*) Hullo . . . Hullo . . .
(*Abandons switchboard as* ROBIN *rushes in; shouts over noise—fast—to* ROBIN.) Tell them to shut the gates on both drives!

... And turn on the searchlight! Run! (*During a momentary cessation of bells, to* MRS. WEBSTER, *snatching up the guest list and holding it out to her.*) Tell the Inspector to check by this list—as the guests come out from supper!

MRS. WEBSTER (*not taking it*): He's got a duplicate. (*She goes as the bells start again.*)

PORTAL (*shouting*): *And tell them to stop the alarm!* (*Immediately they are alone—having waited for the last burst of bells—finishing his question as though nothing else had been in his mind throughout bell-ringing.*) ... in what general shade ... I mean the *tones* of the *luminosity* ...

BENZUTO (*impassive*): In ten deep yellows ...

MRS. WEBSTER (*framed in the open doorway; rigid manner*): They say it's the Renoir, Mr. Portal, that's been taken. (*Disappears.*)

PORTAL (*rushing to door*): Wait—woman! —Not the *big* one? (*Glances back at* BENZUTO *then disappears—shouting up corridor.*) Not *cut*? They haven't *cut* the canvas ...

FERDI-emerging-Benzuto (*alone, softly and with pleasure*):—and the dress—is apricot!

He moves quickly to bedroom door. Key has been forgotten and left in the door. Opens door, disappears inside, returns holding the double picture. Wrenches top open on its hinge, rests it on a table, and uses MATTHEW's *knife to prise up the picture-nails on the inner frame. The canvas of the hidden picture is on a stretcher fitted into a frame, and the frame splinters a little as he wrenches at the stretcher.*

ROSE *appears in the main doorway.*

FERDI (*sharp*): Shut that door.

She shuts it. At that moment the searchlight wheeling over the garden, whitens the room through the curtain, as white as bones. (*With annoyance, ducking slightly.*) That searchlight lights up everything! (*Flinging the half-empty frame-contraption back into* PORTAL's *bedroom, shutting door.*) How do I get past the garden into the woods?

ROSE: Down the grass slope outside. Over the moat by the

bridge—and you'll get into the maze ... (*As he crosses the room fast to window she sees what he is carrying—the canvas stretched on its frame.*) Why—*what are you going to do*!

FERDI: Take back what's mine! Rescue my mother ... (*Throws the fez on the floor.*)

ROSE (*indignant*): If I'd known you wanted *that*—I'd have made stronger terms!

FERDI (*at window*): I brought you Hugo!

ROSE: It's been no use to me! Your shadow's on him!

FERDI (*leg out of window*): I'll leave my shadow for you—in the woods! Tonight's as good as any night for an exorcism! (*Gets through.*)

ROSE (*following to window*): Are you laughing at me?

FERDI (*outside*): With one side of my face! (*Leaning in.*) The crooked one. (*Disappears.*)

ROSE *stands looking out of the window. Main doors open and* OLD TONI *comes in.*

OLD TONI (*reproachfully*): Rosie! Not dancing! (*Looking at her harder.*) ... after all the wear and tear ... Dear child—people will forget you are the hostess!

ROSE (*bitterly*): They never knew it! (*Runs to him.*) Toni! *Toni* ... *You* took me there! You know him!

OLD TONI: Who?

ROSE (*urgent—taking hold of one of his arms*): Hugo. ... Is he one of your kind?

MRS. WEBSTER (*in main doorway. She has come to fetch away the tray*): She can't believe a man won't fall for her!

ROSE (*in anger*): I don't understand women!

MRS. WEBSTER (*putting the tray on a side table*): You understand men.

ROSE: One can only fence with women! One can *talk* to men! (*To* OLD TONI.) You'd tell me ... Wouldn't you? —*Is he*, Toni?

OLD TONI: No.

ROSE (*imploring*): Would you know for certain? (*He nods. She lays her cheek on his coat. Brokenly.*) Then—*why* doesn't he love me? . . . He *did*. Why doesn't he now?

OLD TONI (*stroking her hair*): Don't ask me, love. I can only say—never mind. (*Compassionately*.) Everything gets better tomorrow.

PORTAL(*flinging open the door. Fast; looking round room*): Gone? (*Turns to face them: takes in what seems a sort of complicity about their attitude. Sarcastic*.)—She likes you more than I do, Baron!—Where is he? He was here when I left the room!

OLD TONI (*moving to pick up the fez*): His cap's here! (*Puts it on the table*.)

PORTAL (*as he moves to switchboard*): No head in it! (*A glance— contemplating his daughter—as he stands at the switchboard*.) If Rose were a book—I should say I was illiterate! (*Pressing switch-button*.) And yet, I suppose, she is "written" from end to end . . . (*Into switchboard—sharp*.) Is that the West Lodge? I've had a man here. On business. He should have waited for me. He's gone. Looks like an Englishman. Tall. Ordinary day-clothes. Bare-headed. *He's to be stopped leaving*. (*Listens*.) Yes. And ring the other lodge. Ring me back when you hear. (*Turns and surveys them*.) (*To* ROSE.) Go back to your guests. They're at supper. You should be in the supper room. (ROSE *stands mutinous. Sees gloves—holds them out*.) And put these on. (*For a moment it seems she won't go. Then she takes the long white gloves and, head up, rebellious, sails out. To* OLD TONI, *when she has gone*.) When you came in—was he here?

OLD TONI: No.

PORTAL (*to* MRS. WEBSTER): And you?

MRS. WEBSTER: Who?

PORTAL: The man posing as a dealer!

MRS. WEBSTER: No.

ROBIN (*bursting in*): Mr. Portal, sir—(PORTAL *looks at him*.) It's *there*, sir! In the garden. The picture—

PORTAL: *My Renoir?*

ROBIN: Propped against a wall!

PORTAL (*a moment's thought*): Who found it?

ROBIN: Me.

PORTAL: Who else knows?

ROBIN (*stammering*): The . . . the third housemaid.

PORTAL (*with a sudden brilliant smile, exercising his charm*): Ask her to forget it. Ask her from *me*. *I* ask it. Let the men I pay find it! *You'll* get the credit. Can I trust you?

ROBIN (*hero-worshipping*): Sir—*yes*! Yes, oh yes, sir. (*Backs out of door.*)

PORTAL (*waiting till door is shut*): The Renoir unhooked—and *left*! The alarm set off . . . It's a *cover*! (*His hand on the bedroom door handle. Furiously to* MRS. WEBSTER.) *Unlocked*! (*Throws the door open—stands in the doorway, looking inside. He sees his loss at once. Tense—to* OLD TONI.) Who was this man? (*Silence. Picks up fez from table, balancing it in his hands. Cold.*) Do you know what struck me, Baron?

MRS. WEBSTER (*before* TONI *can answer*): Do you want me here?

PORTAL (*sharply*): Yes. Baron? (*pause*) . . . *that you and he had met before.*

OLD TONI (*delicately facing up to this*): One can't do everything for pay, Mr. Portal.

PORTAL: What have I failed to buy?

OLD TONI: An old man who has had a long life—has loyalties.

PORTAL: Not when he is paid.

OLD TONI: Perhaps you don't pay me sufficiently?

PORTAL (*angrily*): Rich men never pay enough!

OLD TONI (*pursuing*): . . . and when one is called on—suddenly—out of the Past—not to be a spoilsport . . .

PORTAL: I am not a subtle man! Please be clearer!

OLD TONI: I can assure you that if it is he—the Masquerader is beyond suspicion . . .

PORTAL (*sharp*): *Who?*

OLD TONI: And Rosie was even dancing—with his brother.

PORTAL (*smacking his hand hard on the guest list*): *Are the names on this list?*

OLD TONI: No.

PORTAL (*furious*): Are there *two* men here tonight—making a fool of me—*besides yourself!*

OLD TONI (*unperturbed*): In Constantinople—when I knew him . . .

PORTAL (*imperious*): The *name—God damn it!*

OLD TONI: Cavanati.

PORTAL (*silent a moment; then, on an outward exhalation, as though stroking some all-explaining thought*): Ah . . .

OLD TONI: Prince Ferdinand Cavanati . . .

PORTAL: I know. (*Silence. Stepping back from the door.*) Go in there. There's a picture on the floor. (*Back to his desk.*)

OLD TONI (*going to door*): The Sargent . . .

PORTAL: Bring it to me.

OLD TONI (*returning with it*): The frame's broken!

PORTAL (*takes it in his hands; fingers the edge of inner frame, nods with a curious smile*): He too has splintered it! (*To* MRS. WEBSTER.) When I came in—you were with her.

MRS. WEBSTER (*on the defensive*): A minute or two.

PORTAL: What had she been saying to you?

MRS. WEBSTER: A word or two.

PORTAL: About this man?

MRS. WEBSTER: It's not *him* she's after!

PORTAL: How do you know . . . (*Quick—to* OLD TONI.) Get Rose.

OLD TONI (*in protest*): The guests!

PORTAL (*authoritative*): Tell her to come to me.

   OLD TONI *hesitates a second—then goes.* PORTAL *sits at his desk.* MRS. WEBSTER *stands behind him, watching him as he twists and turns small objects on his writing-table . . . a lapsis lazuli seal, an ivory knife etc., setting them out like a "battlefield" of thought.* Do you suppose children know their parents suffer? Or want their good opinion? (*A half-glance over his shoulder.*) You don't comment?

MRS. WEBSTER: I am not a parent.

PORTAL (*gently and dangerously*): No. And if you said you were I would shoot you.

MRS. WEBSTER: You would too.

PORTAL (*idly*): . . . and bury you in cement.

MRS. WEBSTER: You're so efficient.

PORTAL: Who told him about the picture?

MRS. WEBSTER: Not I! (*Then.*) *Rose* knew.

PORTAL: Rose knew . . . (*Doodles on the writing-pad.*) A parent has to be a proud man—and not solicit. If he knows nothing —he is not to admit it. If he wants to know—he can't ask it. (*Silence. Looking up at her.*) Is she in love?

MRS. WEBSTER: It's not a word I remember.

PORTAL: When she is alone with men what does she talk about?

MRS. WEBSTER: Get yourself a son-in-law. Then you can overhear.

PORTAL (*quite simply—with feeling*): It's what I want most in the world! A man of culture! A man who could explain Rose to me!

MRS. WEBSTER (*in spite of herself*): What store you set by her!

PORTAL (*getting up; gravely*): I have made an exquisite thing. It's the only way I am an artist. (*Crossing to main door; rueful.*) —And what a defeat—after the life I've led—that I'm shy of her! (*He opens the door.* ROSE *enters.*)

ROSE (*standing, dignified, in her gloves*): You wanted me?

PORTAL: Shall you be missed?

ROSE (*a shrug*): No.— (*Ironic.*) They know—*each other*!

PORTAL: You can go, Mrs. Webster. (*As she exits, picking up the guest list from the table.*) Did you know that the alarm bells were set off—to get me out of this room?

ROSE: No.

PORTAL: But you knew that . . . (*Hesitates.*) something . . . out of my room might be taken? (*She nods.*) *Why didn't you warn me?*

ROSE (*passionately*): Because I can't *think* any longer! I can't think what should come first . . . (*Stops.*)

PORTAL (*touching the list*): There are two men here tonight— *not* on this list—brothers. You didn't include the names.

Why?

ROSE (*stammering*): I was involved in—a bargain—that had never been put to me . . .

PORTAL: You see how hard it is—between us—to speak plainly!

Where has he gone! (*She is silent. Loud—impatient.*) The *prince!* (*Shouting at her.*) The *thief!* (*Door opens suddenly.*)

OLD TONI: The first dance—after supper!

PORTAL (*a roar*): *Dance it then!* (*Door hurriedly shuts again.*)

ROSE: It was my fault he took the picture . . .

PORTAL: There is more than that at stake. Do you love him?

ROSE: No.

PORTAL (*impatient*): His brother? (*She nods.*) You make a mistake then!

ROSE (*floodgates opening*): And who is to tell me not to make—bitter—mistakes! And why is there never a woman in this house—to talk to me? (*Wildly.*) I suppose—at least—you're my father? (*Silence. Afraid of what she has just said.*) You don't know—you don't know what I ask myself . . .

PORTAL: You have just told me.

ROSE (*frightened*): Father . . .

PORTAL: Don't say it. I never asked you to. Tell me where he went.

ROSE: And if I don't?

PORTAL: I'll prosecute them both. Both brothers. I'll take them to Court.

ROSE (*reluctant*): He went into the maze.

PORTAL: Where does it come out?

ROSE: Where you wanted the tables. In the opening.

PORTAL: The tables for the breakfast?

ROSE: Yes.

PORTAL (*to house switchboard*): *Edwards!*—Give me Edwards! Yes the Inspector . . . (*Listens.*) You have the maze on the plan. The man I want—he's in there. I have information.— Are you looking at the plan? (*Waits.*) You see where the opening is—in the woods beyond it. I'm going to him privately. I'm coming round by the drive.—Bring the men in closer but keep them out of sight. I don't want to see them. Nor be overheard. Wait—stop the searchlight. Keep a watch on the gates . . .

ROSE (*furiously*): Now I *know* you're my father! That's what a father does when you tell him anything!

PORTAL (*suddenly transformed—gay*): Pssht! Silly child . . . (*Flings off his dressing-gown.*) In so many words . . . (*Struggles into his coat.*) . . . since you doubt it . . . (*Smiling—but not at her—to himself.*) . . . you *are* my daughter . . .

ROSE: What makes you smile like that!

PORTAL (*his face lit*): The *Past*! (*Picks up his keys, puts them in his pocket. Goes through window like a boy. Turning and speaking to her through the window.*) Stay here and wait for me. (*He is gone.*)

 She stares a second. Then, struggling with the zip below her arm, which runs far down her dress, she unzips it, the dress falls to the floor, she steps out of it, runs to the black kimono, puts it on, and is through the window and gone.

CURTAIN

ACT III

Time: Near dawn; a paling sky.

Place: the opening in the woods. Downstage centre is a disused woodman's hut, doorless, but still with a window and its wooden shutter,—some sort of rough table, a chair, a barrel, a few shelves. Outside two dead and dried jackdaws, their wings spread, hang upside down from a nail. From another nail hangs a lighted hurricane lantern.

As the dawn grows, the corner of a red and white striped marquee can be seen upstage, masked by the trees.

    FERDI *sits at the table, idly playing with a revolver, absent and in thought. The picture, the Vuillard, is propped on a shelf. His cloak is flung outside on a broken bench.*

    ROSE, *in the black kimono, appears in the doorway.*

ROSE (*breathless*): Why have you stopped here! My father's coming! He knows—he saw at once—there are men all round the woods. . . . (*Suddenly—seeing the revolver.*) What's that for?

FERDI: Not for your father. Besides—it's not loaded.

ROSE: But you have the ammunition.

FERDI: Yes. (*Pulling a cardboard box from his pocket and putting it on the table.*) But I don't need it.—I have a problem. Sit down.

ROSE: He'll be here soon.

FERDI: How soon?

ROSE: I ran. He's walking. He won't go through the maze.

FERDI (*lightly*): Thirty seconds will do it. It's this. I want to die. And I don't know how to. (*As she glances down at the gun.*) No, that won't do. Hugo has one too. Loaded. Now. In his right hand pocket. (*At her exclamation.*) To kill himself if I do. Its blackmail in earnest. (*Gets up and goes to the shutter,*

148

opens it a little to watch for PORTAL. *Turning round.*) He's threatened me and he'll do it. We've tried arguments. No good. He's set men to watch me. What can paid men do? There's so much life that's private. But now what he's done's effective! I can't let him die—and he knows it! He's stopped me in my tracks. (*As she is about to speak.*) Just take it, girl— the situation! He's sworn it. Has he spoken to you about it?

ROSE: No. But I see how it fits.

FERDI: Fits?

ROSE: When he thinks of you I'm blotted out!

FERDI (*a slight laugh*): Death's more important than love!

ROSE (*with anger*): Not for him!— For *you*.

FERDI: Exactly. Of course.— Have you known anyone who's killed himself?

ROSE: Why should I! The people I know live! It's idiotically simple to live!

FERDI: You know nothing about it.

ROSE: I know this! I thought the world had melted for me— after having been like ice! There was this man who . . . this man who . . . (*A sob.*)

FERDI: How far has it gone? Does he love you?

ROSE: He did—He *would*. Yes he did . . . But it stopped. Then I thought perhaps he liked men. But it's not men. It's *you*.

FERDI: How incestuous! Nothing's beyond you! If he loves you we might have pulled off something! Are you too cold? Whip it up! Take him in your arms. Remind him.

ROSE: Of what?

FERDI: The warmth of life. The stupidity of going! Make him feel the sun's out on the other side of the moon!

ROSE: I can't.

FERDI: You can't? Look at you! You're a meal of warmth!

ROSE: A girl doesn't see herself like that. I can't hold him against you! It's like trying to make love through an illness!

FERDI: In normal circumstances . . . (*Stops—looks at her.*) . . . as a wife for my brother I wouldn't think of you. I'm a man you would call—here in England—a snob. I'm a prince. And that's as out of date as bloomers worn on a Penny-Farthing . . .

ROSE: That's out of date, too!

FERDI: I was going to say that I care about my line of birth as another man cares for his cellar! But I'm back to the wall and I'm willing to water my burgundy! I don't know where you come from—but keep him alive and I give him to you! —But "keep him alive's" not easy! It's the reflex I'm afraid of.—The obstinacy! Get him over that first moment— and once dead. (*Breaking off—with a grin.*) Would you be shocked if I shot myself?

ROSE: Yes.

FERDI: Sorry?

ROSE: Shocked.

FERDI: You don't like me?

ROSE: I should like you less if you did that to me. Used that thing in front of me.

FERDI: Well, I'm not going to. It's out of the question. It's not a way I can die. All I meant was that if he loved you enough . . .

ROSE: He doesn't.

FERDI: He's blinded, obsessed, I can't make a movement but I see in his eye . . . At any rate I'll fill it. Fall in with anything I do. Any double cross . . . When it comes to the point it's better done in public. . . .

ROSE (*putting her hand over the box of bullets*): I don't trust you!

FERDI (*astonished*): Don't trust what?

ROSE: Once that gun's loaded you're halfway there!

FERDI: No!—I give you my word!

ROSE: You're not a man any more to give me your word! I can feel death coming out of you. You'll be off—irresponsibly—just because it's loaded. After that—what do *you* care! *I'm* left with the misery.

FERDI: Stupid girl, it's not like that! I'm desperately responsible. Listen. I'll be patient. I've never been patient. No! Don't speak . . . Give me your hand. (*Reaches out. Seizes it.*) I'm not used to being interrupted. (*Pause.*) When my mother died ... (*Breaking off.*) Not a saint. Beautiful, gay, like a girl. I've never said this to any outsider. (*With difficulty.*) He is her legacy. I brought him up. I have the right to accept you for him. (*Takes a ring from his little finger, slips it on hers.*) That's my mother's ring. Help me and I'll get him for you.

ROSE: Help you to die? Then I lose him.

FERDI: Help me to trick him so that you don't. Get him disarmed. So that you have time to do your best with him. So that he doesn't sit under this shadow of mine! (*Still holding her hand he takes the box back from under her other hand.*) Sit back. Don't be a fool. I'll put the bullets in. (*Begins to cram them in the six chambers.*) It gives me something to bargain with. Not as crude as that. More subtle. I'll offer him my life. I'll promise ... (*A shadow falls on him.*)

PORTAL (*stretching out his hand*): What's that gun doing?

FERDI: What's your daughter doing! (*Moving the gun out of reach; a laugh.*) Alabaster fingers! But the tip is missing! No Vuillard ... eh?

PORTAL (*steadily*): No. Not in my collection.

FERDI: But over your bed, you impudent dog! Watching you sleep, dress, pick your nose! And in that dressing gown, Bluebottle! What's it worth—Kutz?

ROSE: Why do you call him that?

FERDI: Old friends, your Papa! Boys of sixteen ... (*To* PORTAL.) What do you put it at?

PORTAL: It depends on who wants it. A hundred thousand pounds. Do you know that if I blow this whistle they will arrest you?

FERDI: And not I— you? (*Levels the revolver.*) Try it on.

MATTHEW (*entering*): Put that down, Highness.

FERDI: Ah ... Matthew! (*To* PORTAL.) Do you remember him? Matthew said you had lice, Kutz, when you knew him!

PORTAL (*gravely*): There was a time when Matthew soiled his napkins. We are all born dirty. (*To* MATTHEW.) How do you do?

FERDI: Old and obstinate. I can answer for him.

MATTHEW: One could speak decently . . .

FERDI: I am not decent! This is Olympus! Anything can be said here! (*To* PORTAL.) Do I hear men in trees talking?

PORTAL (*half humouring him*): I don't think so.

FERDI (*insisting*): Like tree-cutters whose feet are off the ground?

PORTAL (*the same*): I gave no orders.

FERDI: God's footmen discussing our welcome. . . .

MRS. WEBSTER (*appearing*): . . . the caterers' men want to put up the trestle tables for the breakfast.

FERDI (*putting down the gun; rueful*): . . . and there are always explanations for everything . . . (*As a man appears carrying wooden objects.*) Might you be from God?

MAN: Sir?

MATTHEW: Take no notice.

FERDI: Are you carrying the Cross?

MAN: It's the legs for the trestle table.

> The MAN *spreads the legs on the ground during the following dialogue. Two more men bring in the long table-top. The table, once adjusted, the two men go off, but return with a pile of gilt "party" chairs which they stack under a tree. The first man remains stooping to fix the clasps that bolt the legs to the top. The other men go.*

PORTAL (*to* MRS. WEBSTER; *annoyed*): What hour is breakfast?

MRS. WEBSTER: Five.

PORTAL (*looking at his watch*): It isn't four.

MAN: They take time to fix. We got two dozen of them.

> ROSE *suddenly sits down, kicking off her shoes.*

FERDI: Are you tired?

ROSE: My shoes hurt.

FERDI: Hungry?

ROSE: Very.

FERDI (*to* MRS. WEBSTER, *with a dismissing gesture*): Fetch us a dish of eggs and bacon.

MRS. WEBSTER (*offended; addressing* PORTAL): For how many?

FERDI (*forestalling the answer*): For all except me. For me water.

MRS. WEBSTER (*brief icy glance at* FERDI, *to the* MAN): Eggs and bacon—tell the chef. And bottled water. *The* MAN *goes.*

FERDI (*mock polite*): So you're staying with us?

MRS. WEBSTER: Yes.

FERDI: Then we'll have it public! (*To* PORTAL.) Open your wings, Bluebottle, and let the Past fall out of them! The truth about this picture! What happened? Who sold it? Where's it been? When I get curious it's with a howling appetite ... (*To* MRS. WEBSTER.) You've lived in that house and dusted the picture over the gentleman's bed. I mean the picture behind the other! Show it to her, Matthew! There—behind me! What's it to your master? (*Waits.*) Does he set store by it?

MRS. WEBSTER (*grudging*): It's his luck—he says.

FERDI: Then there'll be one less dustable picture!

MRS. WEBSTER: Thank the Lord.

FERDI: Turn it round, Matthew! Turn it *backwards*! I can't shoot at ... *Turn it backwards!* (*Takes up revolver.*)

PORTAL (*hardly able to believe*): You'd shoot. ...

FERDI: Watch the top left hand corner!

PORTAL (*aghast*): You'd make holes in it!

FERDI: Several. It's polluted. (*Levels revolver.*)

PORTAL: Stop!

FERDI: Why?

PORTAL: I would give half my fortune ...

FERDI: A figure of speech!

PORTAL: A quarter then. I entreat you ... I'll give my Cézanne for it!

FERDI: I've got one.

PORTAL: The little Chagall—with the jasmine ...

FERDI: I saw him paint it. Bid higher!

MRS. WEBSTER (*activated by some obscure anger*): Give him the lot—I should!

FERDI: Well said, Housekeeper!—Stand away, Matthew ...

ROSE (*slipping in front of the canvas*): No! (*Turning it round so that the picture shows.*)

PORTAL: Rose! Come back!

ROSE (*to* PORTAL): It was my fault he took it. But why did you have it? (*Hesitating.*) If it's his—why have you kept it?

FERDI: Are you going to tell her?

PORTAL: No.

FERDI (*putting the revolver back in his right hand top pocket*): It comes to this. I'm pressed for time. I have to be abrupt. Rose loves my brother.

PORTAL: I know. She told me.

FERDI: Then I have a right to know some things. For instance —who's her mother?

MRS. WEBSTER (*shrill*): *Ask for the moon—you might!*

ROSE (*turning on her*): What do *you* know then! What do you hug yourself with knowing!

MRS. WEBSTER: Ask *him.*—You've everything in your favour.

ROSE: You're jealous of me?

MRS. WEBSTER: It may be that.

ROSE (*to her father*): I'm not to ask?

PORTAL: No.

ROSE (*hysterically*): But sometimes I go mad with asking!

PORTAL: Who?

ROSE: No one! (*To* MRS. WEBSTER.) And if I *wanted* to know —whatever you know—I wouldn't dream of asking you!

MRS. WEBSTER (*taken aback*): Why do you speak like that . . .

ROSE: Hate, I suppose.

MRS. WEBSTER (*recoiling*): Oh. . . .

ROSE (*sarcastic*): But I thought that was understood between us!—That's how we get on! (*Goading.*) An irritability that's like a relationship!

FERDI (*to* PORTAL): Are you going to tell her?

PORTAL: Not now.

FERDI (*to* PORTAL): Do we buy a pig in a poke? Out with it, Kutz! Her mother? Who's the forgotten girl? An Abyssinian? A Turk? An Arab? Or did you beget her, self-fertilized, like a crab-apple on a Sunday?

MRS. WEBSTER (*with malice*): That's what he'd have liked!

FERDI (*pouncing*): *Ah!* ... Housekeeper! ... *Ah!* It's by the sudden splutter of our Unders—that we're betrayed!

PORTAL (*low—to her*): Be quiet.

MRS. WEBSTER (*voice beginning to rise*): I am quiet!

FERDI: Someone not paid enough ... not *loved* enough. ...

PORTAL (*threatening*): Be silent!

MRS. WEBSTER (*going fast out of control*): *I am silent!*

FERDI: But Mrs. Webster is like a bomb, I can hear the seconds ticking.

PORTAL (*to* MRS. WEBSTER): Do you want to be catapulted into talk by a madman?

ROSE (*aghast at the strange relationship*): Who are you. ...

MRS. WEBSTER (*going fast; tossing her head*): I am what I am!

ROSE: What are you?

MRS. WEBSTER: I am neither fish, flesh, nor fowl. ...

PORTAL (*hand on her shoulder—cruel*): *It suits you.*

MRS. WEBSTER (*all out; shrieking*): "It suits me"—then! ... To hell with everything!—I'm a girl from a brothel that folds the pants of a man that shot his father!

PORTAL *looks over her shoulder sharply, hearing a sound she has not heard.*

(*Hysterically weeping.*) ... and the same blood, brown on his coat, when he kissed me six months later. ...

PORTAL (*catching her, dexterously and intimately, a box on the ear —turns her round to see what he has seen; savage—low*): ... and here in England a drop on a shoelace—serves to *hang a man.*

At that moment OLD TONI *walks in ahead of two men who are carrying trays, silver dishes etc.*

OLD TONI: Your eggs—Prince.

He carries a gold bowl filled with white roses. The men move to the table and arrange the dishes. OLD TONI *places the gold bowl in the centre.*

FERDI (*to* OLD TONI): You walk in on an earthquake!—The trees are upside down! (*Low—to* PORTAL.) Are your detectives out of earshot?

PORTAL: I hope so.

FP-F

FERDI (*to carry on the conversation while the men are there; to* OLD TONI): I allow you to remember me.

OLD TONI: I am overjoyed, enchanted.

FERDI (*impatiently watching one of the men putting a match to a night light under a silver heater. Absent—to* OLD TONI): You must be old.

OLD TONI: I tremble to think of it!

FERDI: And ... how has love been. ... (*Makes a gesture to the men to go.*)

OLD TONI (*also watching the men*): As long as I can remember ... humiliating ... (*The men go.*)

FERDI (*instantly—to* MRS. WEBSTER): Is it a relief, woman, to have spilt the beans on him?

MRS. WEBSTER (*miserably*): No. It's an emptiness.

PORTAL (*so bemused that her Christian name escapes him*): You have lost your power, Clara. No need to mince matters. As she says—I killed him. It was an accident. I hit him and his gun exploded.

FERDI: When?

PORTAL: After the valuation.

FERDI: Where?

PORTAL: Two miles from the border. Twelve from your home.

FERDI: Was it there, Matthew?

MATTHEW: The body? That's where they found it.

FERDI: Robbed?

PORTAL (*intervening*): I robbed it. There was forty pounds in the coat's lining.

FERDI: And a picture worth a fortune.

PORTAL: I didn't know it! As you see I never sold it. I never saw a Vuillard, that I knew of, till years later sheltering in a Paris gallery from the rain ... (*With passion.*) *I* took it! It was my doing! I cut it from the frame on the third morning ... That night as we lay down to rest he saw it. I had wrapped it under my vest. He ripped my coat back over my arms to bind them ...

FERDI: You fought?

PORTAL: That's when it happened. Yes.

FERDI (*silent for a moment*): Out of strange sources come the fragrant drops. Here's a man saw my home three days before he killed his father. I should say something bloodily appropriate. Instead I ask ... How did it look—my home?

PORTAL (*shortly*): A castle. Flags flying.

FERDI (*eagerly*): What weather?

PORTAL: Hot. A dusty day.

FERDI: What hour?

PORTAL: Midday.

FERDI: From the gap—where they change horses ...

PORTAL: We walked.

FERDI: The money ran out?

PORTAL: As always.

FERDI: From the gap there's an early-morning miracle. The palace floats. Mist blots out the lower windows... I have come home a thousand times and seen it! You stayed—how long?

PORTAL: Three days.

FERDI: What rooms did you go into?

PORTAL: They had laid out the gold snuff boxes and the objects to be valued—on the long library tables ...

FERDI (*interrupting*): Did you hear talk? ... I find myself a beggar ... was there a sentence ... (*Waits.*) Something called out ... something overheard ... a habit of the house? ... Did someone call out ... "tea time" ...

PORTAL: No.

FERDI: Wood burning? A scent? A smell? ... Paradise must have a smell of its own!

PORTAL: We were in the servants' quarters.

FERDI: Servants! But I am more democratic than you! We have been there six hundred years! Upstairs, downstairs—the long continuity—of grandfathers of grandfathers of grandfathers! We were the Town Hall of their deaths and weddings! The same talk, the same jokes—made in affection ...

PORTAL (*ironic*): An old race.

FERDI: An old race—impervious to money. People rich enough—I apologize—never to have been hungry! Leisure, learning, erudition carried on a bubble ... (*Breaking off. Attemptedly off-hand.*) You saw my mother?

PORTAL: Yes.

FERDI (*suddenly maddened*): "Yes-no-yes-no-*No*!—*yes*!" ... What do you find difficult about words!

PORTAL (*a shrug*): I stammer.

FERDI: Not noticeably!

PORTAL: Deeper—where you can't hear it.

FERDI: If I can't be deep I want no other relationship!

PORTAL: I understand you.

FERDI: I forbid you!

PORTAL: You can't. It's *my* experience. It runs through my life as a wave from Japan hits Kent. Sun lay on the tables. It was the afternoon stillness. You came in from the garden with your mother ...

FERDI (*sharp*): Keep it light!

PORTAL: Am I too serious?

FERDI: Out of key!

PORTAL (*sombre*): I am a man, you may have noticed, without light virtues. You crossed the room talking. She had a green brooch like a fir branch. And these bracelets (*Pointing at the picture.*) slipping down her arms. People talk, without knowing what it is, of good temper. I saw on both your faces so divine a temper ... (*Pause.*) You were my age. Do you remember me?

FERDI: Vaguely. As someone standing in your father's shadow.

PORTAL: Listening. Envious.

FERDI: Of what?

PORTAL: Words. I had never heard the charm of conversation. I had never heard gaiety before. My father was a rag and bone man. He became a valuer. I have been with him often when he broke open shallow graves. We lived like rock apes. Bestial—without noticing. It's not terrible to live like

that. It's *unnoticeable*. But what I want to explain to you is
—that we did not use words.—Or only for shorthand communication.

My life was changed that afternoon. I followed you in the
passages and in the garden. Once through an open door I
heard you discussing love. I had never guessed that people
allowed themselves to open the heart and turn it into talk.

It was as though we broke through a hedge—and heard
old Greece talking!

I fell in love ... No! Not with your mother! With your
relationship together. I vowed to grow rich. I didn't
think it could be done without it. And that when *I* had a
daughter. . . .

FERDI: You were a boy!

PORTAL: A Jewish boy often thinks of his unborn child.
(*Glancing at* ROSE.) Rose was to be—my single-handed
facsimile ...

MRS. WEBSTER: And *I* was the way he got her!

FERDI: You have a malady for interjection—Skeleton-in-the-
Cupboard!

ROSE: You ...

MRS. WEBSTER: Me.

ROSE: What a night to find a mother! What shall I say, having
known you for years, and having been enemies?

MRS. WEBSTER: I shouldn't say much.

ROSE: What shall I call you?

MRS. WEBSTER: The same as before. (*Nervous glance at*
PORTAL.) Ten minutes doesn't change everything.

ROSE: What made you do it?

MRS. WEBSTER (*low*): Temper.

PORTAL (*sternly*): It's like drink. It makes one break promises.

MRS. WEBSTER (*flaming*): And what have *I* got out of them!

PORTAL: Me.

ROSE (*in deep surprise*): You? (*As the answer grows on her.*)
You're not ... fond of her?

PORTAL: She's a woman of limited mentality but I'm fond of

just a corner of her.

ROSE: And ... (*Swinging round to* MRS. WEBSTER.) ... *you?*

PORTAL: Don't ask her complicated things.

MRS. WEBSTER (*with simplicity*): Women like me attach themselves to a man. And when the man allows it it's for life. (*Pause.*) I'm best left without feelings. They disturb me.

ROSE: I want to *know*!

MRS. WEBSTER: You can know then! (*With real love, real passion.*) I worship and adore him! (*She has shattered them. She walks away up the woodland path. Turns, her face irradiated; romantic—like a girl.*) And look at the figure he cuts—though he's had his whack of sin!

ROSE (*winded*): Where can a girl look—when the grown-ups make love in front of her ... I thought you were afraid of him!

MRS. WEBSTER (*with dignity*): A woman doesn't mind being afraid of the man who's married her. (*She has shattered them. To* PORTAL.) Do you want ... further of me?

PORTAL (*a slight pause; his forgiveness for his strange wife*): My tea. At seven.

ROSE (*as* MRS. WEBSTER's *dress disappears in the trees; rueful*): Toni. . . . I'm legitimate.

OLD TONI (*comically*): Never mind, dear.

ROSE (*ironic*): But I'm as pretty—and as young—as I was before I heard it.

PORTAL: *And* as rich.

ROSE (*as the music swells for a moment from the castle*): But the ball's an irony and the guests are swindled ... (*To* FERDI.) You made a promise.

FERDI: Do you hold me to it? (*To* MATTHEW.) My head aches. Get me an aspirin. They're in my cloak. (*As* MATTHEW *goes to fumble in the cloak* FERDI, *moving a step forward, is lit so that his shadow lies across the stage.*) Look at my shadow! It's the moon!

ROSE: It's the sun.

FERDI: How you notice things! Men cut their hair and their nails—why not their shadows? (*Low.*) If he comes—and I ask you to take it from me—remember where I put the gun. (*Louder.*) Have they brought the water? (*She picks up the Evian bottle.*) Pour me some. (*He takes a glass, holds it up to the light.*) There's a spider in it! (*Tosses the glass into the bushes. Looks round the table, seizes the gold bowl.*) This will do. (*Empties water and roses on to the ground, and holds out his hand to* MATTHEW *who tips some tablets into it.* ROSE *fills the bowl and* FERDI, *holding it up high. To Rose, her evening!*

ROSE: No one would think it!

FERDI (*bringing the bowl near his lips*): . . . and before I make myself light as air . . .

HUGO (*strolling in past some bushes, his right hand deep in his trouser pocket*): How are you?

FERDI (*lowering the bowl*): At the top of my form! A little euphoric . . . and as always too hilarious . . .

HUGO (*abruptly*): Is this a rehearsal?

FERDI: And if I were to tell you it was the play itself? (*To* PORTAL.) Would you take my brother for a son-in-law?

PORTAL: I had sooner it had been you.

FERDI (*with a laugh*): Too short notice! (*Lifts the covers on the table, sniffs in the coffee pot, clatters forks and spoons, violent, like a maitre d'hotel in a mania.*) . . . and I have other plans (*Heaping the plates helter-skelter with food, thrusts a plate at* ROSE.) Rose? (*She shakes her head. To* HUGO, *holding out the plate.*) If Rose won't have it . . .

(HUGO *takes the plate automatically, but using his left hand. Puts it down on the table.* MATTHEW *pushes up a gilt chair. Tyranically*): Sit! Eat!

(HUGO *sits. And, as in a kind of absorption he picks up a fork with his left hand and begins to eat,* FERDI *puts the tablets in his mouth.*)

FERDI (*raising the gold bowl high again*): To the bride!

HUGO (*as* FERDI *drinks*): What bride?

FERDI (*setting down the bowl*): If you look closer she wears your mother's ring. (*Nodding at* HUGO's *plate amusedly.*) Is that good?

HUGO: Excellent.

FERDI: And eaten with one hand?

HUGO: That's how it's eaten.

FERDI: Don't be an ass! She knows you have a gun.

HUGO: What can she do about it?

FERDI: Rose—ask him for it.—*No*—take *mine*!

HUGO (*as* FERDI's *hand goes up*): *Don't move!*

FERDI: If you shoot too early you may have taken your life for
nothing . . . Hugo—she loves you. (*Waits.*) Are you blind?

HUGO: No.

FERDI: Deaf?—What then?

HUGO (*taking the little gun from his pocket and holding it on his lap,
the muzzle facing up to his chin*): It's up to you.

FERDI: Rose . . . (*She moves a pace towards him.*) The idiot's
trigger-happy. Like one of those small dogs that waits on the
throw of a stone and moves on a reflex . . . open my coat . . .
careful . . . it's loaded. In my inside breast pocket. (*She takes
it.*) Give it to your father. (PORTAL *takes it and, walking up to*
HUGO, *holds out his hand for the other gun.*)

HUGO (*sharp—to* MATTHEW): *See if he has two!*

FERDI (*as* MATTHEW *comes towards him, relaxed, to* HUGO):
Don't trust him! He's sick of me! (*He holds his arms straight
out on either side.*) Flush me . . . frisk me . . . I am the Holy
Cross! (*As* MATTHEW *feels him up and down, looking down at
the old man, comically.*) Hairs on your coat, old man, and
scurf on your collar . . .

MATTHEW: There's nothing, Mr. Hugo.

HUGO *puts his gun slowly into* PORTAL's *hand.*

FERDI: . . . before you go to God you'll need brushing!

MATTHEW: Ye're profane.

FERDI: I am not. . . . (*Sways; supports himself with one hand on
the table.*) I am a postscript. . . . One of those remarks people
call from a moving train . . . (*Passing to the back of the table.*)
Goodbye, Mr. Portal. Thank you for the party. Before I
go home—abdicating and fretful—can't you stop my
brother making a fuss about death?

PORTAL: I can't help you. I adore life.

FERDI: I can hardly believe it! You look so gloomy! Well . . .
(*swaying*) . . . it's born in one! (*He reels, catches at a branch, as though it alone supported him.*)

PORTAL: Are you ill?

FERDI: Ill? (*He considers.*) No. I see double. It's the sudden stereoscopic effect . . . of putting on distance glasses! The Near and the Far . . . (*A head-to-foot shiver takes him.*) Fetch me my cloak, Matthew, there's a chill. (*Pointing.*) Look!

HUGO: What?

FERDI (*swaying, ecstatic*): The forest close-up! . . . Green fires. . . . God blazing away! Magical . . . the veins in the leaves . . . Knock out the middle distance! I could put my finger in the moon's eye!

ROSE: It's the sun.

FERDI (*a shiver*): The heat's gone out of it! (*To* MATTHEW— *who holds the cloak.*) Put it on.

MATTHEW *wraps it well round him and stands back.*
(*Doing up the neck-clasp himself.*) Do you know why men wore cloaks in old days. . . . (*A long shiver, like a rigor, from head to foot; getting the better of it. To* HUGO—*gently.*) I've stolen a march on you. I drank my travel ticket.

ROSE: The bowl. . . .

FERDI (*smiling at her*): The hemlock.—Socrates died in his cloak.

HUGO: Why have you done this to me!

FERDI: There are extraordinary explorations . . . to permitted people . . . (*Breaking off.*)
(*Brotherly, intimate.*)
I wanted my own way!—I've always had it!

HUGO: Ferdi . . .

FERDI: My name . . . I shed it! (*No longer looking at them.*) Nails, hair, nose . . . and all the glories of this world . . . I shed it! I'm off! I'm sea-mad!—Not even for you, dear fool, on this bright morning. . . .
Staggers, nearly falls across the table, supports himself with

both hands; then with a sudden resurge of strength and waggish gaiety he lifts HUGO's *plate up in the air. Loud.* I call your bluff, dearest! No man goes to God—with an egg in his stomach! (*Crashes forward. The plate shoots downstage on to the grass. Then he slips back, drawing plates, glasses and the cloth with him—and is seen no more.*)

There is a quick movement, instantly quelled by MATTHEW— *who has not glanced down to see if he is dead.*

MATTHEW (*with authority*): I have his order. Leave him.

OLD TONI (*under his breath*): Dead. . . .

MATTHEW (*with pride*): He wouldn't fail.

HUGO (*facing downstage—he doesn't want to see*): Lift him on to the table.

MATTHEW: He was to lie as he fell.—*You are free, Mr. Hugo.*

HUGO (*always with his back to them*): Did he tell you to say that?

MATTHEW: In the car. Coming down.

HUGO: You knew?

MATTHEW: I gave it to him. I'm old. I've always obeyed him.

HUGO: You're sure? Beyond finding? (MATTHEW *nods*.) . . . Into the absolute marble . . . What a gift death gives one!

MATTHEW: The only one ye didn't expect?

HUGO: Yes. . . . No more apprehension. . . . What else did he say?

MATTHEW: Ye were to offer. For the girl.

HUGO (*half turning, wooden*): I ask you for Rose, Mr. Portal.

There is a long silence. PORTAL *stands upstage looking down at the fallen prince.*

ROSE: Father. . . .

PORTAL: I heard. (*Pause.*) I don't care for the terms.

ROSE (*her face radiant*): I take responsibility.

PORTAL: He doesn't love you.

HUGO (*looking at no one*): You can't ask a man you've pulled out of a lake if he loves.

First . . . (*Exhausted.*) . . . you've got to dry him.

CURTAIN

The Chinese Prime Minister

THE CHINESE PRIME MINISTER was first presented by Roger L. Stevens at the Royale Theatre, New York City, 2nd January 1964. Setting by Oliver Smith. Costumes by Valentina. Lighting by Jean Rosenthal. Associate producers Lyn Austin, Victor Samrock. Directed by Joseph Anthony. The cast was as follows:

BENT	Alan Webb
OLIVER	Peter Donat
SHE	Margaret Leighton
ROXANE	Joanna Pettet
ALICE	Diane Kagan
TARVER	Douglas Watson
RED GUS RISKO	James Olson
SIR GREGORY	John Williams

THE CHINESE PRIME MINISTER was presented in London, in an altered form, by H. M. Tennent and Roger L. Stevens at the Globe Theatre on 20th May 1965. Dame Edith Evans played the principal role with Alan Webb as her butler. The play was directed by Vivian Matalon.

The action takes place in the drawing room of a once fashionable house in London.

TIME: Any year in which the actress is sixty-nine. One hour before she is due to leave for the theatre for her evening performance.

ACT I: SCENE 1: Late Autumn.
SCENE 2: Early Spring.
ACT II: The same evening.
ACT III: Five months later.

CHARACTERS

BENT
OLIVER
SHE
ROXANE
ALICE
TARVER
RED GUS RISKO
SIR GREGORY

ACT I

Scene I

THE SET: *A bay window which overlooks what has been success-*
ively a stable yard and the mews cottage garden. The window is
full of the leaves of a very old plane tree. Green light filters
through. There is also a window on the street. There are three
direct doors, one to HER *bedroom, one to the kitchen quarters, one*
to the hall. But there must in some way be a method of reaching
the rest of the house—perhaps by a vestibule seen between
columns at one side, so that anyone coming from upstairs can be
seen as they go to the hall door. Somewhere in the room there is
an empty birdcage.

When the CURTAIN goes up: SHE—*the lady of the house—in*
a dressing-gown, is finishing her breathing exercises at the open
window facing the plane tree in full leaf, her back to the audience
—raising and dropping her arms—while her son, OLIVER, *aged*
twenty-nine, counts aloud for her. A freshly opened note—and its
envelope—lie on a small table by the sofa.

OLIVER (*idly—as he reads a book*): . . . forty-four . . . forty-five
. . . forty-six . . .
SHE (*impetuously turning*): Just imagine!—*No description at all!*
It shakes me!
OLIVER: Go on. Forty-seven . . .
SHE (*coming downstage, but still moving her arms automatically*):
He just indicates love! . . . (*Breathing.*) leading to marriage
. . . —That's all!
OLIVER: . . . forty-eight . . . forty-nine . . .
SHE (*spitting it out*): *Fifty! This* isn't a day when I can breathe!
(*Seeing old* BENT *in the doorway.*) What is it, Bent?

BENT: Sir Gregory, m'lady—

OLIVER: *What!*

BENT: Your husband again on the telephone. I've switched it up.

SHE: Then switch it down.

OLIVER (*impatient*): Who do you mean by—"Sir *Gregory*"?—my father's dead.

BENT (*imperturbable*): At the Savoy, he said.

SHE: And I don't take calls from unknown men!

OLIVER (*casually stretching out an arm to the telephone*): I'll see what it is—

SHE (*sharply urgent*): *I'll* see! (OLIVER *looks up astonished at her tone. Half-excusing herself.*) I know what it is—it's about a hat. . . . (*He gives telephone to her.*)

BENT: No, it isn't.

SHE (*holding* BENT *with her eyes over the telephone*): Who's speaking? (*To* OLIVER.) Well—don't stand over me! (*He strolls away.*) Ten—what? Ten—*orchids?* (OLIVER *smiles.*) Ten—*DOZEN!* (*Putting her hand over the telephone she holds it away from her a moment. Then, suddenly.*) I wish they *were* for me—but I'm afraid they're not! (*Replaces instrument on stand.*)

OLIVER: Is it love?

SHE: Of course it's love—but he had the wrong number. (*To* BENT.) I'd *forgotten!*—It's your afternoon off!

BENT (*grim*): But it's gone.

SHE: If it's gone you could stay and boil my egg.

BENT: Mr. Oliver said he'd boil it. (*Pulling out his large turnip watch on its chain and consulting it.*) I'm off now. (*Breaking off—*) The gin's running short.—It's my young lady—meeting me. (*Obstinate, as he turns to go.*) It *was* Sir Gregory's voice on the telephone.

SHE: So you said yesterday—and it wasn't! (*Reasoning with him.*) Look, Bent! When one gets old—as you and I get old —people long dead— (*But he is going.*)

OLIVER: Take it from me! My father's been dead twenty years.

BENT: I know it. But that doesn't stop him ringing. (*Goes.*)

SHE (*carelessly*): It's an *obsession*! (*Picking up the note again—washing out the subject of* BENT.) Telling me *nothing*! Does Tarver think I like a total surprise!

OLIVER: Tarver hates to be embarrassed. You sent him to school too early.

SHE: I never know anything about him!

OLIVER: He doesn't mean you to.

SHE: I used to.

OLIVER: If you look back—not since he went to school when he was seven.

SHE: Those schools!—Thank God I never sent you!—Settle me, Oliver. (*He arranges the cushions on the sofa.*) My handkerchief. In my bag. Over there. (*Curling up on the sofa.*) And he knows—before the theatre—things upset me! And *tonight*!—The last night of the play!—after twenty-three months—(*Suddenly, conventionally, dropping a small false wreath.*) it's so *sad*.

OLIVER (*walking over to the secretary on which lie a pile of those yellowish envelopes that contain scripts. Mocking, over shoulder*): But you're *glad*.

SHE (*a conventional rebuke*): We are loyal to our plays.

OLIVER (*holding about six of the heavy envelopes up between his two hands as though weighing them*): And the next play? What about these?

SHE: I haven't read them. I haven't *opened* them! Those lines —those words! (*Pushing them away as he holds them near her. Touching her forehead.*) I feel a muscle in my forehead that's carried words for forty years! Oh—why does no one write *real* plays—about the fascination and disaster of being old!

OLIVER: What's the fascination?

SHE: What might lie ahead of me! If I had the daring . . .

OLIVER: What's the disaster?

SHE: What you all expect for me! That for me it's the end of surprises! For me it's the final run-in.

OLIVER: It may be the winning post.

SHE: My horse, if it wins, runs past the post into the fog. (*Reverting again, toying with note.*) *Telling me nothing!* Not one word about the girl! Not even a surname! —She's called Alice. That's all!

OLIVER: You can expect she'll be beautiful. That's the prime thing my brother demands in a girl.

SHE (*vexedly*): So do you. (*A door opens.* ROXANE *comes in dressed to go out. Very chic, very young, very lovely—she crosses the room, or the vestibule. They watch her. Surely she will speak? Not a word! Giving her every chance. At the last ditch.*) Good morning.

ROXANE (*immediately stopping, polite*): Good afternoon, Mama.

OLIVER (*involuntarily*): How sweet you look!

ROXANE (*gravely*): Thank you. (*Stepping forward as though about to say something of importance.*) Mama . . .

SHE: Yes?

ROXANE (*with her special good manners*): I shall be out tonight. (*Goes.*)

SHE (*a moment's silence*): "Mama"—as *she* uses it—is like a sword! Her manners are so beautiful they're like an armour! I should like to have seen her as she was being born— exquisitely thanking the doctor!—Do you know where she's going?

OLIVER: No.

SHE (*angry*): You *ought* to know!

OLIVER: *I* ought to? Or is that a general rule?

SHE: *You* ought to!—It's laughable!

OLIVER: Those in love are always laughable.

SHE: She's obviously dining with some man.

OLIVER: She may be.

SHE: Don't you care! She's your wife!

OLIVER: She hates to be asked. It's a kind of adolescence. In a way I understand it.

SHE: Understand her, if you like! But *hide* it!

OLIVER: I'm not that kind of man! I'm not inscrutable!

SHE: It's she who is inscrutable.—She isolates herself from you because you don't try to master her, and she isolates herself from me because she guesses I know it. I thought she could be a daughter. And so she is. But an enemy-daughter! The truth is—that I ought not to be able to watch your troubles as I do! The truth is—you ought never—once you married —to have lived on here with me!

OLIVER (*lamely*): She's not grown up.

SHE: But she will be!

OLIVER: Couldn't you be charitable?

SHE: I could. But I'm not that kind of woman. You think I've done badly by her? I began by trying hard. But it's dishonest to make friends with the next generation.

OLIVER: Then what about me?

SHE: You were born when your father left me. You and I have a language of intimacy.

OLIVER: She knew that. She knew she wasn't elected to the club!

SHE: You promised you'd bring her last night. The tickets were waiting.

OLIVER: I know.

SHE: She hasn't seen me play since you were married.—She avoids my triumphs!—she keeps me in a single focus—as a mother-in-law! (*Dismissing the subject.*) How soon will they be here?

OLIVER: Five minutes.

SHE: And *now* what sort of girl is Tarver bringing to me! Who else do I have to be unselfish for? (*Smiling.*) I used to look at my daughters-in-law—in their prams in the Park— and *hate* them! . . . What will—"Alice" be like?

OLIVER: She'll be at least twenty-five. And sophisticated. A cool, pale, marble girl—and a catch socially.

SHE: Is Tarver a snob?

OLIVER: No, but he doesn't undervalue his world. . . .

The door opens. TARVER *comes in, the elder son, with* ALICE.

TARVER (*giving* ALICE *a push as she hangs back*): Go on, Alice.
   ALICE *is seventeen, a hobbledehoy. Awkward. Hair-trouble.*
ALICE: How do you do.
SHE (*rising ceremoniously*): Can I call you Alice?
ALICE: Please do.
SHE (*drawing* ALICE *to a chair beside the sofa*): Sit here. Let me
   look at you. (*Smiling ravishingly. Taking* ALICE'*s hand.*) I don't
   kiss you. Things ought to come gradually! (*Her smile belying
   her words.*) It's a relationship—of enormous danger—my
   little girl! (*Putting a hand up to* TARVER.) I think she ought
   to have come *alone* to see me!
ALICE (*eager, blurting*): That's what I thought, too! (*With a
   gulp.*) I've been dying to meet you! (*Another gulp.*) You've
   twice signed my little book—did you know?
SHE: *I* have?
ALICE: Once outside the Duchess Theatre at the stage door.
   Once outside the Haymarket . . .
SHE: You're one of the girls with little books and pencils!
ALICE: I'd never have dared to ask you if Tarver hadn't come,
   too!
SHE (*bowled over*): Tarver!—I can't believe it! *Tarver*, at the
   stage door!
TARVER (*changing the subject*): This is Oliver—Alice.
OLIVER: I've seen you somewhere.
ALICE: So have I you. You came down with . . . (*Rapturously.*)
   your mother—when she gave the prizes at school. I got one
   for gym.
TARVER (*his hand on her shoulder*): My *darling*!—You sound
   like a goop but I love you!
ALICE (*to* OLIVER): I was so envious! You brought a marvel-
   lous girl with you!
OLIVER: That was my wife.
ALICE (*to* HER): So you've got a daughter-in-law already?
   I couldn't take my eyes off her. She was so well dressed she
   made me feel a slob.
TARVER (*to his* MOTHER): This is a divine girl but she takes

knowing! I've *done* with all my sleek ideals! I've remade
my taste in girls. This one's *not* my type ... (*Puts an arm
around* ALICE's *waist.*) She's *not* well dressed—she's *not*
beautiful—but I love her from scratch! Look at her hair!
(*Rumples it:* ALICE *dodges out from his hand, displeased.*) She's
as newborn as a chicken!

SHE (*gravely—to* ALICE): Do you feel so young?

ALICE (*carefully*): Not as young as that. (*Eagerly.*) Will you
let me marry him?

SHE: And have my daughter-in-law my fan?

ALICE: Is that against me?

SHE: We won't let it be! (*To* TARVER.) Leave me alone with
her. (*To* ALICE.) Will you talk alone with me?

ALICE: Thank you.

TARVER (*going to the console table*): I'll give you both ten
minutes. And I'll take a drink with me.

SHE: There's whisky. And a syphon.

TARVER (*holding up bottle*): There's not much gin!

SHE (*looking vaguely round*): I don't know where it goes ...
I never touch it! All the old girls get drunk on gin now—in
my world.—Put on the egg—Oliver.

TARVER: Is it Bent's day out?

SHE (*vexedly*): Yes, it is. (*To* ALICE.) Bent's my butler. Fifty
years my Impresario!—and pokes his nose in too much!
(*To* OLIVER.) And one of these days I'm going to retire
him! I can't stand his nostalgia another minute!

TARVER: Nostalgia for what?

SHE: Even served at dinner I have to hear it! Nostalgia for
girls! *He* wants to get married—too!

TARVER: At his age!—For *girls*!

SHE: He calls all women girls up to sixty. But this one really
is a girl. (*Pause.*) And much too developed for him!

TARVER: Are you inventing this? Just to feel good at getting
rid of him?

SHE: No. This is true.

ALICE: Do you invent things?

SHE (*amused*): If life is annoying I do. (*As* OLIVER *goes to the kitchen door.*) Take Tarver with you.

TARVER (*carrying his whisky. At kitchen door—to* ALICE): Got courage enough?

ALICE: Yes, thank you.

SHE (*getting up—shutting door after* TARVER—*turning to survey her new* DAUGHTER-IN-LAW. *At last*): This will be like talking from two sides of the world! (*To console table.*) First —you must stop worshipping me just as soon as you can. (*Takes what remains of gin, looks at it, puts it away on another table.*)

ALICE: How does one?

SHE: You may be marrying Tarver because you are infatuated with me.

ALICE: I may be.

SHE: Tarver's my son. But I don't *know* him. I can't help you in dealing with him.

ALICE: Oh, Tarver's easy to know!

SHE: Do you think so? (*Pursuing her own line of thought.*) And then—as you get to know *me* better—you may hate me.

ALICE: Why?

SHE: Because we shall never have been neutral. You have begun by adoring me, and for the wrong reasons. And when you stop adoring me you'll take it out on me.—Don't interrupt!—After that—you may further divide Tarver and me—by complaint of me. (*As* ALICE *is about to protest. Overriding.*) I don't say it *will* happen. I say it might. One is sweet to one's daughter-in-law in the first year because one is sucking up to one's son. Quite soon she may become an enemy. In the end there's a chance she may become a friend. No, don't interrupt me! ... Then there are other complications. (*Turning and facing* ALICE.) I require a great deal of attention. I'm used to it. A woman who is successful on the stage isn't easy. Oliver manages it. But Oliver's the tender one. (*Suddenly remembering—faintly put out.*) I should be having my egg in a few minutes! (*Returning across the*

room. ALICE *just sits and looks at her.*) I suppose you would
call me a selfish woman. But self-expression takes doing.
Especially on the stage. An actress must be an egotist. Her
personality is so important to her! And that's the real truth
about people! They are not types. They aren't mothers-in-
law and daughters-in-law! They are creatures ardently engaged on themselves! I say all this to show you that you
and I have got to stand up to each other.—It won't be
roses! (*Walks up and down.*) Another thing . . . (*The TELE-
PHONE rings. Picks it up.*) Who is speaking? (*Listens.
Smiling.*) Always the same wrong number! (*Presses instrument to her breast so that it is muffled.*)

ALICE (*timidly*): What other things?

SHE: I don't want to seem ridiculous. In your eyes no doubt
. . . (*With a half smile she lifts the telephone from its muffled
state and holds it not far from her mouth.*) But my private life
isn't run on age. It may surprise you, Alice, but men still
fall in love with me. . . . (*Puts the telephone back on its stand
—touches a flower in a gilt basket. Takes off card from flowers.*)

ALICE (*devoted*): I should think so!

SHE: Yes, there's a glamour hangs about a woman of power
and success—yes. But that's not exactly what I mean—what
I want! What I'm trying to say—but don't answer me—is
that my life is still full of surprises. I have an extra vitality
and extra expectations! I can't imagine living on when there
are no more expectations!—I don't know why I say this to
you—except that it may be a revelation for *your* old age!
Though by then you will have forgotten it! Oh, Alice, how
young you are! Are you sure you can be happy with Tarver?

ALICE: Absolutely! He's the kind of man I've always dreamt
of. He's a bully and I love that. I always longed to marry a
bully.

SHE (*crumpling card in her hand*): Then you can understand
more than I!— (*Inward smile.*) His father was a bully.

ALICE: Tarver thinks he can remodel me.

SHE: And can he?

ALICE: No. But I love to see him trying.

SHE: It seems to me that at first sight I underrated you!

ALICE: Can I ask you one thing?

SHE (*cautious*): It depends.

ALICE: On the whole—and quite apart from difficulties—do you like me?

SHE: Yes, I do. But don't count on it lasting!

ALICE: I worship you. But I quite see that to worship you is a kind of puppy-fat. Tarver says—that you criticize him—

SHE (*vexed*): He talks about me!

ALICE: Only with me.—Only because he loves you.

SHE (*sarcastic and still hurt*): Thank you.

ALICE: You don't like my saying that. But you *did* want to know. (*Struggling on.*) As a matter of fact—and to be honest . . .

SHE: Go on.

ALICE: It's a message from him. He says you *don't* know that he loves you. And he wants you to know. (*Hurrying on—afraid of being stopped.*) He wants our marriage to be started like that. With you knowing. So that you would never think . . . (*Choking with difficulty.*) that I had . . . more love than you. I mean—I've not stolen him from you! (*Pause.*) Would you think it fearful cheek—if I warned you? (SHE *is silent because she is thinking of what has been said.*) There are things in me—that you ought to know. I get bursts of rebellion. It's my growing pains. I've got a temper like the devil. I can't cure it. And a sort of mutiny. If you try to push me I go hard and something rushes over me. A terrible obstinacy. I can't help it. And then—what Tarver *doesn't* know—but I'm telling you—is that I mind terribly, terribly —that I look as I do. I could have killed Tarver when he said just now—and in front of you—that I wasn't beautiful. Though I know I'm not.

SHE (*absent*): Oh, but I'll dress you—so that you won't know yourself!

ALICE (*in dead earnest*): That's just what I don't want you to do!

You're so powerful that you could change me! And I
mustn't be changed! It must be *my* business! That's what I
used the word "warning" for! I want to warn you to let
me do my growing by myself. (*Trying hard to get over what
she means.*) If the *wrong* face—looks out of *my* face— (*Breaking
off.*) Oh—a girl's looks are *agony*! Do you remember it?

SHE: It seems to me I said the same five minutes ago! But I
couldn't have said it—as you do—so clearly!

ALICE: I've got a sort of back-to-the-wallness that makes me
clear. (*As the door opens—loud, to* TARVER.) All right! We've
made a fist of it.

TARVER: Is that my magical hockey girl?

SHE: Yes, Tarver. And she and I understand everything!—
Except that I don't know her name!

ALICE: Alice Feathers.

SHE: *Feathers!*

ALICE: I'm afraid so. And in case you want to know, I have
an aunt who drinks. And my father and mother are
separated.

TARVER: So were mine.

OLIVER (*coming in with the tray*): The sacred moment has
come!

   (SHE *sits down on the sofa.*)

TARVER: The moment of the egg. From now on, Alice, my
mother is hardly human.

SHE (*grave*): I have to leave in half an hour for the theatre. I
always sit alone before I go. The play comes off tonight—
and I have to say something.

ALICE (*with bated breath*): Make a *speech* . . . to the *audience*!

SHE: I suppose so. I expect so.—Turn off the lights, Oliver.—
Except this one.

ALICE: Oh, I wish I could be there!

SHE: You *can* be.—You arrange it, Oliver.—*You'll* be coming?

OLIVER: Well, no.—But I'll ring about a seat for Alice.

ALICE (*worshipping*): When can I see you again?

SHE (*smiling*): When you want to be disloyal to your husband

—with his mother! Look in my engagement book, Oliver.

OLIVER (*picking up a small scarlet engagement book. Turning pages*): The whole of next week ... *full.*

SHE: Not a chink—not a corner for a new daughter!

OLIVER (*looking ahead in the book*): Nor the week after.

SHE (*indignant*): So it has been for forty years! It creeps ahead of me! It strangles me! (*To* ALICE.) I'll ring you! I'll tear a living minute from that book!—Goodbye.—And don't have a moment's doubt, Tarver. I adore her. (TARVER *and* ALICE *go out. To* OLIVER.) I feel in love myself. I feel included. I feel ... (*Looking far away.*) the meal might be for me! (*Reminded of her egg, she attacks it.*)

OLIVER: Don't go too far!

SHE: I thought I would be jealous. And very critical.— And God knows there's room for criticism!—She's a grave pudding of a child. But she won't be a pudding long.

OLIVER: Were you kind?

SHE: Yes, I was kind. But kindness is so fugitive. It comes like a gust into the heart. And blows out again. (*Putting down her spoon and looking up.*) A girl as young as that brings one to one's senses! She looked at me as though she thought I *knew* about life! And I know nothing!—And I play— tonight—that "wise woman" who knows *all* the conclusions! What do I know of a private life! I've been defrauded! ... I wish I could meet ... (*Smiling at him.*) a Chinese Prime Minister. (*Pause.*) Before the coming of Christ. In the East —when age was near paradise and not a prison ...

OLIVER (*in the same tone—humouring her*): A Prime Minister still in office?

SHE: No! He makes a triumph of his retirement! He writes poems that will outlive his achievements!—He carries a birdcage. We go up in the mountains together ... (*Her voice stops.*)

OLIVER: ... very faintly etched on the landscape ... Is it love?

SHE: Of course! And why not—why shouldn't it be! (BENT *comes in but she pays no attention.*) I suppose the car is round

—and my big coat in the hall? (*As* OLIVER *goes.*) Call me in fifteen minutes and I'll start. (*As the door shuts on* OLIVER, *she gets up and picks up the red engagement book that has fallen to the floor. Straightening herself after stooping.*) What am I doing here—with *fifteen* of them! (*As* BENT *looks a bit taken aback.*) Minutes!—Unique!—Fifteen! What are they *for*!

BENT: Not for resting. (*Coming near her.*) There's a bit of life coming.

SHE: Yes. I know. (*Suddenly aware* BENT *shouldn't be there.*) I thought you were *out.*

BENT (*sour*): She gave me the slip. (*Sour-meditative.*) To hell with women, m'lady, I'm fed up. (*Picks up her tray.*)

SHE (*rising, intent on herself*): And *I'm* fed up! (*Paces away—turning round.*) Or shall I say it nobly?—I want to change my life—absolutely! Suddenly, publicly—so that it *can't* be taken back!

BENT: I should think twice.

SHE: I want to get *out*! (*Picking up and shaking the engagement book.*) *Out* of this book—with its procession—moving me on! *Out* of the theatre! What am I doing playing these —fabricated—women!—Running north, south, east, west— inside a playwright's brain!

BENT: There's many'd give their eyes to do it.

SHE (*moving downstage*): In the spring it's my seventieth birthday. Like a Roll-Call. "Stand up," saith the Lord, "and call your number! Your time's up!"—Thus saith the Lord. (*Completely to* BENT—*but not aware of it.*) And then He takes me—at my weakest corner. Breaks me—where some screw or bolt's not doing its job. I shall be laid suddenly on a bed that I despise! Not my own bed. Not chosen by me. But the last bed. Dragged off into the Infinite, as it were, from a pub.—Like the one with curtains on the doors—where you fetch sandwiches.

BENT (*eyes shining—after all, what an audience he is!*): That'd make 'em sit up!

SHE (*echoing—bemused*): "Sit up." . . .

BENT: Among the Curtain Calls!

SHE (*still half there and half not*): Tonight?

BENT: Pub and all—just as you said it!

SHE (*sharp—alert*): *How long have I got?*

BENT (*pulling the turnip watch out on its chain and holding it for her to see*): I can't see it.

SHE (*stooping a little to see it*): Ten minutes. (*He picks up tray and goes to kitchen door.*) I could say it—lightly . . .

BENT (*turning in surprise*): Eh?

SHE (*to herself*): . . . almost as a joke. I'm so afraid of a grandiose ending. (*Pause.*) And after all, it's a wild thing to do!—Put down that tray.—I mean one could suggest— without making it certain. Tell Mr. Oliver. . . . He said he wasn't coming. But tell him—*most particularly*. . . . Say it like that! Say that I *beg* him to come tonight. Give me— still—ten minutes. . . . I want to try and remember . . . what I said just now. . . . (BENT *goes over to the door to go out. Coming downstage in the half darkness, trying out her voice.*) Ladies and Gentlemen . . . (*Clears her throat.*) old friends of so many years . . . (*Haltingly.*) (BENT, *fascinated, lingers.*) when one puts things in one's own words . . .

BENT (*low—sly*): . . . and no author to help you . . .

SHE (*appearing to take no notice—but made firm by opposition*): Ladies and Gentlemen . . . old friends . . . I have come to a decision. In the Spring it's my seventieth birthday. Like a Roll-Call. "Stand up," said the Lord, "and call your number!" (*CURTAIN begins—either here or a little earlier—to come down as she says:*) "Your time's up! . . . but the lucky ones have a margin. . . ."

CURTAIN

Some months later. Very early spring. In fact, The Birthday. Before luncheon. The room is much the same. The sofa has either gone or is in the background. In the foreground is the armchair; and a small table of wrapped-up presents. Plates, glasses, etc. are on the console table.

BENT *is discovered sitting on the sofa, a cheap paper bag beside him. A pink and white iced birthday cake is on the low table. He is rapidly sticking birthday candles into the icing of the cake. When he has got in half a dozen he pulls out a fresh bundle—realizes the size of his task, reverses gear on the undertaking, throws the bundle back in the bag and pulls out the six candles, and as* SHE *comes in from her bedroom, he rapidly shuts up the bag and hides it. Rises—presents candle-less cake to her.*

SHE (*with distaste*): *Seventy!*
BENT: Well, you knew you would be.
SHE: What!
BENT: One sees it coming.
SHE: You've been so surly since I left the theatre!
BENT (*a grumble*): Why did you?
SHE: It was an act of folly! What have I gained by it! Seventy was a mountain I wanted to survey! To make an exploration! But I've been a woman in public so long—this gift to myself befogs me!
BENT: *Gift* to yourself?
SHE: Of a private life. I don't know how to lead it!—Without the theatre I feel diminished. Caught in so small a programme! I put on clothes. I take them off. Eat. Sleep. And in between . . . No sense of God!
BENT: Had you expected one?

SHE: One would have thought—some brush of a wing. ....
He might have winked. (*Pause.*) The engagement book is
there just the same—but the appointments are meaner! (*To
the window.*) Nobody here! How late they are! It's only the
Old who are punctual! I'm more vulnerable to petty things!
Your mind on your wife—the house not running—fewer
flowers!

OLIVER *comes in in a hurry with flowers.*

OLIVER: I'm late— Oh God, one's always kept by something.
... *Happy* Birthday! (*Glancing around.*) Hell, I forgot the
cake! Who ordered it?

BENT: Her ladyship remembered. *She* ordered it.

OLIVER: No candles?

BENT: *I* remembered. But I decided against them.—Sooner
or later one's got to stop counting. (*Goes.*)

SHE: I hate that trick! He gets it out of plays!

BENT: What?

SHE: Those postscripts at the door. Is Roxane coming?

OLIVER: I reminded her. (*Avoiding.*) Open your presents.
(*Stooping.*) That's her writing!—Open it!

SHE (*taking the parcel, weighing it in her hand so that she can both
hear and feel that it is a bottle. Handing it back*): I'm afraid to.
(*He takes it.*) I asked you.—Is she coming?

OLIVER (*reluctantly*): She stayed last night with a friend.

SHE: Is *that* your married life? (*Waits.*) Having your own house
has made no difference?

OLIVER: It's made this difference—that I've started to write
again. (*With surprise.*) It's a bottle of gin!—Why should she
send you that!

SHE: She knows I like my tipple.

OLIVER: How much do you drink?

SHE: Too much for me.

OLIVER: For your health?

SHE: I shall take a lot of killing.

OLIVER: When did you begin?

SHE: Don't talk about beginning! It's a respectable habit—

that grows less respectable with time!

OLIVER: But *when*?

SHE: When I needed mystery at sunset. When the cards grew dim.—*She* came in—your wife—it was the day you left here —and I obscured the bottle.—It wasn't what I had drunk that caught her fancy!—It was the gesture!

OLIVER: She is jealous of you. She says it isn't fair that you are past the age of beauty—and still in it.

SHE (*delighted*): It was always a trick I played on people! I was never beautiful.—I invented it! Does she know how beautiful *she* is?

OLIVER: She can never be sure of it. I watch her as she dresses and undresses feverishly in front of the mirror. It's painful! —I love her.—Every dress she wears—*ravishes* me!

SHE: Do you know that I feel guilty?

OLIVER: For what?

SHE: I have made you defenceless against her. I have made you so specially a woman's son.—In a way—you hardly had a father!

OLIVER: Biologically difficult!

SHE: Psychologically easy!—Roxane—*jealous* of me! Is it because she has married the son of my heart?

OLIVER: She was afraid of you—and she doesn't forgive it. She said when I brought her to you that she was frightened of a woman with sons.

SHE: I was willing—in theory—to have them taken from me. I was prepared to open my narrow charmed circle. But it took me by surprise to have the circle broken!

OLIVER: She said you were on the lookout for bandits!

SHE: No, I could have stood a bandit.

BENT *comes in with the midday papers.*

OLIVER: You've got a bandit in the other one!

SHE (*sharp*): *Alice!* What's Alice been doing?

OLIVER: I was going to tell you. It's in the midday papers—

BENT: It's *headlines*!

OLIVER: Shop-lifting.

FP—G

SHE: *Shop-lifting!*—Alice! (*To* OLIVER.) What's Tarver doing?

OLIVER: He won't do anything. I've just stood bail for her.

SHE: Why you? Why not Tarver?

OLIVER (*rueful*): Because you have decreed I am the tender one!

SHE (*as* BENT *brings her the newspaper*): What shop was it?

BENT: Fortnums. (*Exits.*)

SHE (*to* OLIVER): Ring Cazan. The solicitor. He gets everyone out of scrapes. No—wait. He was buried yesterday. . . . That's why I thought of him! Who do I know who could help? Don't *you* know anyone?

OLIVER: Take my advice. Don't pull strings. Today everyone relies on something else—that everyone forgets everything.

SHE: Is she alone? Where is she?

OLIVER: I offered to drive her home. Home—or anywhere. She went into a pub.

SHE: Why didn't you go after her?

OLIVER: By the look she gave me she would have bitten me.

TARVER (*in doorway—grim*): Happy Birthday.

SHE (*turning*): No—a shocking one!—Why didn't *you* go bail for her?

TARVER: I'm finished with Alice!—I'm for my career.

SHE: Have you thought what's to become of her?

TARVER: She's been headed downhill ever since I married her.

SHE: Is it your fault?

TARVER (*crossing to her*): Who knows? (*Stoops and kisses her.*) Who knows when the evil starts? When I married her, I suppose I married all that's behind her.

SHE: Nonsense! You and Alice are responsible together for her vices! Why does everyone blame the ancestors? Before I can turn round the failure of both your marriages will be on *my* shoulders!

OLIVER: Mine hasn't failed yet. (*To* TARVER.) Had you a row?

TARVER: One of many.—She asked me for money.

SHE: Why didn't you give it to her?

TARVER: She has enough.

SHE: Enough for what?

TARVER: To run our lives together.

SHE: She must have wanted more for her own life.

TARVER: Are you against me?

SHE: How should I know! You exclude me from knowing.

OLIVER (*turning the point of pain. Smiling*): He preserves you from crossing his married frontier!

TARVER: Well, of course! Because you'd say you had heard it all before.

OLIVER (*lightly*): And the battles of a man and his wife should be as fresh as dew! (*To his* MOTHER.) Does Tarver hurt you?

SHE (*absently—she has been pursuing her own thought*): I've been thinking—if Tarver is half my immortality I shall have to rely more on Oliver. (*Suddenly coming-to.*) Yes. Tarver hurts me. I *so* hate blame! At my age the charming thing would be to be above criticism! (*To* TARVER—*direct.*) Remember! She's still your wife.

TARVER: Until I can get rid of her.

ALICE (*in doorway*): That'll be difficult. (*She walks unsteadily. She is followed into the room by an enormous man with a flaming head of red hair.*) Hullo, Oliver.

ALICE *has a new rebel-surface. She wears whatever is the anti-uniform when this play is finally produced.*

MAN: Are you all right now, madam?

ALICE: No. Stay with me.

MAN (*to* OLIVER): She wasn't well.

ALICE: I was sick in the pub. I owe him the taxi, too. Could you settle it, Tarver?—No. Better, Oliver. He's easier with the purse. (*To* MAN.) Wait a minute. Sit down. . . . Mama . . . can he have a drink?

SHE: Of course. Why don't we open the champagne now?

ALICE: I see you've got gin there. (*Picks up bottle.*) It's quicker to open. (*Sees card attached.*) From Roxy!—Funny present! (*Strips off the lead cover round the top. Offers bottle to* MAN.) Help yourself. Glasses over there.

MAN: I don't drink. Which is your husband?

ALICE: Him.

MAN (*to* TARVER): She's in trouble. You ought to look after her.

TARVER: Mind your own business.

MAN: She *is* my business. I brought her here.

TARVER: D'you want me to punch your nose for you?

MAN: You'd get nowhere. This is a straight girl in straight trouble. I'm watching to see how you treat her.

TARVER (*to* ALICE): How fast you make friends!

ALICE: He's religious.

TARVER: Does that explain it?

ALICE: He does a good deed every day.

MAN (*showing a huge doubled fist. Calm*): I don't find it difficult with this behind it.

TARVER: You're nothing but a bully.

MAN (*calm*): Say that again.

TARVER: No. I prefer once only.

MAN (*to* ALICE): Shall I take you out of here?

SHE (*to* MAN—*suddenly*): And where would you take her? (*Looks at him—waiting.*) She's got her own home. And her husband's here to take her there.

MAN: That's up to her.

SHE: No, it's up to *me*. This is my house and these are my relations. You can't punch me at my age. So it's safe for me to talk to you! I don't like people as simple as you are! It's no good hammering life into black and white because you've got a fist like a sirloin!

ALICE (*in laughter*): Oh, I do like Mama! Oh, God, I like Mama when she gets going!

SHE (*gathering momentum*): And what's more—you are complicating life for me! I don't like strangers taking sides! There are enough sides taken with my own children! I don't like brute force simply walking into my drawing-room! I don't like Boy Scouts when they are as big as you are! Accept the money for the taxi and please go.

ALICE (*her hand on the* MAN's *arm*): Go along. You've had it!

Our romance is over!

MAN (*as* OLIVER *comes up to him with a "paying for taxi" face and gesture*): Keep your half crowns. I've got a yacht and a Bentley.

ALICE: You've got a ... *What* have I let slip through my fingers!

MAN: Red Gus Risko.

ALICE: The one on the placards outside the Albert Hall! The *Boxer*! Oh, I ought to have known! Why didn't you tell me!

MAN: Because I like to do my good deeds quietly. (*He goes out, followed by* OLIVER.)

ALICE (*to* TARVER): So you were talking of getting rid of me.

TARVER: I'll speak to you when you're sober.

ALICE: I'm not drunk. I had a glass of beer and it made me sick, owing to emotion. I'm faint now. I could eat ... (*Seeing the birthday cake.*) Oh! ... Mama! Of *course*! It's your birthday!

SHE: Cut it and eat it. (*Crossly.*) *I* had to remember to buy it.

ALICE: No, *you* must cut it! (*Carries cake and knife to her. To* TARVER.) You can't get rid of me—unless I'm mad or unfaithful. And even then it's legally difficult. I'm going to remain your wife and damage your career.

TARVER: Well, you've done it.

ALICE (*taking a piece of cake*): Not sufficiently.

TARVER: What lies did you tell that creature?

ALICE: I said you kept me short of money and you beat me. He's very chivalrous and gets inflamed very quickly. But Mama's right. He's too simple.

TARVER: So when you took the bag in the shop it was aimed at me?

ALICE (*mouth full of cake*): That's right.

TARVER (*to his* MOTHER): I'm glad you hear it.

SHE: I had no idea that you beat her.

TARVER: Nor I, either! It must be nearly luncheon time.

SHE (*swiftly*): I had expected you to lunch here!

TARVER: You never said we were to come!

SHE: Yes, I did. I asked all four. Formally. By letter.

ALICE: I never got any letter.

TARVER: Nor I. . . .

SHE (*to* TARVER): Couldn't you dine tonight?

TARVER: I am dining with a client.

SHE: Put him off. The birthday of a woman who is old and famous . . . is sad and important. Alice? Or shall you be in prison?

ALICE: I'm out on bail. I don't think the law works as fast as that.

SHE (*suddenly seeing the letters*): *Gracious!* . . . *Here they all are!* —*stamped*. And never posted! (*Puts her finger on a bunch of envelopes.*) You see what it is—Bent is so old! He's totally forgotten them! Well—stay all the same. We can picnic in here.

ALICE: And Roxy?

SHE: Roxane's not coming. (*To* TARVER.) Where's Oliver? Go and fetch Oliver. (*Directly he goes out. To* ALICE—*with urgency.*) Is your marriage worth mending?

ALICE: He doesn't try to understand me!

SHE: He knows by instinct that he mustn't!—Quick! Is it worth mending?

ALICE: I can't . . . all in a minute . . . I shouldn't think so. I don't know. What's the real heart of him? What's his breaking point? Can I win by fighting? What's he made of?

SHE: I don't know, either.

ALICE: But you . . . you . . .

SHE: Yes, but they change so. I'm afraid of him. The baby isn't the boy and the boy isn't the man and when he's old there'll be no link, either.

ALICE: Did you say—afraid of him?

SHE: Out of my reach then! He has something implacable and male that's grown. . . . Hush.

(BOTH MEN *come back*.)

OLIVER: Tarver says he won't stay if Alice is staying.

(TARVER, *side-tracking by the writing-table, looks down on to it.*)

ALICE: Tarver can't eat while he's hating.

SHE: Nonsense!

TARVER (*to his* MOTHER): They're *not* addressed to us! (*Picks one up.*) They're bills you're paying! You've invented those invitations! Why?—Is the food a myth, too?

SHE (*dignified*): There is champagne. And the cake there.

TARVER: You *can't* ride out on that! . . . (*Enter* BENT, *carrying a small tray delicately laid for one, probably a vegetable and egg salad in a pretty bowl, perhaps sticks of celery in a glass, obviously for one person.*) What's that?

BENT: Her Ladyship's luncheon.

SHE: You know very well I told you to arrange for four! In the dining-room!

BENT: No, you didn't.

> As SHE *puts her hands over her eyes.*

OLIVER: What's the matter?

SHE: I don't feel well. I feel giddy. (*Sits down: eyes closed. Waving her hand at the tray.*) Take that food out of my sight! (*He puts the tray down on the side.*) If I sit quietly here . . .

OLIVER: Get her champagne, Tarver!

SHE (*faintly*): Didn't Alice say—gin acts quicker? (*Fans her face with a newspaper.*) Give me—Roxane's . . . horrible present. . . .

OLIVER (*to* BENT): How often has my mother had an attack like this?

BENT: Hardly . . . (*Stuck between two loyalties.*) ever.

ALICE (*smiling—low*): In fact never.

BENT (*to nobody*): But on one's seventieth birthday—why shouldn't something begin? I mean—we've got to get the door open, haven't we? *Something's* got to start coming undone. . . .

SHE (*annoyed—to* BENT): Nonsense! Every thread and stitch and lock and hook of my life's in place—whatever simile you are using! (*As he picks up the tray.*) Leave that there! I may want it later.

> (BENT *goes.*)

TARVER (*waiting till he has gone*): What was all that about lunch, Mother?

SHE: It was an impulse!—Use your imagination!... I wanted to see if you would stay! I *wanted* you to stay! For that matter I wanted you to want to *come*!—You all send me flowers but ... What I wanted was for you yourselves to be here!

TARVER: Well, we are!

SHE: But only for a morning visit. I wanted you all to want that ... little festivity of a meal. *Together*. As we used to have it.

TARVER: Why didn't you ask us?

SHE: I thought *you* would have done the asking. And—when you didn't... I didn't, either! And when you came I wanted to see if ... to know if ... (*A little break in her voice*.) when I asked—you'd *accept*!

TARVER: Well, I didn't! (*Pause*.) And now you get a son back.

SHE: What do you mean?

TARVER: You said you saw me oftener before I married. Now I'm going to be *un*married.

SHE (*in a wail*): It won't be the same! You've outgrown me! You will be looking for women and it will be all to do over again! The love and the disappointment and the unadjustability! And the sense of silence and the things you think I shouldn't say!—And the false sweetness to the new woman! And her disapproval of me. I hate disapproval more than anything! I should like to be a miracle—as I used to be! (*To* OLIVER—*a quiver in her voice*.) You must find me the Chinese Prime Minister!

OLIVER: Tar—it's her birthday.

SHE: You think I'm going to cry? Well, it may be. The dearest thing in the world to me is my vanity. (*To* TARVER—*who is on the point of going*.) Aren't you going to drink my health! —*Do* stay! I want to talk of *me*!

ALICE: Tarver's right. We can't be nice to you on a private volcano.—*I'll* go. (*Moves to near door*.)

SHE: No! I want you more than anyone! You're such a woman!

(TARVER *picks up his document bag.*)

ALICE: "Such a woman"?

SHE: Violent, and selfish. And desperate to live for herself. It's a relief to have someone here—like me.

ALICE: Like you? But I've no fame in front of me—

TARVER: Must you have your eyes always on yourself?

ALICE: Always—always on myself! Like all of us here!— Except Oliver. All of us wanting to leave some mark! Even Mama. . . .

SHE: Most of all Mama—God help her! (*To* ALICE.) I see no hope for you with Tarver! Stay—as a young woman stranger, who is going to have another life!

ALICE: Ten to one I'm going to prison—if that's a life.

SHE: When I was a girl . . . I *wanted* to go to prison! (TARVER *smiles at her.*) Well, all right. I wasn't always a mother! Nor even chiefly a mother! You seem to forget! I was what they call spirited. I thought then that no harm could come to me that I couldn't turn into a triumph.—*What are you thinking of, Oliver!*

OLIVER: Roxane.

SHE: No wonder I prefer Alice to be here and Roxane *not*! Daughters-in-law unloved by their husbands are my cup of tea!

OLIVER: The expression is unlike you!

SHE: I thought of grist to the mill and discarded it. I find I don't lay my hands on words as nimbly as I used to do. Open the champagne, Tarver! I am seventy—I am famous —I am your mother.—Talk about me as in an obituary! How do you consider me? It seems a pity that for once . . . Or am I maudlin?

ALICE (*thoughtfully*): I don't believe we *can* consider you . . . until you're gone.

SHE (*note of panic*): So while I live I shall *never* know what you think!

TARVER (*to* ALICE): There's no need to be so frank that you're cruel!

ALICE: I thought Mama and I were on a very high wind of truth.

BENT (*to nobody in particular*): The wind was too high for her.

SHE (*disregarding—to* ALICE): So to you—what I *am* doesn't matter?

ALICE: Yes, it does.

SHE: But not what I have *been*?

ALICE: I suppose you can become history. But you can't make us *feel* what you have been.

BENT: It's blowing gales.

SHE: Where are you going, Oliver?

OLIVER: I think I shall ring her.

SHE: In my bedroom? Well, ring her. You look vacant.

OLIVER: No. I won't ring her.

SHE: Oh, I hate vacillation! Is Roxane to stand in the wings —I have a sense of being understudied till I am nearly off the stage. I want to speak about the Past—which Alice says is gone. I want to tell you both about your father—

OLIVER (*lightly—he is on the whole bored*): *What* about him?

SHE (*lamely*): He left me.

OLIVER: Well, of course.

SHE: Why "of course"?

OLIVER: Of course we know.

SHE: It came out in a curious manner!

OLIVER: Was it for another woman?

SHE: No! He adored me!

OLIVER (*lightly*): Then were *you* in the wrong?

BENT: Don't egg her on, Mr. Oliver. Ask for the Past . . .

SHE: *Leave the room!*

BENT: . . . and you never know what you'll get. . . .

SHE: . . . *this minute*. (*He goes. Immediately—to* OLIVER.) What did you mean?

OLIVER (*smiling*): One can't ask one's mother if she had lovers!

SHE: D'you think I've forgotten!

TARVER: I hope you can't remember!

SHE: Why that tone?

TARVER: Respect.

SHE: Can't I get *out* of being a parent? Can't you listen to a woman!—Does love change?—And jealousy?—And torment—and possession? The *power*—the *fall* from power!—The reverse situation!—A whole landscape of love about which I am talking!

OLIVER (*completely undercutting, intent on his own love. Nearing bedroom door*): If I don't ring her now I may miss her. ...

SHE: *Oliver!*

OLIVER (*disappears into bedroom*): I won't be two minutes. ...

SHE (*rising and crossing swiftly to the bedroom door*): Can one shout the Past after a train in motion?

OLIVER (*reappearing in doorway*): What's the matter!

SHE: I feel embalmed!—Like a bishop in stone—or those kneeling women like vases—with seventeen children! Yes —Oliver, yes! You were embarrassed to ask—*Yes!*—I had lovers!

OLIVER: I don't believe it.

SHE: Do you find it incredible?

OLIVER: No. Not incredible. I hear you say it.

SHE: Well?

OLIVER: Well, I must examine ...

SHE: What?

OLIVER: Whose son I am.

SHE: Your *father's!*

OLIVER: Of course. But which?

SHE: That's *not* what I meant!

OLIVER: You said it. So I am illegitimate. It might account for my nature and its complications. ... And your domination of me. And my inability to master her!

SHE: Stop, Oliver!

OLIVER: And why I had to be the tender one.—And for *whom*! (*Bitterly.*) I'm the one who is so aware of the heart

I can't move in any direction! (*Postscript thought.*) I think I shall take orders.

SHE: From whom?

OLIVER (*savagely*): Holy Orders.—I'm going home.

SHE: Wait! I'm prepared ... D'you want the truth! Can you bear the truth ... Oh, for God's sake, I'm not in the dock! Must I call across the room!—I told you I was unfaithful to your father. I had no idea he was a good man!

OLIVER: Why?

SHE: I had never met one. (*Invention flowing better now.*) I had lived on my wits since I was fifteen.

TARVER: Your wits!

SHE: Would you rather I had lived on my appearance! (*Pause.*) I did that, too. (*To* OLIVER—*quickly.*) Oh—long before you were born! I ran away from home—I was as pretty as sin! (*With satisfaction.*) As pretty and evil as an adder! I had nowhere to live—I'd have gone on the streets—but ... (*Pause.*) I was *rescued* by your father!

TARVER: I seem to have heard ...

SHE: What?

TARVER: ... that line before. ... (*Searching memory.*) Mrs. Warren's Profession!

SHE (*quick*): Why not! *I knew the author!*

TARVER (*smiling*): Is that—accurate?

SHE: How can the Past be accurate—on demand! As though it was the gas bill! I was the rage in Bloomsbury! I knew *all* the authors! They sat at my feet—singers and poets and actors—here in this room! I remember ... (*Pause.*) *six brothers.* ... (*Recollectory pause.*) Six—identical—brothers.

ALICE (*fascinated*): Why *identical*?

SHE: They all had the same reactions to me. Instantaneous, unmistakable!—And then—that other—*unrefusable* man! It was with him your father caught me! (*She begins to laugh.*) It was in this chair—with the mended leg. Your father broke it! Bent was just bringing in coffee. ...

OLIVER: Don't laugh like that!

SHE: I *do* laugh like that! I'm laughing at my seventieth birthday!

OLIVER: *Stop!*

TARVER: Go *on*. We may never hear this again.

OLIVER: I don't want to hear it!

SHE: Nor ever asked for it—oh, this absorbed generation!

OLIVER: There's something *wrong*! About *all* of it!

SHE (*pious*): Of course it was wrong.

OLIVER: I mean the *way* you tell it!—The way you *warm* to it!

ALICE (*slyly inserting her words like velvet*): But all the same——you see—she has got your attention.

SHE: *You* don't believe me?

ALICE: No.

SHE: Was I so absurd then?

ALICE: I took your Past away. You are putting it back again.

SHE: And if I tell you truth or lies—isn't it the need that tells them?—I *meant* to be absurd! I wanted to bring home to you—that nobody ever asks!—And I *need* to be alive—as I was then—and *am*! *Now*—as much as ever! (*Picking up her glass.*) To Alice's rebellion—which was also mine!

ALICE: You felt that too—in your time. . . .

SHE (*indignant*): "In my time"! . . . The thing's a ribbon—not a set of beads. It's joined—it flows. What is this egotism called "Modern" which, like the hymns, becomes "Ancient" before you can turn round! What you feel—I felt. And so did the Greeks. And so they will in the moon! But I shall be gone—and there'll be no trace of me! I shall be ashes—and you won't admit that there were embers.—And I care—I *care*—not what you think of me—but that you should know what *kind* of woman I was!—Go! All of you!—I want my *own* Contemporary! The man to whom I mattered! Who knew . . . who *knows* . . . (*Absolute change of tone to the practical.*) Bent! Ring *Sir Gregory*!

   They are frozen.

BENT: There you are, you see!

OLIVER: My . . . *father* . . .

SHE: The Savoy. Temple Bar 4343.

BENT (*as he dials*): All the dead are at the Savoy.

SHE: Extension 217.

TARVER: *This* is hysteria!

SHE: It is *not*. I am only *frantic*.

OLIVER: You can't bring back the dead, Mother.

SHE (*crossing the stage to the telephone—takes it from* BENT): Can I not? (*Into telephone.*) Gregory! Are you alive! (*Follows the longest pause ever made in the theatre. Various expressions follow each other across her face as she listens.*) I relent. Eight o'clock. Tonight. (*Pause. She walks to her bedroom door. In doorway.*) Will you all dine with me tonight—and meet a ghost for dinner? (*Goes into bedroom; door closes.*)

CURTAIN

ACT II

Before dinner the same evening.

BENT *is in full evening butler's rig. Though now married to his "girl", he still keeps some clothes at the house.*

BENT (*mutinous—insisting*): But there's the dining-room, m'lady!

SHE (*in an evening dress of splendour*): We can't have dinner in there. The fire smokes. There's a bird's nest in the chimney.

BENT: But it's a warm spring evening.

SHE: There should always be a fire burning. It makes the silver flicker. Do as I say ... (*Suddenly encountering a more obstinate look.*) and pull yourself together!—Or I shall telephone to *Mrs.* Bent to come round and help me.

BENT (*trembling with instant rage*): That young woman doesn't put her nose in here!

SHE: You should never have married so young a woman. It always brings a loss of dignity.

BENT (*muttering*): There's other things to marriage.

SHE: Don't make me blush for you.

BENT: With that dress, m'lady, it *should* be the dining-room.

SHE (*flat*): It's a fork supper.

BENT (*disgusted*): What am I here for, then!

SHE: To hand plates out and take them back again. Odd jobs and no ritual.

BENT (*etherealized*): I don't exist, m'lady, without ritual. I'm an empty coat—hanging on a line.

SHE: Ah, Bent—your preoccupations with images!

BENT: Snatches of 'em—snatches of 'em come back, Madam.

SHE: Why—"Madam"?

BENT: I was thinking back, far back, to when you were Madam. To when you first engaged me—I came to you to study life. I had literary aspirations. I should have written a book.

SHE (*absently*): What would it have been about?

BENT: Upper class life. But the life vanished. (*Ferociously and suddenly.*) And *sex*.

SHE (*startled*): Sex . . .

BENT (*still fierce*): It's a big deterrent! It's brought me to battle with unworthy women!

SHE (*glancing at herself across the room into a mirror*): How do I look?

BENT (*mechanically*): No different.

SHE (*turning round in surprise*): Nonsense!

BENT: To tell you the truth, I can't see.

SHE (*sitting down*): Nor can I. It was charming of God! I never expected it! . . .

BENT: Eh?

SHE (*glancing again at the mirror from where she sits*): . . . That as beauty vanishes the eyes grow dimmer. I look in the glass and the outline seems as good as ever! In the illusory haze . . . (*Sits bolt upright moving her head to loosen it on the shoulders.*) . . . I make for mystery! (*Breaking off.*) But one must keep the spine straight! (*Stretching her neck and feeling the neck muscles with one hand.*) There's the hall door!

BENT (*going slowly to the door. Turning with his hand on the handle*): Are the young gentlemen of an age for love?

SHE (*impatient*): How you forget! They're married! . . .

The door opens. TARVER *has let himself in.*

TARVER (*impeccably dressed—black tie. Coming in quickly—urgent*): Mother . . .

SHE (*stately—dignified*): It was good of you to come.

TARVER (*impatient*): Naturally I came! But before the others—and it's why I've come early . . .

SHE: I don't want to answer questions to you alone!

TARVER: I must know where I stand! (*Going near street window —evidently anxious to get something out before the others come.*) I'm the elder! How long have you been in touch with . . . this man?

SHE: "This man"! I won't answer!

TARVER (*extreme annoyance—looking out of window*): It's Alice! Good God. . . . That creature! He's brought her in his Bentley! (*Turning back from window.*) You must forbid her!

SHE: What?

TARVER: Oh, good heavens, you must see that if it's my father . . . is that boxing creature to be in the room?

    The door opens. ALICE *comes in. The* BOXER, *being nervous, keeps out of sight behind her for a moment.*

SHE (*outraged—to* ALICE): You've not *changed*!

ALICE (*rebellious retention of ego*): No. This is how I *am*.

SHE (*now aware of* BOXER *in doorway, carrying box*): Good God —again?

ALICE: He's brought you foie gras.

TARVER (*furious—to* ALICE): This is *too* much!

ALICE (*wilfully getting him wrong*): Much too much! It cost him twenty pounds. I *dote* on extravagance!

SHE: So do I—more plates, however.—Tell him to come in but warn him not to use his fists. (OLIVER *appears, properly dressed.*) (*Sharp.*) Where's Roxane?

OLIVER: She hasn't come back.

SHE: Thank God for that! I want *all* Oliver here!—And not half!

OLIVER: All of me *is* here!—I want to speak to . . . Sir Gregory —with a clear mind.

TARVER (*to* ALICE—*angrily*): It's monstrous of you to have brought that man!—And *frivolous*!

ALICE: You'll find a stranger a help in what's coming.

TARVER: What's coming?

ALICE: Awkwardness.

TARVER (*sharp*): Bent!—The bell!

BENT: Yes, Sir Gregory.

TARVER (*as* BENT *goes to the door*): Don't you know who I am!

BENT (*at door*): Not just at the moment. (*Goes out.*)

TARVER (*in the apprehensive silence. To* OLIVER): Are you prepared!

OLIVER (*grimly*): For *anyone*.

ALICE (*mocking—to her* MOTHER-IN-LAW): Who have you persuaded . . . (*Cocking an ear at the door.*) into taking off his coat out there!

SHE (*smiling*): Still not convinced!

BENT (*scared—returning, holding door shut against someone behind him*): It's Sir Gregory's . . . father, m'lady. . . . (*Fumbling with relationships.*) It's your ladyship's . . . father-in-law. . . .

SIR GREGORY (*a very personable strong old man. Nearly pushing* BENT *down as he bursts door open*): I should need to be a hundred and twenty, you silly ass, to be her father-in-law! (*Half crossing room.*) My wife! At last!

BENT (*recovering his balance—mumbling*): I remember that voice . . . "you silly ass". . . .

OLIVER (*urgent—suspicious*): But do you remember *him*?

BENT: I remember the night he went . . .

    SIR GREGORY *stops dead.*

SHE (*imperious*): Bent—go and sit in my bedroom!

BENT: Is there a bell?

SIR GREGORY (*shouting at him*): No, there isn't! Just *go*!

TARVER (*suspicious*): How did you know?

SIR GREGORY: Because I pulled the bell out of the wall a long time ago!—Do you doubt it?

OLIVER: *I* do.

SIR GREGORY (*over his shoulder as he goes to his* WIFE): Who are you?

OLIVER: Another . . . son.

SIR GREGORY: Impregnable woman! It's been a siege! (*Taking her hand.*) You haven't changed!

SHE: The only man to whom I seem young!

SIR GREGORY: The only man in the world who *knows* you

are young!—I have remembered your birthday—but I
haven't remembered your age!

SHE: What can happen to me after seventy?

SIR GREGORY: *I* have happened to you! Do you remember?

SHE (*smiling*): No!

SIR GREGORY (*gay*): But I remember!—And, oh, she was a
handful!

SHE: *That's* what I wanted to hear!

SIR GREGORY: *And* Lausanne! And Paris!—and Roumania!—
And the row in the canal—at Emms!—I've brought you
diamonds. (ALICE *pushes up to see.*) Who are *you? Opens a
small case he carries.*

ALICE (*on guard*): Don't you know?

SIR GREGORY: Yes, I do!—Shocking!—Your face was in the
newspapers. (*To his* WIFE.) How beautifully you touch
jewels! (*Glances at* ALICE.) But keep them away from the
Shop-Lifter!

ALICE: Are you rich?

SIR GREGORY: Very rich.

ALICE: How rich?

SIR GREGORY: I am Advisor to the Sheik of Mwelta, I guard
his interests while he prays by his oil wells. I see they don't
chisel him out of his royalties. We are all rich there but the
Sheik and I are the richest. Keep it dark. But in the family
I let you know.

ALICE: Do you come often to London?

SIR GREGORY: Last autumn was the first time in twenty-nine
years.—I live in the Sheik's pocket! It's not safe to leave it.
(*Pause.*) And when I *do* come—my wife won't see me!

SHE: That's how we arranged it.

OLIVER: Why couldn't you have come here—if it's your own
house?

SIR GREGORY: That's my business! (*Cold-shouldering him. To
his* WIFE.) Did you get the caviar?

SHE: I did indeed.

SIR GREGORY (*complacent*): The best Beluga. Two jars.

SHE: I sent them back. (*At his look of surprise.*) How could I have explained them!

SIR GREGORY: In your own house you could have explained an octopus! (*Wrathfully—to* TARVER.) Do you bully her?

   SHE *begins to laugh.*

TARVER: Certainly not!

SIR GREGORY (*to* OLIVER): And *you*?

OLIVER (*polite*): Have you come back to the wrong wife—Sir?

TARVER: My brother means that perhaps you are not the right husband.

ALICE (*as* SIR GREGORY *is about to explode on* TARVER. *Flattering him*): You look so young for someone so long dead, Sir Gregory.

SIR GREGORY (*mollified*): Then why did old Bent think I was a hundred and twenty!

SHE: He slipped up among the generations!

OLIVER: After twenty-nine years are you *sure*, Mother?

SHE (*lightly. Smiling up into* SIR GREGORY'S *face*): How can I be!

SIR GREGORY (*instantly—stooping*): I haven't kissed you yet. . . .

SHE (*dodging the kiss—waving it away*): Pay a little attention to your sons!

SIR GREGORY: I remember a little boy—touching and manly. . . . —*Tarver*—I gave you your name!

OLIVER: Do you remember *me*?

SHE (*introducing hurriedly*): Oliver!

SIR GREGORY (*wary*): I remember a baby. (*Pause.*) When I dine out and meet men—I don't necessarily feel tender towards them. I employ a great many men. I like a few. But not many.

OLIVER: Are you warning us?

SIR GREGORY: I am only saying that as I haven't watched either of you grow up, we are meeting on the level. I mean —neither side is weakened by affection. (*To* TARVER.) Are you in oil?

TARVER: The Middle Wells.

SIR GREGORY: How curious. The Sheik owns that one.

TARVER: Then—must I conclude—that it is through you— that I am where I am?

SIR GREGORY: I seem to remember making some such suggestion.

ALICE (*aside, to* TARVER): Does that clinch it?

TARVER (*very short*): Yes, it does. And I feel *enormously* irritated.

OLIVER (*with cold sarcasm*): What have you done for me, sir?

SIR GREGORY: Nothing.

OLIVER: Why do you discriminate between us?

SIR GREGORY (*a half laugh*): Some sort of natural vexation.

OLIVER: My mother says I am like you.

SIR GREGORY (*they seem not to get on*): I see nothing like you in me or like me in you.

OLIVER: I am struck by it!

SIR GREGORY: A man doesn't care for his sons to be too like him.—As with dogs—who *seem* so individual until you visit the breeders! (*Changing the subject.*) Who's the guest in the background?

ALICE: Another rich man.

SIR GREGORY (*delighted*): But I *know* him! (*His hand out.*) I know who he is—at any rate! It's Red Gus Risko! (*To* BOXER.) You've got your Championship fight on your hands in four days! (*They shake hands.*) My God, I wish you well! Have you shed that last two pounds?

BOXER: There's four days still. And he's an easy touch! I'm not losing sleep over that left-hand artist! Things don't look too rosy for him!

SIR GREGORY: There's something about a heavyweight that's magic to me! You can have all your middle chaps and your little chaps, But a heavyweight fight is the most terrible breathless thing! Is it being televised?

BOXER: They won't allow it. May I send you ringside seats?

SIR GREGORY: I have to go back tomorrow to my Sheik.

OLIVER: This is unbearable! This talk—from a man we thought dead! From a dead father!—I don't speak for Tarver but for me!—I'm *giddy*! I'm as giddy as if north and south were abolished! *Much* giddier! Look, Sir! Let's come to grips! In a single day—*today*—at the age of seventy—my mother reverses everything! She tells me she's not a widow—

SIR GREGORY (*chuckling*): Nor she is!

OLIVER: —that she's not the mother we've known—that she's as evil as an adder—that you left her in disgust—that she behaved worse than Satan. . . .

SIR GREGORY: Women exaggerate, don't they?

OLIVER: That's no answer!

SIR GREGORY: She always told me lies! I loved 'em!

    As they talk, SHE *takes out a small vanity case, toys with it, opens and shuts it.*

OLIVER: If nothing will move you—she tells us she had lovers!

SIR GREGORY: So she did!

SHE: Gregory—

SIR GREGORY: I threw one of them out of the house! That damn singer!

SHE: Get your father a drink, Tarver!

ALICE (*as if it were to herself*): It seems shocking, doesn't it, that one should be old . . . and yet have slept with someone?

SHE: It seems shocking . . . (*Deliberately lifts the open vanity case and contemplates her own face in it.*) that there should be no record of it!

SIR GREGORY (*looking at* OLIVER): No *record*!

SHE (*hastily*): That is *not* what I meant!

SIR GREGORY: If I hadn't promised—

OLIVER: Why are you glaring at me, Sir?

SIR GREGORY: But I never broke a promise in my life!

SHE: If you fight an old battle—where are the witnesses! And the evidence—obliterated!

SIR GREGORY (*a glance at* OLIVER): Not all of it. (*Suddenly inflamed.*) I could have the same blazing row now—

SHE: So could I!—You always insist on yes or no!

SIR GREGORY: Very normal.

SHE: No, it is *not* very normal! It doesn't take into account—the inner need! The urges of fantasy ...

SIR GREGORY (*to the* OTHERS): Your mother's mind slides from the centre to the periphery!

SHE: And with your *yes* and *no*—standing up like two lamp-posts—what about the invisible army behind them! The lies one tells oneself! The self-delusions! The lacks—for which one is compensating? The ache for conquest, the bragging, the ambition ... Whatever I said then—*Yes*—or *No*—had no meaning! You would *never* admit that there are two sides to a quarrel!

SIR GREGORY: It doesn't get you anywhere *to* admit it!

SHE: But to be got anywhere isn't what one's after! There's the delicate question of—what *happened*!

SIR GREGORY: Well, *what* happened?

SHE: What—here in this room?

SIR GREGORY: They are old enough to stand it!

SHE (*loftily*): I remember only the *outlines* of the situations!

SIR GREGORY (*quite recovering*): It isn't the wicked sides of women that inflame a man!—It's the nimble way they side-step when you blame 'em!

SHE: So you haven't changed! And you admit no faults. ....

SIR GREGORY: Yes, I do. (*Picks up her hand. But she withdraws it.*) But I react fatally to contradiction! (*Seizes her roughly by the waist. Kisses her.*)

SHE: Oh ... (*Touches her eyes with her handkerchief.*) That hasn't happened for ...

SIR GREGORY (*sitting down beside her. Teasing and tender*): ... how many years? (*To them* ALL.) Whatever have you been doing to her to bring all this about? Haven't you learnt how to treat her!

ALICE: I told her her Past was dead. ....

SIR GREGORY: Don't you know she can't stand oblivion!

ALICE (*protecting herself*): The Past she invented is dead—for none of it's true!

SIR GREGORY: What's true is that I worshipped her! She was the Burning Bush and the Apple of Eden and the silver snake on the Tree! (*Pause.*) And then all of a sudden she was like eczema to me!

SHE: What a horrible simile!

SIR GREGORY: Your mother-in-law is an exceptional and extraordinary woman!—She is outside rules!

ALICE (*to* TARVER): Would you come back to me—after half a lifetime—and say that to me, Tarver?

SIR GREGORY (*to his* WIFE): Don't they get on?

TARVER: We are fighting to the death, if you want to know. She defies me to get rid of her.

SIR GREGORY: Walk out of the house on her!

TARVER: But it's *my* house!

SIR GREGORY: What are a few possessions! You must be gentlemanly.—*I* left your mother. (*Chuckles.*) She never thought I would!

SHE (*murmuring*): Hackles are rising.

SIR GREGORY (*patting her hand*): The old yeast stirring . . . (*To* ALICE.) Why did you pinch the bag? Was it insanity?

ALICE: No. It was revenge.

SIR GREGORY: Revenge for what?

ALICE: His superiority.

SIR GREGORY (*to* TARVER): You simply can't keep 'em down unless you break them. It's no use—half measures. It only maddens them. They want to be right with a kind of passion. If you let them be right—well and good. But if you don't want them to be right you must half murder them.

ALICE: There speaks a husband!—I wish I'd married *you*!

SIR GREGORY (*meditatively—a reply at a tangent*): What a horrible relationship.

TARVER (*taken aback*): Ours?

SIR GREGORY: Marriage. The beginning and the end are wonderful. But the middle part is hell.

SHE: Shall we call Bent?

SIR GREGORY (*with a smile*): Side-stepping?

SHE: But he ought to be carving the turkey. (*To* TARVER.) Call Bent for me.

TARVER (*going to the bedroom door*): Bent! ... Bent! ...

BENT: I'm coming! (*Stands, his hair a bit on end, in the doorway, supporting himself against the door jamb.*) I had a dream in there.

SHE: Carve the turkey.

BENT: I dreamt everything was still to come.

SHE: Carve the turkey.

BENT: Let me finish! There was ice on the pond in the village. She was the first girl I ever loved.—She was fourteen. (*He begins to skate.*)

SHE (*annoyed with herself*): Oh! I'd *forgotten*!

TARVER: What?

SHE: I left it behind the looking glass. But he always found things!

BENT (*skating about the room as in his dream, his hands behind his back*): She said she had tripped over a star. And when I looked she was right! The stars were in the ice, too!

SHE: Oh, Bent—Ah, Bent. Marvellously elliptical! Evocative! —The night ice and the girl!

SIR GREGORY (*muttering*): Silly ass! Night-ice-nothing!

SHE (*to* TARVER): Carry him back to his dream again. Put him on my bed.—And *bring away the bottle.*

BENT (*as* TARVER *comes up to him. Turning truculently to face him*): Hands off, Sir Gregory! (*Moves back a pace and in doing so upsets a chair which falls backwards. Turning sharp, pointing to it—his old finger shaking.*) You know what happened. ...

A burst of laughter from the real SIR GREGORY.

OLIVER (*quick*): *What* happened?

SHE *rises: warns* BENT *by a look to shut up.*

BENT (*vague*): There was a lot of love then about the house—

OLIVER (*sharp*): How much of it did you see?

BENT (*still trying to keep it general*): Cries behind doorways and arguments and high words and quarrels that burnt from room to room like marsh fires—

SHE (*very sharp*): Bent!

BENT (*same technique*): And she so taking and lively, with that shine of love like diamonds—

SHE (*furious and helpless*): That's the *bottle*!

BENT: And the two of them fighting. Fisticuffs. Words of murder—

OLIVER (*cutting across this—to* SIR GREGORY): *What* happened?

SIR GREGORY: I hit him.

OLIVER: What for?

SIR GREGORY: Something insufferable and not important.

BENT (*goaded*): Not important! Me nearly throttled. And Her Ladyship flat on the floor!—You tried to get his name out of me!—But you never got the card!

SIR GREGORY: What did you do with it?

BENT: I ate it.

OLIVER: Was that the night he left?

BENT: It was like the ringing of the fire engines crowding down the street. There was a sense of something dreadful somewhere.

SIR GREGORY: Did she cry when I was gone?

BENT: She was in a hurricane of temper. Cry she might have done. But I didn't see it.

SIR GREGORY (*tenderly*): Did you cry?

SHE: I wept oceans. But my temper kept me going. Well, let him carve the turkey.

BENT *pulls himself together and walks with shaky dignity to the console table, examines the turkey, turns to count the number of people.*

BENT (*mutters*): No need to ease out the legs. . . . There'll be sufficient with the breast alone. (*Picks up carving knife and long steel and sharpens the knife, a little vaguely.*)

OLIVER (*to* BENT): Whose name was on the card?

SHE: Get on with that turkey!

BENT (*querulously*): Don't hurry me! I nearly can't do it. . . .

(*Drops the carving knife. As he picks it up he makes an extraordinary noise like the bark of a dog beginning with "B".*)

SIR GREGORY: What's that?

SHE: A word one can't say. He says it often.

ALICE (*to the* BOXER): Come on, Red Gus—give me a hand.

    The BOXER *gets to his feet and lumbers to stand beside* ALICE *near* BENT.

OLIVER (*crossing hurriedly to Her bedroom*): Do you mind if I telephone?

SHE: Yes, I do.

    But OLIVER *disappears as though* SHE *hadn't spoken.*

SIR GREGORY (*taking this in—with a half-smile to her*): Who's he in love with?

SHE: His wife.

SIR GREGORY (*joining group near* BENT): That's one mercy!

BENT (*who is carving—now pauses. To* SIR GREGORY): I know who you are now! It's come back to me.

SIR GREGORY: Does it make any difference?

BENT: That's what I've been thinking. It doesn't!

ALICE: Get on, Bent!

BENT (*abandoning the carving. Turning to* SIR GREGORY): And if it doesn't—who are we? I mean, I don't know why we have names. (ALICE *gets round him as he talks and gets hold of a filled plate.*) I seem to see more than I used to see! Call it auras. But auras is a lot of nonsense! I get *glimpses*!—I know who you are by your naked soul—hanging where your face should be! (*Brandishes the long knife with the steel almost in* SIR GREGORY'*s face.*)

SIR GREGORY: Pay attention!

BENT: —But I've no name for it.—Perhaps I'm near death.

SIR GREGORY: Cut more slices, Bent. *Keep* cutting. Always employ your hands when you catch yourself thinking about death.

BENT (*carving again*): Oh, I don't look death straight in the face. But sometimes he gets round and looks at me. (*Putting two slices on to a plate.*) Like that, Sir Gregory?

SIR GREGORY (*taking the plate to his* WIFE—*the* BOXER *follows, having lifted the mustard pot off the small silver tray it was on.* ALICE *takes the tray and gives it to him, but he holds the tray in one hand and the pot in the other.* SIR GREGORY *taking the* BOXER's *hands and, as it were "mating" them so that the pot is on the tray*): Like that! (*The* BOXER *stoops to offer the mustard.*) What do you do with your money?

BOXER (*In "stoop-difficulty"*): Buy things.

    SHE *takes an unconscionable time helping herself to mustard.*

SIR GREGORY: Who advises you?

BOXER (*back nearly broken*): I've got six of 'em. (*At last upright again.*) Very clever tax gentlemen. They work out the dodges.

SIR GREGORY: Put some in my companies.

BOXER: What I like is loose money.

SHE: So does everyone! (*Patting the chair next to her.*) Sit down and talk to me!

SIR GREGORY (*leaning down to her*): Are you happy?

SHE: I'm *basking*! (*To* BOXER.) If you've got a girl—buy her diamonds!

BOXER: I haven't got a girl.

SHE: You *haven't*!

BOXER: When I fight I'm not allowed them. (*Mumbling.*) I have to save things.

SHE (*at a loss*): *What* things?

BOXER: To keep my mind off them.—A girl would have to be—*extra*—to knock me!

    Now the hall door opens and ROXANE *comes in hurriedly. She is breathtaking. The effect exquisite; very personal. She has dyed her hair since we last saw her—in various shades of bronze, gold and buttercup. It hangs down like a child's. The* BOXER *slowly rises to his feet with tray and pot. He is hit for six. Perhaps forever. He never takes his eyes off her. She half crosses the stage —guilty about not having been here in the morning, about being late now, and alarmed and remorseful about the bottle of gin.*

ROXANE (*not seeing* SIR GREGORY): Happy Birthday, Mama!

SHE (*icy—the battle is joined*): Why did you send me gin?

ROXANE (*halted; reincased in reserve and politeness*): You spoke about my hair.

SHE: For or against it?

ROXANE: You don't understand. .... A girl's hair ... (*Now she sees* SIR GREGORY. *He is silent. She is silent.*) A girl's hair ... is like her soul waving! (*Slowly turning her face to her* MOTHER-IN-LAW.) It's something personal and not yet said!—And may *never* be! It's like her handwriting!

SHE: In my day we just had it brushed and arranged. It wasn't this burning, vulnerable, yes-or-no to success.

ROXANE: But in *our* day it's our signature-tune! If it isn't— we're lost!—There are so many of us! All trembling to live! Most of us trembling. .... (*To* SIR GREGORY.) What are you doing here?

OLIVER *comes in from bedroom.*

SIR GREGORY: I'm the husband and the father—"here".

ROXANE (*to* HER): I thought he was dead.

SHE (*deceptively casual*): I have revived him.

ROXANE (*a step further into the room*): I love a bombshell.—He picked me up in Bruton Street yesterday near the evening.

TARVER (*behind her*): What do you mean—picked you up?

ROXANE (*not turning*): It's well known—the expression.

OLIVER (*hotly*): Not to *me*!—About *you*!

SHE: This party has exploded in my face! (*To her* HUSBAND.) Did you know who she was?

SIR GREGORY: Of course I didn't! We walked the length of Bruton Street. No more—on my honour! Cairo, Mwelta, Israel—I never saw such a girl! She seemed, even as she walked, to know men wanted her, and be sorry for them.

ROXANE: I don't like things *said*!

ALICE: No, but you do them!

SHE: Roxane—come here to me. (ROXANE *crosses to her. Deliberate.*) Sir Gregory—though my husband—is perfectly free. (*Pause.*) I should have thought you were *not*.

ROXANE: But I want to be.

SHE: Well—I've tried patience and abdication!

ROXANE (*slight smile*): They aren't for you, Mama! I shouldn't try them!

SHE: Do you want to leave us?

ROXANE: Yes.

No one had quite expected that flat answer.

SHE: And—Oliver?

ROXANE: I'm fond of Oliver but I don't want to be.

OLIVER: Couldn't you have said that first—alone—to me?

SHE: No, because she has brought her life—into my drawing room.

ROXANE: Poor Oliver.

OLIVER: Poor Oliver is *not* what I want to be!

SHE: What do you want, Roxane?

ROXANE: I want to be . . . (*Hunts for a word.*) thought more of!

SHE: So did I! But there's no short cut! It took my life to achieve it.

SIR GREGORY (*a bit mealy-mouthed*): And now she deserves respect.

His WIFE *throws a sharp look at him: not pleased.*

ROXANE: I don't know whether by respect you mean admiration!—Women grow downhill!—I'm at the top! If I can't get it now—when do I get it?

SIR GREGORY (*not quite able to resist her*): What are you at the top of?

ROXANE: My good looks.—It's all I have of my own.

BENT (*without emphasis*): Oh, she's pretty.

ROXANE *gives a tiny bow.*

SHE: What can you want—more than that Oliver adores you!

ROXANE (*low*): It's not enough.

OLIVER (*to his* MOTHER—*with anger*): Leave that to me! (*To* ROXANE.) *Where* have I failed you!

ROXANE: It's not your fault. But I have to have more . . . (*Stops.*)

OLIVER: More what?

ROXANE (*humbly—hanging her head*): . . . men around me.
(*He makes a small exclamation of pain.*) You know those things
—stuck to rocks . . . that wait for the sea. . . .

OLIVER (*who can never resist her loss of a word*): Sea anemones.

ROXANE: Yes—I'm only alive when the tides come in and
men admire me.

SHE (*sweeping to sideboard to put her heaped plate back*): Uneatable.

ALICE: Oh, Roxy—how *yourself* you are—absolutely! With
your own laws . . . and your own innocence . . .

SHE: . . . But your own manners!

OLIVER (*harsh*): So even an old man . . .

ROXANE: Old men know better what they are admiring.
(*Slips her little hand through* SIR GREGORY'S *arm.*)

OLIVER: *Take your hand away!*

ROXANE (*obeying*): It meant nothing!—He's nice to women.
Oh—if you hold on to me you'll find—suddenly—nothing,
nothing, in your hand!

BENT: Oh, she's pretty.

ROXANE: *Can't* you understand me?

OLIVER: Not without pain.

ROXANE: But I don't want to have remorse or sorrow!—
I want to go out floating in my best dress in the streets in
the early morning—not responsible to anyone—not responsible to you! The happiness I shall get is the looks of the
men and the being the fountain for everything! I'm only the
breath that—makes the flute play!—And I can only make
the flute play—for strangers! (*She is staring at the* BOXER *as
she moves towards him.*)

SIR GREGORY: Have a little decency! Things have to be
impalpable!—Not on a Tuesday or a Wednesday—but on
some day never named in the week! In my day things had
to have mystery! *Unthinkable . . . discussing* it. . . .

ROXANE (*low—to* BOXER): Have you a match?
The BOXER *looks wildly round—no matches.*

ALICE: In our day . . . (*Mercifully the* BOXER *finds matches and
lights* ROXANE's *cigarette.*) we discuss *everything*!

SIR GREGORY: Do you think a million years have gone by—
to arrive at *your* day!

TARVER: That's *just* what she thinks! (*Carries his empty plate,
passing* ALICE, *back to the sideboard*.)

ALICE (*holding out hers*): Take mine—

TARVER: Carry your own.

SHE: Oh, Alice! Oh, Tarver! This was meant to be a night
with a difference! I had meant to bring the Past into the
Present! But back—back—back we go, Gregory, to you
and me!

SIR GREGORY: Nonsense!

SHE: The same chemistry! The same sparks and flashes!—And
the fire as hard to put out as it used to be!

ALICE: Did you never think that there would be a daughter-
in-law?

SHE: You never crossed my mind when he was young!—But
life goes on and I accept you.—I love my sons. And even
the girls they married. But I should love them better if their
marriages were broken!

ROXANE (*softly inserting*): Alice! Shall we give her back her
sons?

ALICE: Give her back!—Leave *Tarver*! ... —When I hear
you talk—as really I never have before—you might be an
ant, with an ant's language! Or a silver mackerel! Or a hare
from the North Pole! I'm a *woman*. If I leave Tarver it will
be with agony! And a need to tear him to pieces—and come
back and *look* at the pieces!

SIR GREGORY (*to* TARVER): She'll fight you to a standstill.

ALICE (*shouting*): Yes, I will!

SIR GREGORY: Well, fight her to her knees!

ALICE (*rounding on him*): Tarver and I have each married
people with not one thing in common. . . .

TARVER: Nothing, nothing that we agree on! (*To* ALICE.)
You are not my type nor my kind of good-looking! You
are a badly dressed girl and I hate a badly dressed girl! You
argue, you are not accurate and if I ask you the time

you tell me the wrong time—

ALICE (*furiously*): And if you marry again you'll choose the same wife again with the stupidity of a buffalo!

SIR GREGORY (*getting up*): My God, what a house of baboons! (*As he crosses room to the bedroom door. He observes the locked looks of the* BOXER *and* ROXANE.) *Look out, Roxane!—Look out for that man! He's got to fight in four days!* (*Opening the door.*) Shut the current off, girl! It's not fair to him! (*Disappears through door, leaving it open.*)

TARVER: He seems to remember his way about.

ALICE: It must be pleasant to reach that age when one can go to the lavatory without explanation.

SHE (*who has been floating, restless and impatient, about the room —now returns to her chair*): There are many pleasant things about age, but listening to the young is not one of them.

OLIVER *bangs the bedroom door shut ferociously.* SHE, *having closed her eyes, gives a start.*

TARVER (*ruefully—to* OLIVER): I'm thinking of his company— in which I hold a high position!

OLIVER: Well, it wasn't you who banged the door on him!

BOXER (*in a heaven of his own. Staring into* ROXANE'*s eyes*): A chap has thoughts. . . .

ROXANE (*same heaven*): What are they?

BOXER: That you're as pretty as a little moon on its first night out.

OLIVER: How *dare* you!

BOXER (*astonished that there is anyone else in the room*): What— me?—The very first words I've spoke!

OLIVER: You could keep them to yourself!

BOXER: It seems a pity. I had it in my head and the words flew out.

ROXANE (*softly—to* OLIVER): You have to change men *all* the time.—Don't you *see*?

OLIVER: *No.*

ROXANE (*sighing*): It would be so clear to a woman!

ALICE: No, Roxy! It's not clear to me!—You are very

extraordinary—only you don't know it!—It must have cost you the earth to come out into the open! I've hardly ever had a crack out of that lovely secret mouth! (*Suddenly facing* TARVER.) I *talk* when I'm in pain! So that I can *bear* the pain! I *shout*!

SHE (*restlessly altering her position*): Now we have the other one.

ALICE (*disregarding—to* TARVER): I shout! But you don't answer! And when you don't answer I rebel like murder! Oh—that little ounce more of hate that's needed!

BENT (*fetching a dirty plate*): But none of 'em dare.

TARVER (*jumping up*): I've had enough of it!

    SHE *opens her vanity case.*

ALICE: Back to the flat, then, Tarver! Oh, these flats, oh my God, where there's no room to hate!

SHE (*considering her features in the glass of the little case*): A look of age has appeared in the last five minutes.

ALICE: I ran out into the street yesterday after the row between us—I ran *counting*! Counting the cost of what I'd have to pay in remorse!

SHE: Are there no new lines for two people in anger? I'm appalled at what you *feel*!

ALICE: Well, that's being old.

SHE: It seems to me God knows more reasonable! I should think I was nearer the Almighty and His Everlasting Conundrum than two people wrapped in madness like white silk cocoons!

ALICE: But Tarver and I are not near the Almighty by forty or fifty years! And we have to settle something and with whom to pass the time!

SIR GREGORY (*appearing*): The bathroom has become very feminine! (*Walking over to his* WIFE.) Asleep? (SHE *turns her head and looks up.*) It seems to me that you were asleep.

SHE (*bolt upright*): It seems to me that I am being used up and wasted!—Asleep!—I was *not* asleep! You said it was a house of baboons! But the lions are roaring! I close my eyes—but my ears grow more sensitive! I close my ears but

I feel them in my toes!—ASLEEP!—I'm in the Zoo!

ALICE: You don't do much for the animals!

SHE: I can love a human being but I can't love a battle!

ALICE: You can tell us how it can be won!

SIR GREGORY: I can tell you who will be defeated!

ALICE: What *is* this puzzle—that's so well known and never solved! What is this ghastly *difference* between men and women?—What is this closeness that works—and doesn't work! That boils, that burns and blisters, and is so *near* love!

TARVER (*sarcastic*): You call that love?

ALICE: I shan't call it that twice—if you can't see it!—Do you know, Tarver—one word would change our life!

TARVER: What is the word?

ALICE (*desolate*): There are several that might do. It would have to be a light word—like idiot, or . . . It would have to be said with indulgence . . . or . . . humour. It would have to be said without a rifle at my breast. Just saying "idiot" won't do. I don't want it said with pity. . . . (*Suddenly turning to* HER.) You're his mother! Can't *you* tell me what to do!

SHE: You ask advice of my heart—but you know you will throw it back unused!—No, I *can't* tell you!

ALICE: What's the point of being here seventy years—unless age gets you somewhere?

SHE: It doesn't.—*I* made a mess of things.—And now so do you.

TARVER: And what about me! You isolate me! You defend Alice—because it's yourself you're defending!

ALICE: You must come down one side or the other!

SHE: Whatever side I come down—I find I am left alone on it! Roxane is leaving Oliver! I am to see his pain. You and Tarver fight like street dogs. I am torn again! There is *nothing* I can do! Oh—when I had you growing round my skirts it was, as you said, a club! I spun a web—of things we laughed at together! I *knew* your secret wit and chuckles of delight. . . .

OLIVER: And now you know your sons—better than they know their wives.

SHE (*stabbed with pain*): Oliver! (*Hitting back in self-defence.*) I *said* it was wrong—to make friends with the next generation!

TARVER: No, it isn't!—But you use us simply to fill your days!

SHE: I *live* for my children! Is that wrong?

SIR GREGORY: Take care, my girl! Women who outstay their motherhood—become damn boring women!

SHE (*her face lighting up*): Gregory!

SIR GREGORY (*with energy*): And what's more—it's a self-indulgence! (*More energy.*) And what's more—it destroys the children! Let them get on with their own lives! I came back to find my wife! Not the mother of my sons!

SHE: It only needed a touchstone to explode! (*To* ALICE.) I have been in as many scrapes as you and as many fixes and I have *never* discovered what to do! If I knew, I wouldn't tell you because it may be I don't want to make you happy! Every time I help either of you girls to happiness I am helping my sons away from me! It's graceless in you to think I can turn into an advisor because I am seventy! I wish there was another adventure before me and, good God, there may be! But not while I am pulled down by the pressure on me of what you think I am! In your very manner as you speak to me another minute is added to my age and taken from my confidence! I begin to walk slowly because of you. I could skip if I chose! I could run if I chose! But there is something in you that dreads that I should seem young, that deplores it! I don't know what I am doing here at seventy being a mother!—The *sheep* knows better than that and the *tigress* knows it!

SIR GREGORY: Bravo!

SHE: Why bravo?

SIR GREGORY: I want you to pack.

SHE: *Tonight!*

SIR GREGORY: Yes. Have you a maid?

SHE: Good heavens, one can't get them!

SIR GREGORY: Then I'll help you. . .

SHE: What . . . *Now!*

SIR GREGORY (*opening bedroom door*): It's the only time to do it.

SHE: Come away—with you? (*Looking round.*) The house . . . and its lifelong things . . .

 BENT *seems to try to get up; but can't.*

SIR GREGORY: . . . will be dust-sheeted. (*Something about his prompt authority ravishes* HER.) I shall take you away to Mwelta.

SHE (*low—conspiratorially to* OLIVER): It might be . . . the Chinese Prime Minister. . . . (*Her hand fingering the birdcage. To* SIR GREGORY.) Do we go up into the mountains together?

SIR GREGORY (*slightly at a loss*): Well—the hills are enormous. (*Shrugs.*) But float as though they were light!—Take one suitcase only.

SHE: Can't I get all I want from the Arabs? (*Going towards door.*) The resolve's very light—so the baggage had better be!—My *make-up* box! (*Goes through door.*)

SIR GREGORY (*calling after her*): And your jewellery!

BENT (*in his chair. Centre stage. Desperate*): *I can't sit here and see it happen!* (*Struggles to get up, but can't.*) It'll be the same thing. . . . M'lady . . . m'lady . . . all over again! (*Struggles again to get up. He doesn't see that* SHE *has heard him and is now in the doorway behind him. She wears her sables. Carries long blue gloves, and her make-up box.*) Sir Gregory and Her Ladyship were like two wild animals fighting. The ground was all over blood and hair! The first words came up like lighted matches! The room was on fire before you could turn round! I can't get up. . . .

SIR GREGORY (*not listening to him*): We must blow out of this house like an explosion—(*To his* WIFE.) if you're to come! Arrangements and plans and alternative plans. . . . (*To* TARVER.) Send me on bills and I'll settle them. I leave the hard work of the care of the house to you, Tarver. (*Suddenly seeing that his* WIFE *is leaning over* BENT.) You're not packing!

SHE (*looking intently down at* BENT, *who is strangely still*): He's asleep!

SIR GREGORY (*looking*): Are you sure?

SHE (*note of panic*): Tarver! (TARVER *comes up.*) Take his pulse. . . .

    And it is true that BENT *is in a very odd position. They are all suddenly still in the presence of death.* TARVER *pulls up the old man's cuff and feels his pulse.*

TARVER (*as they wait with bated breath*): None. (*Pause.*) None at all.

SHE (*leaning closer*): So that's death. No sound.—No pain.

ALICE: You are thinking of yourself!

SHE: Everyone's death is a sample of the medicine we'll soon be taking. (*A note of fear.*) I feel the threshold! Gregory . . . (*Looking round for his support. As he comes up to her.*) Oh, what bad timing! (*Leaning over.*) Bent!—I must *beg* you to live again!

    BENT *stirs.*

BENT: I've been dreaming.

SHE: We thought you were ill.

BENT: No, you didn't.—And now I know what will happen. No sooner dead than your minds will be trotting away from me. And then galloping. But I'm not dead now!—And to see your faces and your warm living bodies and the shine on the silver like I never saw before . . . (*Looks searchingly round.*) and the most beautiful young thing of all . . . (*Closes his eyes again. In a tired voice.*) She was pretty.

OLIVER (*sharp—strangled*): Where's Roxane!

SIR GREGORY (*half aside*): And where is that Boxer?

BENT (*opening his eyes*): I frightened her. And it *was* a near thing! I felt the wonder!—If someone cut my throat and I died this minute—I'd have *lived*—like a spark of crystal!

SHE: This decides me. . . .

BENT (*gets to his feet. Stumbles towards the hall door*): Let me get home—while I feel it!

SHE (*anxious*): Hadn't you a coat?

BENT (*walking straight on*): No.

OLIVER: Shall I call a cab?

BENT (*walking on*): No. (*At the door.*) Good night—good night. . . . This doesn't come to everyone. (*Goes.*)

SHE: Go after him, Tarver! No coat! And like that! He might die in the street. . . .

TARVER *goes towards the door.*

ALICE (*wrought up*): Tarver! Wait! (*He doesn't look round.*) Tarver! . . . Forgive me!—It was *love*! *Be* merciful! . . . If you were once merciful . . . If it were once not taken all out of me . . .

TARVER (*looking at her*): Every farthing of your beastliness?

ALICE: . . . so that I lie awake hating myself and hating you for hating myself . . . (*But he goes. Louder in the hope it may reach him.*) and hating my weakness as I sail to perdition. . . .

SHE: *Alice!*

ALICE (*wildly—as she goes*): I'm for *one* man—even though I hate him. . . . (*Goes.*)

SHE: *Nothing* stops them! They'd quarrel through my funeral. . . .

SIR GREGORY (*hard—to* OLIVER): Where's your wife?

OLIVER (*bitter*): Away.—Changing men.

SHE: Gregory . . .

SIR GREGORY (*peremptory*): Don't upset your mother! Face it. Solve it—You should have solved it sooner!

SHE (*expostulatory*): Gregory!

SIR GREGORY: No.—Let *me* talk to him. (*To* OLIVER.) You've lost your wife. You must decide why.—And whether you want to find her. (*Putting out a hand to stop interruption. To* OLIVER.) It's your affair. Don't talk it over. —*Do* something.

SHE (*handing make-up box to her* HUSBAND. *Suddenly frantic. To* OLIVER): You're not going! (SIR GREGORY *stoops and*

picks up something.) You're *not* to go!—Come to the airport!
—I can't have this on my mind! I shall be haunted! Oliver!
—*Say* something!

OLIVER: Disagreeable as it is—disagreeable as I find him—I
shall take his advice, Mother. (*Goes.*)

SHE (*instantly flaming*): You hate him!

SIR GREGORY: I don't hate men. I manage them.

SHE: You're *worse*! You're more tyrannical than ever!

SIR GREGORY (*instantly*): Then don't come! (*Looks at her like a
man of iron, then, like a small boy, bangs the make-up box
violently on the table.*)

SHE (*a little scream*): The *bottles*!

SIR GREGORY (*opening lid—sheepish*): Nothing's broken.

SHE (*looking inside*): My *face*—I couldn't go without it! (*Suddenly abandoning this line, looking up at him.*) Are we mad!
... Is this my second folly? (*He looks down at her.*) Aren't
we too old for warfare? (*His face is inscrutable. No doubt he
too has a few doubts.*) What shall I *do*?

SIR GREGORY (*neutral voice*): Toss a coin. (*Fishes in a pocket.*)

SHE (*watching him, fascinated*): So (*sarcastic*) clever with your
fingers! ... Naturally ... (*Her eyes follow coin in air.*) you'll
make it come down. ...

SIR GREGORY (*as the coin has descended he has put one hand over
the other. Removing the hand*): Heads. (*Looking at her with a
faint smile.*) We go.

SHE (*uncertain—moving about the room. Pouncing on the birdcage*):
You must take *this*! (*Holds it out to him.*)

SIR GREGORY (*aghast*): Carry *that*!—Take that damn thing!

SHE: Or I don't come!

SIR GREGORY (*reaching for it. Under his breath*): Women ...
(*But he marches to the hall door, birdcage in one hand, make-up
box in the other.*)

SHE (*hunting about the room—here—there ...*): I've lost a glove.
... I've only got one glove! (*He turns, puts birdcage on a
small table. Rebelliously.*) I won't go! I *can't* go—without the
other one! (*Without a word he draws the second long glove*

slowly from his pocket and holds it up. She walks across the room and takes it. He picks up the birdcage.) Are you so certain of me?

SIR GREGORY: No.

SHE: Are you certain of yourself?

SIR GREGORY: No.

SHE: Is it forever?

SIR GREGORY (*a half smile*): We'll see. (*Turns and walks out. She follows him.*)

CURTAIN

ACT III

Probably late afternoon. The same room, but under white dust-sheets. The strangest disorder. The oddest lighting. Broken light in shafts crosses the room from a Venetian blind which hangs down in a "fan"—its cord hooked up one side but free on the other. White linen blinds pulled down. A look of twilight-in-daytime. The chandelier has a linen dust cover. The dust-sheets are scuffled. Have cats or panthers been in here?

The BOXER *wanders in in the half darkness. Gazes round. Sees no one.*

BOXER: Was it *this* room that night—that had all that light? —It looks like a graveyard. . . .

BENT (*removing a bit of dust-sheet from his face. He is lying completely covered by sheets on the sofa.*) Am I dreaming? (*Stares at the ceiling.*) (*On a small tray on the floor are a bottle of milk, a mug, bowl of sugar.*)

BOXER: No more'n I am. (BENT *turns his head and sees him.*) Have they quit—the lot of them?

BENT (*swinging his legs off the sofa, his knees still covered with the dust-sheet.*) She'll be back! My Lady! With or without her gentleman! Fifty to one. . . . (*Chuckle.*) Sixty to one— they'll split.

BOXER: Split?

BENT: What the lightning does to the rock. (*Suddenly alive to situation.*) Who let you in?

BOXER: You left the street door open.

BENT (*vigorous*): That's a lie! (*A small doubt.*) The lock's weak. (*Shuffles towards hall door.*)

BOXER: I rang the bell here yesterday.

BENT (*complacent—not to say ecstatic*): I heard it. (*What a pleasure to have chosen not to answer it.*)

BOXER: I saw that girl ... (*Goes to the window with the plane tree and looks into the leaves, but it is too dense.*) wandering down here back of this house day before yesterday. She went into some gate. That's what I came for! Someone ought to look after her.

BENT: If it's young Mrs. Oliver—it's *your* affair!

BOXER (*with sudden violence*): Yes, it is! It's my whole career! I lost that fight because of her! She drove me mad! She's *poison.*—She don't undertake ...

BENT (*a tiny thin passion like an insect*): I'd knock you down if I was young!

BOXER (*bitterly*): Oh, God, that isn't the answer! Knocking people down! It's *me* that's down—down for the count! It's me that's crashed. And all those chaps humming round me wanting me autograph—like smoke they've gone! I'm *out.* D'you know what they said to me? That I'd gone into that fight like a piece of old mutton.

BENT: Pah! *Women!*

BOXER: I hope to God I never see one again. Three days did all that mischief! (*Gloomily.*) I was a virgin.

BENT (*deprived of speech for a moment*): You give me the pip.

BOXER (*violently*): *SEX!*—They warned me!—A breathless mass of blood and lumps—that's what it's done to me!— *Me!* That's hammered my way through sixty wins in nine years from Liverpool to Utah!—Crazy I was for her! Took her round the town, never went near the gymnasium, slammed down the telephone on the manager!—And then what! *Then* what!—What did that two-fisted bacon-slaughterer do to me!—A demolition-job! *Sex!*—If I'd known what would happen I'd have fled to the Altar!

BENT (*with deep contempt*): You chaps that got religion!

BOXER (*innocent astonishment*): Haven't you?

BENT (*stooping to attend to his bits of crockery on a tray*): Me?—

I'm *there.* I'm *in* it. Me and the Lord walk up and down this room. (*Suddenly.*) Voices down there! ... (*Listens.* BOXER *starts to go to hall door.*) Not *that* way! Get out the back. ... (*Points to pantry door.*)

BOXER (*obeying him—muttering as he goes*): It isn't that *I* want her ... (*On exiting.*) But it's my *good deed.* ... (*He is gone.*)
        BENT *hides under dust-sheets. Enter the* LADY FROM ARABIA *in travelling things.*

SHE (*wandering in*): The end of Arabia. ... The end of the flight. ...

BENT (*starting up—indignant*): You never *said* you were coming!

SHE (*unsurprised*): My old house dog ... what are you doing here?

BENT: I came to die here.

SHE (*indulgent*): Why in the drawing-room? Have you forgotten that you left me?—That you're married?

BENT: I found the key of the back door in my pocket.

SHE: *That* doesn't turn Time back. ... How long have you been here?

BENT: Five months. (*To her—with strange joy.*) Five months of my own—what I never had before!—The sun and the moon passing over me. ... And nobody saying to me the dinner's ready—nor the morning's come!—And it isn't being *alone* that makes the difference!—It's being alone— *without Time!* (*Suddenly—taking in that* SHE *seems alone.*) Didn't it do?

SHE (*very straight*): No. It didn't.

BENT: *That* was a mistake—you going! He's mortal meat! (*As* SIR GREGORY *comes in.*) You're *not.*

SIR GREGORY (*astonished*): Why are you here, Bent!

BENT: I'm caravanning.—I mean I'm squatting.

SIR GREGORY: That's what it looks like! Have you fallen out with your wife?

BENT: Fallen foul. You know how it is in marriage, Sir Gregory.

SIR GREGORY: No, I don't.

BENT (*sly*): I've *seen* you knowing!

SIR GREGORY: That's enough! Clear a chair. Bring a chair up. (*Looking round.*) Everything so unready. ... We're ahead of the cables, perhaps. We have come back to sell the house, Bent.

BENT: Sell the house ...

SIR GREGORY: We're going to travel.

BENT: Whatever for?

SHE: The idea is Sir Gregory's.

BENT (*suddenly agonized*): And what about the plane tree? Would they cut it down? There's voices in the plane tree— evenings. I hear things.

SHE: Are you ill, Bent?

BENT: Wearing thin.—And you don't have to be holy to hear them. Any old chap that's wearing thin—if he keeps still enough—can hear a chap speaking.

SIR GREGORY: Is he talking about God?

BENT: No, I'm *not* talking about God.—There's other things in heaven.

SIR GREGORY: That reminds me! I've never checked the luggage! (*Goes out.*)

BENT (*muttering*): Cut the Mother of God out of the branches! It couldn't be done! (*To her—direct.*) You remember that night I went home—carrying my wonder? She dragged me in the dust!

SHE: Why should she?

BENT: Because like an old fool I had a need to tell! And that night I was stuffed with rare stuff—hard to come by! And only having the relationship of bed—she didn't value it!—So—when at the last lip of my time—that *woman*— (*Stops.*)

SHE (*startled*): Bent! What have you *done*!

> SIR GREGORY *returns with the suitcase.* BENT *takes it into the bedroom.*

ALICE (*bursting in*): Mama! (*Turning round and shouting through the door.*) She's here! (*Back to* MOTHER-IN-LAW.) We thought it was *tomorrow*!—The cable said tomorrow! *Nothing's ready!* (*Crossing the room in a rush.*) But I'm *first*! I'm first with the news! (*Pause—triumphant.*) I'm going to have a baby!

SHE (*involuntarily*): Not by Tarver!

TARVER (*hard on* ALICE's *heels*): Why not by me!

SHE: Well, I knew there must have been co-operation.— But I left you hating.

ALICE: Lots of babies are got by hating!

SHE: And what about prison?

TARVER: She got let off.

SHE: So there was pull again!

TARVER (*kissing his* MOTHER): Are you pleased—about the baby?

SHE: Oh, Tarver—dear Tarver—and dear Alice ... (*Taking his hand.*) do you think it's the beginning of the world?

ALICE: For me it is.

SHE: So it was for me.—And isn't it wonderful how hope is renewed and one can put up with repetition! ... With the autumn and the spring—and the foolishness of tulips who think they are the first ever seen! (SIR GREGORY *stands looking out at the plane tree. Slyly.*) And to *think*—even though I was painted by the best men of my day—my portrait will end up in the *attic* of that baby!

SIR GREGORY (*suddenly pulling up another blind. The room floods with light. He turns and looks at the room.*) How charming the room looks—so nearly empty! (*Pause.*) I'd forgotten the charm of this room! (*Crossing to his* WIFE.) I can't think ... I can't think why we're selling it!

SHE (*smiling at her own repetition*): The idea is your own! (*She picks up a large conch shell.*)

SIR GREGORY: After all ... there's no pressing need to travel. ...

SHE (*putting the shell to her ear*): And I can hear the sea just as well from here! (*Toying with the shell.*) I was told as a child— "Jehovah inhabiteth the shell."

SIR GREGORY (*blowing up—for no reason—but there probably is a reason*): How I hate whimsey! Women love it! I hate implication ... without precision. ...

SHE: I know!

SIR GREGORY (*sticking to his new idea*): *How about one more London Season?*

SHE: One *more*? We never bothered with one!

SIR GREGORY: We should have done!

SHE: I was too busy! It was a bit of a rush getting famous!

SIR GREGORY: It was a bit of a rush getting rich.

TARVER: Why did you sell your companies, Sir?

SIR GREGORY (*turning on him instantly*): Sell!—Who said *sell*?

TARVER (*taken aback*): I'm ... in one of them.

SIR GREGORY (*angrily*): My God, how they gossip—the underlings!

SHE (*alerted*): *Sell?*

SIR GREGORY (*overriding*): One doesn't sell—one refloats and reorganizes. ...

SHE: Is *that* what happened?

SIR GREGORY (*but he knows*): When?

SHE: The night of the Sheik's great party. When you suddenly decided to come home!

SIR GREGORY (*defensive*): Why not? The world's our oyster! (*To* TARVER.) I feathered the nest—and kept the power, my son! Remember to do that!

TARVER: I'll bear it in mind!

ALICE: Will they be old or young, Sir Gregory?

SIR GREGORY: Who?

ALICE: If you have a London Season!—If you entertain?

SIR GREGORY: It's only the Old who are at the top of things! Would you like to sit next the Prime Minister?

ALICE (*shaking her head*): The gap would be too wide between what I am and what he's done. There's something unfresh about fame—! But Mama knows.

SHE (*with a start—from abstraction*): What do I know?

ALICE: You told me once that not much could be done with adulation.

SHE: I told you that when I still had it.

ALICE: Do you still miss it?

SHE (*absently*): As one misses love.—Only at odd moments.

SIR GREGORY (*to* TARVER): Are you in touch with architects? ... (*Looking round.*) We must get decorators ... *swells*! Always go to the top man! I'd never trust my own taste! ...

SHE: Not even mine?

SIR GREGORY (*going to window*): A lot has happened to taste since we were young! (*Using his umbrella as a measuring rod to test the height of the window seat.*) Personally I'd have the windows lowered. ...

OLIVER (*in doorway*): And why should *you* be measuring the windows with your umbrella? (*To his* MOTHER.) If you meant to come back and live here *together*—why did you telegraph for *me* to come!

SHE (*softly*): Because there's a crisis. (*Even more softly.*) But it's *my* crisis.

ALICE: Ah.

SHE: Why "ah"?

ALICE: Nothing.

SHE: Do you see Roxane?

OLIVER: No. (*Bitter.*) But sorrow doesn't last!

SHE: Yes, it does—it *does*—Is there somebody else?

OLIVER (*bitter*): Yes. And always will be! (*The truth.*) But never another Roxane ...

SIR GREGORY: There's a young fool—if ever there was one. (*To* TARVER—*tapping on a wall.*) There's a room through this wall we could throw in.

OLIVER: What for!

SIR GREGORY: For large scale entertaining.

TARVER (*pointing to the window with the plane tree*): And the little garden? And the mews cottage—that was the stables?

OLIVER: *I* want it.

SIR GREGORY: What for?

OLIVER: To write in.

SIR GREGORY (*offhand*): Is that what you are—a writer?

OLIVER: Have you something against it?

SIR GREGORY: No. I read books. Though you mightn't think it. But you have to know where you are with a man. I never trust writers, poor devils. It's like sinking a shaft in quicksand.—But on with our plans. (*To* ALICE.) How about a swimming pool—and the mews as a dressing room?

ALICE: If you're altering the house—how about the top floor that's shut?

OLIVER: I suppose it's not struck anybody ... (*They look at him.*) that my mother plans nothing?

SHE (*on the periphery, yet lying in wait*): It seems not to have.

SIR GREGORY: Your mother needs putting back into life!

SHE (*softly*): Whose life?

SIR GREGORY: Mine. (*Searching in a pocket.*) Where's my little book? (*Pulls out his engagement book. Flicking over pages.*) When's the season? ... May? (*More pages.*) What are we now?

SHE: We're seventy.

SIR GREGORY (*startled*): Why should that make one behave differently!

SHE (*to* BENT, *who returns from the bedroom*): Bent,—would you like to see the house alive again?

BENT: It's been so beautiful—dead. Excuse me, m'lady. May I have a moment of your time? (*She looks up in surprise. Is he going to give notice? Yes, he is.*) Might I ask permission to sit down? (*She assents.*) I am afraid I must give my notice. —You remember that night—sitting here—that I nearly died? I have the same feeling on me now. This time I think I shall make it.

SHE (*intensely interested*): Bent—are you going to *die*?

BENT: I think I am. (*Pause.*) You'll find it's nothing. (*Pause.*) Most people die murdered.

SIR GREGORY: Good God, what's he mean!

BENT: I mean by disease or some accident. I'm at the age when I'm merely withdrawing. If everybody arrived— where I've arrived—there'd be no fear of death. The legend would be finished. It's like taking trouble . . . over a bubble. (*Pause.*) So few people achieve the final end. *Most* are caught napping. (*Silence. Then shockingly clear.*) *My last advice— Don't do things twice!* Put a screen round me. So you can go on talking. (*Dies.*)

SHE: Dear me.

TARVER: Good God.

SIR GREGORY: Is the chap dead?

OLIVER (*who has taken his pulse*): Snuffed out like a candle.

SHE: And much left unsaid.

TARVER: We must ring someone!

SHE: Who is there to ring?

SIR GREGORY: We must ring the police!

SHE: And if we don't ring the police for ten minutes, Bent won't tell them. He has told you what to do. Put the screen round him. (OLIVER *carries the screen and puts it round* BENT.)

SIR GREGORY: You can't *do* such a thing!

SHE: Yes, you can. He'll be dead for so long.—He said the only way to—*enjoy death*—was to— (*Pausing to give emphasis as she slowly chooses her words.*) exhaust life!—And not be caught napping!

SIR GREGORY: Have you gone off your rocker?

SHE (*nodding at the screen*): No, but my warning's come! There are things to be seen—that are the things we have always seen—but different! There must be more in the moment itself! And less in the programme. . . . Now that I am without Bent . . . (*They all look apprehensively at the screen.*) He may be playing some trick on me. Go and look.

OLIVER (*looking*): No. Still dead.

SHE: As I was saying—now I am without Bent—there may be *another* way to live. . . .

OLIVER: Then what's all this talk of entertaining?

SHE: He made plans. (*Smiling.*) I listened.

TARVER: But you let him run on!

SHE: That was my irresolution.

SIR GREGORY: All I ask is to live as I've always done! I'd like every bloody minute of the same thing over again?

SHE (*pause*): Then will you go back to Arabia?—And leave me to try living alone?

OLIVER: You haven't quarrelled again!

SHE: Yes, we have. In the back of the taxi that took us that night.—In the plane . . . and— (*With a sweeping gesture.*) all over the mountains of Arabia!

TARVER: What on earth d'you want to live alone for?

SHE: I want to be attentive to . . . (*Slight smile.*) trivial things.

SIR GREGORY: And weren't you before!

SHE: Never without that guilt—peculiar to women!

SIR GREGORY: How do *I* produce it!

SHE: By being you, Gregory! Women are so dutiful!—And the best men make them work so hard for them!—By the time-table married life imposes . . . by this little book we carry! (*Waving the little scarlet book at him, that she has kept in her hand.*) I have yet to find out what a day is like when I am not planning the next one!

ALICE: I can't imagine not looking ahead!

SHE: That's how I've turned Saturday into Monday and Monday into Saturday—and become seventy!

SIR GREGORY (*suddenly intensely irritated*): They hit you where you can't get 'em—those nebulous answers of women!

ALICE: Mama wants to get free from every responsibility!

SHE (*murmuring*): Except one.

ALICE: Who is on your conscience?

SHE: There is always someone.

ALICE(*fiercely*): I should like to think that it's my unborn son!

SHE: Well, it isn't.

SIR GREGORY (*boiling over*): Get out—the lot of you! Get out—the next generation!

ALICE: What—*me*?

SIR GREGORY: Yes—*you*!—I want to talk to my wife! (*Waits, glaring as they go out. When the door is shut he helps himself to a cigarette which he does not light.* SHE *goes over and looks out of the window. After a pause—a change in tone.*) So—you don't want to sell the house. And you don't want to travel. And you don't want me here? Is that it? (SHE *turns, saying nothing.*) See if I can understand you! (*Slight laugh.*) I can understand men!

SHE: Men wouldn't say what I'm saying!—That I want the whole of myself—and not half again! "I am as I am!" you used to say. We were so different that when two rooms separated us for half an hour—we met again as strangers. It was I who was told to change!

SIR GREGORY: That's a tussle that nobody sees plainly till they get into the deeps of marriage! Hasn't it worked—these five months?

SHE (*coming near him*): Has it?

SIR GREGORY: Of course it has! I want a woman with the faults I know!— (*Coming up to her.*) where I'm either enchanted—or bark my shins on the furniture! . . . The battle of two people who won't leave each other—

SHE: But you did!

SIR GREGORY: I was wrong.

SHE: You're stout as an old stick one leans on!—You know we waste each other! But you won't be the first to say it! We're two old lions when we're together!—The old answers —to the old vexations! The battle to be right . . .

SIR GREGORY: And some sort of rule about forgiving?

SHE: Yes. The sun going down. Gregory, it's here we speak the truth! (*Pause.*) And the heart has no part in it!—I'm going to be cascaded into eternity! (*Ruefully.*) I'm more interested in the full moon!

SIR GREGORY: Don't be arrogant, my old girl! You were always arrogant! There's a ceiling *there* (Points up.) and a floor *there*— (Points down.) and no one gets beyond it!— Not the clever chaps more than the stupid chaps—but the clever chaps grow paler! (*He walks away a little—something on his mind.*) That night I came to dinner—what made you suddenly give in?

SHE: My ... (*Hesitating.*) my femininity!—I wanted it con-
firmed!

SIR GREGORY: Before I came ... (*Now he pauses to light his
cigarette.*) those tales ... (*Slight effort.*) that stuff about a
lover! What made you spill the beans?

SHE: They thought I was boasting.

SIR GREGORY (*casual*): And were you?

SHE: Does it matter?

SIR GREGORY: You damn maddening woman!—What was
that fellow's *name*?

SHE: The singer?

SIR GREGORY: Of *course* the singer.

SHE: Can't you remember?

SIR GREGORY: *No!*

SHE (*pause. The incredible truth*): Well, I can't either.

SIR GREGORY (*winded*): It was in *that chair* you told me!

SHE (*fingering the arm of the chair*): In the momentary hate of
love I might have said anything!

SIR GREGORY (*menacing*): *Was* he your lover?

SHE (*simply*): I had the wish. (*Musing.*) But did it happen?
    A pause.

SIR GREGORY (*a sudden roar of laughter*): So what the hell do
you tell Oliver!

SHE (*instantly alarmed*): Gregory—you'll never—no matter
what happens—or under what circumstances ...

SIR GREGORY: Throw a doubt?—No, never! God, I'm glad
I've seen 'em!

SHE (*can she have heard the plural*): *Them!*

SIR GREGORY: *Both* of them. Now it's the *plant* that matters!
What a fuss about a seed!—The desire for a son was only
present after seventy. I'm an old egotist.... (*He finds himself
in front of the mirror. Pause.*) What a *monstrous* thing. ...

SHE (*startled*): What?

SIR GREGORY: *Age* is a monstrous thing! Just when a man's
at the top of life—off they want to tip him! (*Shakes his fist
at the face in the mirror.*) I've learnt the whole bag of tricks!

I know the weakness of a man as quick as you can feel a drop of rain! I can see in an Arab's eye which way he's heading! I can feel the flow of money like a fish in the river! (*Turning round on her.*) To be old is *magnificent*! But damned if they'll admit it!

SHE: What do you want *most*, Gregory?

SIR GREGORY: You.

SHE: It's too late for gallantry. (*Softly.*) Think again.

SIR GREGORY (*with sudden violence*): I want my own way! (*Not looking at her.*) I want what I've always had!

SHE (*insisting*): But ... most? (*There is no answer. Then—*)

SIR GREGORY: Power!—Respect! (*Bitterly.*) Or *fear* will do!

SHE (*shaking her head*): Still not the truth. . . .

SIR GREGORY (*walks away from her. Turning, violently*): Blast the end of life!—And the way men take it! (*Halts. Through clenched teeth.*) And *blast* the Sheik!

SHE (*low—but he hears*): I knew it.

SIR GREGORY (*more quietly*): He's making ready to die and he's gone out of my range.—He wants Arabs about him.

SHE: At the party? Was it *that* night he told you?

SIR GREGORY: Huh! Arabs never tell you things! But suddenly—there's more dignity and less intimacy—and your hold's gone! I was to sell my companies. *He* wanted them. Thirty years we'd been together. Same age as I am. (*Pause.*) I said I wouldn't. Then he turned his eyes on me. And his eyes upset me. I flung out of the doors.—I thought he'd send for me.

SHE: And he didn't.

SIR GREGORY: He sent his emissary. It was that night, yes, I knew what it meant.—It was done in the form of a present. A jackal ... (*Holding up thumb and finger to show the size.*) in gold and jade. (*Pause.*) I threw it in the sea at Gibraltar when we changed planes. (*Pause.*) Once more the Arabs have disgorged the English! (*Sits down as though his legs have given way.*) I can govern men, my girl!—But I don't know what life is about! (*Knowing there are tears in her eyes.*) Take my handkerchief—the top pocket one!—It always ended like this—didn't it?

OLIVER (*in the doorway. He sees it as a farewell*): Are you going out of our lives again?

SIR GREGORY: Yes. Are you glad of it?

OLIVER: Oddly enough—no.

SIR GREGORY: I remember you in your cradle—with your writer's eyes screwed up against me!—A mother's son from the start.

OLIVER: *I* had no hand in it. (*Pause.*) Whether you are my father—or not . . .

SIR GREGORY (*instantly—ablaze*): I am!

OLIVER: If I may be allowed to say so . . . *Nonsense*, Sir!

SIR GREGORY: You are *not* allowed! You think you know, puppy, why I parted from her!—You think some chap fathered you?—Well, he didn't! When your mother fell in love I knew how to forgive her! It isn't the faults on the grand scale that matter. It's the little fault, the rubbish of life, the damn thing that crops up too often! (*Glares for a moment. Then.*) A million to one you don't know why I left her! I wore *boots. Patent leather.* She swore she had put the laces in and she damn-well knew she hadn't!—The room blew up. I threw my glasses—they broke. She threw her slipper. I shook her chair as she sat and it went over. . . .

SHE (*again touching the arm of the chair with her fingertips*): You *tipped* me over.

SIR GREGORY: Well, whether I did or not I went blazing across the sky to Arabia! (*A sudden impulse. To* OLIVER.) If I go back . . . I've other irons in the fire. . . . Come with me!

OLIVER: You have Tarver.

SIR GREGORY: He's too like me! What a man wants is a surprise-packet! (*Chuckling.*) What Joseph must have felt—in Jerusalem! (*Looking and nodding at* OLIVER.) I could do something with you! (*Pause.*) Put that girl out of your mind! (*Pause.*) Do you know where she is?

OLIVER: I have her followed.

SIR GREGORY: What do you hope to gain by that!

OLIVER: Only the sad knowledge that she wants for nothing.

ROXANE (*standing in the doorway to the kitchen. In an exhausted voice*): Or that what she wants—she *has*!

OLIVER (*unsurprised*): Roxane . . .

ROXANE: I came through from the mews cottage. . . . (*Struck by his attitude.*) You didn't *know* I was there!

OLIVER: I knew it

SHE (*low—she understands what Bent heard*): "The voices in the plane tree . . ."

ROXANE (*using the curious, unaccustomed word*): Mother . . . in . . . law. . . .

SHE (*startled*): You *never* called me that!

ROXANE: It holds me to life a little.

SIR GREGORY: What were you doing there?

ROXANE: I sleep where I can.

SIR GREGORY: Alone?

ROXANE: With a stranger.

SIR GREGORY (*indignant*): Couldn't the chap afford—?

SHE (*interrupting—tilting up* ROXANE's *face—tenderly*): How tired you look. . . .

OLIVER: But *pretty*.

ROXANE (*looking at him a moment*): Isn't it sad that I should be so pretty . . . (*Low.*) and any man can have me.

SIR GREGORY: Good God, what a thing! What do you get out of it that *one* man can't give you?

ROXANE: Only—saying—"yes".

SIR GREGORY: It seems damn little!

SHE: Roxane . . . Roxane. Who's to look after you!

ROXANE: Nobody. I'm like one of those . . . (*Looks helplessly at* OLIVER, *who has always found her words when they failed her.*) *you* know . . . that die at dusk.

OLIVER (*gay—as though it was a game they were playing together*): Dragonflies! (*Moves a small step towards her. She starts back, alarmed*.) Keep still, my love. (*Another step*.) How sweet you look. ... (*Imperceptibly moving—as though she were a small wild animal*.) don't move ... keep still ... how pale. ... (*Nearer. Close—but not touching her*.) I love your hair like that.—Sweet and untidy!

ROXANE (*a whisper*): I can't come back.

OLIVER (*tenderly, soothing—matching her tone*): You shan't come back. ... (*Slips an arm round her gently*.) Is that your waist?—Slender.

ROXANE (*lifting her face—murmuring her new found truth*.) I have no sex, Oliver.

OLIVER: Nor has a child, my lovely! (*Over her shoulder he puts a finger to his lips—for silence. Moving her gently*.) Where shall we dine? (*Persuading. Stooping to her ear*.) I'm hungry. (*Step by delicate step they go towards the door*.)

ROXANE (*stopping a moment*): How can you be like this?

OLIVER: It's what I was born for.

They move on again—and disappear. There is a moment's silence. SIR GREGORY *crosses the room and shuts the door carefully.*

SHE: I have escaped by a miracle! *She* is the one! He will forgive me.

SIR GREGORY: To be plain about it—the girl's on the streets. (*Going back to her*.) How can he live with her?

SHE: You can live with anything human.

SIR GREGORY: Then why can't you put up with me?

The door bursts open and ALICE *comes in, holding a yellow envelope in either hand.*

ALICE: A cable, Sir Gregory!

SIR GREGORY (*taking it. Dully*): Goddamn 'em.

ALICE: And another!

SIR GREGORY (*taking the second cable*): Goddamn 'em twice over. (*Cables in hand, he gets up, slams them down on a table, leans over, glaring at* ALICE.) And who's to see *me* off—as an old man! (*Grim*.) Has she thought of that?

Pause.

SHE: Yes . . . I think of it. . . .

SIR GREGORY: I shall die sooner than you will. (*As he speaks he picks up one of the envelopes.*)

ALICE (*cheekily*): But supposing you don't?

SIR GREGORY (*sharp*): You keep out of it! (*Slitting envelope open. More mildly.*) Threescore years and ten is all they give us! (*Pulls out a three-page cable: one page flutters to the floor.*)

ALICE: But if there's a bit over . . . (*Stoops to pick up the page. Intuitively.*) it's her own.

SIR GREGORY (*taking the page from her*): What should she want to do with it. . . . (*His eye catches something: his voice trails to inattention.*)

SHE (*low*): What should I want to do with it . . .? (*Moves away. He takes no notice. His hand goes to his coat pocket for his reading glasses, changes glasses, spreads the three pages flat on the table, leans over them, reads. To herself—as he reads.*) I want to find out who I am. I can wear the personality of anyone—why else have I been an actress? Thirty authors— or thirty lovers—have made thirty women of me . . . (*Suddenly—to ALICE.*) How *much* does he need me?

ALICE: He isn't listening.

SHE (*watching him—as ALICE also watches. Pause*): What is it, Gregory?

SIR GREGORY (*upright. His old eyes blazing*): Oil again! (*Smashing his hands down on the cables.*) Oh my God—oil again! Where they've never found oil before! And that damned old Moslem kneels and prays to Allah!—

SHE (*breathless*): They want you again. . . .

SIR GREGORY: No pipelines—no anything! My desert bursting—on the far side of the mountains!—"*Want* me again"? They can't do without me! They want a new Concession!

ALICE: Does that mean money?

SIR GREGORY: It *does* mean money! (*Gay, whirling. Opening dispatch case to make sure of wallet, passport, etc.*) They're squealing for money! (*Zips it up again.*) And they know I can whistle up money—with a fortune behind me like mine!

(*To* TARVER.) Remember *that* when you're rich—that money finds money!—And get me a taxi—*quick*. We'll go down to the City. . . .

TARVER *rushes off.*

SHE: His coat—Alice! (*She herself picks up hat, scarf, gloves.* ALICE *holds the coat ready.*)

SIR GREGORY (*getting into his coat. Struck by a thought*): And what about you? (*Suddenly turning his head and looking at* HER.) Why don't you travel? Take Bent!—(*Suddenly turning his head and looking at the screen.*) My God . . . I'd forgotten him! (*Exasperated. As* SHE *hands him gloves.*) Now—who's to look after you! . . .

SHE (*wildly hunting for his umbrella*): Like the poets and the drunks . . . (*Looks in another corner.*) I shall end the appointment with food—(*Pounces on it.*) and the appointment with dressing. . . . (*Dusts the umbrella with her hand.*)

SIR GREGORY: Very uncomfortable!

SHE: It wouldn't suit a man!

SIR GREGORY (*another thought*): And—come to that . . . you may die yourself!

SHE: I don't think I shall. I can't be bothered with it!

SIR GREGORY (*at the door—going*): I shall come back. (*Suddenly opens his arms wide to* HER.)

SHE (*smiling*): Your umbrella, Gregory.

SHE *pops it into his opened arms. So he kisses, instead of her, the hand that holds it.*

SIR GREGORY (*going through door*): I'll look in on my way to the plane. (*Disappears.*)

SHE (*calling through the open door after him*): If you have time. . . . (*Waits. Gently closing the door with finality. With a curious triumph.*) He *won't* have time! (*Crosses to window. Now a complete change of manner.*) He is looking forward again! (*Throws up window and waves down.*) But I am going to make Time stand still! (*Turning back into the room.*) It is *I* who am the Chinese Prime Minister!

ALICE: What do you want, Mama?

SHE: To be alone. (*Moving majestically towards the central armchair.*) For after death I shall never know him again. (*Sits down.*) And I may have to know myself. (*Silence. Then:*) You think, Alice, that I have duties. (*Musing.*) And in my way I have done them. But I inherit the dual sex that the centuries have slowly brought me. I am a modern, not an antique woman. And there is a Me in me that I have never lost.—And don't intend to.—Without it nothing has importance.

ALICE: We are so close, Mama!

SHE: Not yet! You are still a woman!—But I am a rock three parts submerged. I shine on the skin of the sea—waving my seaweed. The rock below is common ground. (*Pause.*) Had you thought of living on the top floor yourself?

ALICE: It did occur to me.

SHE: With Tarver—and the baby?—And other babies?

ALICE: Would you like that?

SHE: Would you think it unsuitable if I said no?

ALICE (*stung*): I thought women liked being grandmothers!

SHE: It isn't the grandmothers who say so! The using-up of grandmothers is not for me. It was pre-Christian! Now only the Latins and the natives do it! I admire you, Alice, and I know what's in your mind!—But I won't help you with the nursery, my dearest! I won't fill-in for you with the harness of the kisses at six. I *had* my babies—it was like love! But I won't do things twice! (*Suddenly throwing out both arms to their length—stretching, as though waking.*) Alice!— Above all things . . . I want a cup of tea! (ALICE *slips away at once to the kitchen door. Calling after her.*) Everything must be there—in the kitchen. . . . (ALICE *is now gone. Now* SHE *gets up.*) Free me. . . . (*Pause. Walks up and down.*) From the expectation of tomorrow—free me! From the eye of the clock—free me! From the habits of a lifetime . . . but they are as strong as *harness*!—I shall have to *exaggerate* . . . to get them off in time! (*Looks around the room.*) Let the house burn! Let me *not* . . . (*Speaking rapidly—counting her fingers.*)

have to remember to turn the gas off, make sure of the insurance, ring for the fire engines, save my jewels!—I will go out into the garden and think how *beautiful—are the flames!* (*Pause. Seeming to wake up.*) But I can't talk to *nothing*! Even on the stage—one can't do that! Or not in the plays. ... *I* was brought up to play in!—A second actor makes a dialogue!—Even a dead one! (*She sweeps the light screen to one side. There is time to see that though* BENT *died with his arms hanging at his sides—his hands are now folded in his lap.*) Bent!—are you alive?

BENT (*eyes shut*): Just about.—Hardly.

SHE (*murmuring*): Like a watch that one shakes—you've gone on again.

BENT (*his head tilts forward; his fingers seem to count his waistcoat buttons*): Back in the old carcass.—It don't seem to fit. (*Looking up—his eyes now open.*) There's things going on you wouldn't believe!—Like Easter on a farm with the cocks crowing! A whistling—very old—that I should have heard before.—And cries and catcalls—of the gods.

SHE: Where?

BENT: Threading through the traffic. And in the yard. It's thick as Derby Day. Everything is everywhere. ... Even a spoon I'd lost—let alone the people.

SHE: Would you rather have died?

BENT: No, I wouldn't. (*Pause.*) And *I'd* like a cup of tea.

SHE *starts, looks at him with suspicion. Crosses to kitchen door and calls down.*

SHE: *Alice!* (*Waits.*) Bring two cups. (*Pause.*) Or if *you* want one—three. (*Walks slowly back, her eyes on* BENT.) Bent—we are alone.

BENT (*shutting his eyes again. Cautious*): But how are we sure of anything?

SHE: That night she threw you out—*did something happen?*

BENT (*pause*): How are we sure? (*Thinks.*) I had the wish. (*Thinks harder.*) But did I put it into action?

SHE: My very words!—So one can eavesdrop from heaven?

BENT (*anxious*): What'll you do?

SHE (*moving away—forgetting him*): Reverse the habits of a lifetime.

BENT: I mean—about *me*?

SHE: About you?—Nothing. When the unplanned day is before me . . . (*Stops.*)

BENT (*in his cunning manner*): How'll you fill it?

SHE: I shall indulge the pleasures of the senses. (BENT *cups an ear. Can he have heard aright?*) Heat and cold—for instance! And make *sure* I feel them!—Like Alexander—who changed a cold stone from his left to his right hand, that each hand in turn knew it was living.—I shall cut down sleep. . . . There are pills to keep you awake, and I shall take them. . . .

BENT: You may pop off doing that.

SHE (*replying—but not to him*): And if I die in ten years—or ten minutes—you can't measure Time!—In ten minutes everything can be felt!—In four minutes you can be born!—In two minutes God may be understood! And what one woman grasps—all men may get nearer to. . . . (*Pause.*) When I stir my coffee at dawn . . .

BENT: Who's going to give it to you?

SHE (*tart*): You.—A man who can die twice can do anything! I shall get up in an ecstasy of no-responsibility—as though it was the beginning of the world—and toss the grass with my rhinoceros horn—and be barbed with words like Saint Sebastian!

The door opens. ALICE, *her eyes glued on the tray she is carrying, walks in.*

ALICE: Why the third cup?

SHE (*gay*): Show no astonishment. Take it as a miracle!— There are lots of them! Pour it out. For me—no sugar. (ALICE *pours, filling two cups.*) I have always been a punctual women. I have never glanced at the sea as I drove to the station. If God had been stoking the engine I wouldn't have seen Him! There are continents around and about us . . .

(ALICE *takes her own cup and walks two steps into another life.*)
and wild, unharvested things. . . . (*Fills the third cup.*)

ALICE (*hypnotized by her own dreams*): What . . . things?

SHE (*adding sugar. Gay*): Why the grey parrot talks—and not
the green! (*Crossing the Stage with the cup, flinging each line
back as she crosses.*) Why a sea lion—out of the cold sea—
can come into a circus and understand fame! How a dog
can establish with me the mystery of humour!—I want to
think of these things and find the springs in common there
may be. (*Puts the cup down by* BENT.)

BENT: I should like to know what happened between you and
Sir Gregory?

SHE: We parted again.

BENT (*fishing up a light thought from his crumpled surface*): I am
glad you are back.—You were meant to be a single woman.
—For that is how you were born. (*Second light thought.*)
And I'm glad for Sir Gregory. Women of individuality—
are damned uncomfortable for men.

SHE: And I'm glad you are alive.

BENT: Hardly worth mentioning. I'm an old leaf—from an
old tree. And even the tree cut down.

SHE: Oh, Bent—ah, Bent! What did I always tell you! If you
hadn't drunk and you hadn't fornicated—what a poet you'd
have been!

CURTAIN

Call Me Jacky

AUTHOR'S PREFACE

Twenty years ago the writing of plays became for me a passion, an opium, an addiction. I obstinately loved the hard form of the three hoops. Life being too huge an animal to put through them (you can't dig deep and jump nimble) I have to lighten the creature. I have to distil. I hold a fan up in front of life, and the fan is—words. Hints, understatements, winks, ellipticalities—all infinitely worked-on for comedy. "A comedy that is funny without making laughter its sole concern" (thesis on my play, *The Chalk Garden*, by Gerald Weales, *Tulane Drama Review*, called "The Madrigal in the Garden".)

When a play is (at last) finished—and I (at last) go into the theatre—I need comedic co-operation. I need a director who knows that the serious things I say are less serious than those said in fantasy. The animals must be let out gaily like gazelles —though they be lions. I need a movement governed like ballet—not up and down the stage but in the mind. And the play needs hard work, obedience, discipline, and at least ten weeks' rehearsal.

I have written eight plays. Seven have been put on either on Broadway, in London, or both. All have had to fight to get on. Having a success makes no difference. It's on the cards (so the managements think) that you won't have two.

The stage is a curious country with its own language, where a "foreigner" (the author) has very little power. I am a writer, not a general. I can't get the troops to obey me. They give me a general to do it for me; but not one who knows how to win.

Except once.

The Chalk Garden was refused in London over a week-end. It had taken me four years to write: and a fifth in battle with my New York manager, Irene Selznick. Fury, exhaustion, crossings of the Atlantic, differences of opinion like two tigers. But finally we closed ranks and wanted the same thing. Irene then stood behind me, inexorably bound in my cause, to every word, every comma. The play was played as I had worked on it—in couplets of remark and response sharpened like a pencil. The candles for laughter were lit where I had placed them—to form a long ripple. Some were "lit" backwards as the audience "got" the language.

I don't mind telling the truth. I'm too old to mind. The "direction" in America was not only negligible but finally antagonistic. Irene and I "brought it in".

That play had the kind of success you dream about. It got the Arts *Award of Merit* in America, it is played there in summer stock and repertory, it is in the drama libraries of most American colleges. In London it ran twenty-three months, and it is played constantly by amateurs. Yet it has never been revived in London, nor asked for by Chichester or the National Theatre: though the National Theatre's Literary Manager, Kenneth Tynan, once wrote of it: ". . . It may well be the finest artificial comedy to have flowed from an English (as opposed to an Irish) pen since the death of Congreve."

But he also wrote: "We eavesdrop on a group of thoroughbred minds" . . .

Is this the trouble? Well . . . temporarily. For inverted snobbery must be nearly over. Each attitude has its day.

Here is *Call Me Jacky*, my eighth play; the first that never reached a capital. I wrote it through 1965–66–67, three years.

What's the story? That one thing leads to another.

What's the theme?

Does it have to have a theme? I don't believe playwrights have to have themes. Not watertight-Arthur-Miller ones. I believe that's why John Osborne won't be interviewed, and Harold Pinter says, "I won't explain."

If *Call Me Jacky* must have a theme it is—roughly—that the old lady, Mrs. Basil, was more permissive than they thought.

I started like that. And it hung itself with a lot of thoughts as I went on.

The theatre critic, T. C. Worsley, once said to me: "Don't worry about your theme. The critics will pull it out."

There is something lucky that happens to writers—a mixture of invention and memory that runs down the arm. If that doesn't happen, nothing happens. My plays are dense with things that have happened to me. And they need a willingness, a participating audience. And a critic willing to hear.

Frank Hauser directed. He did his very best in the time given him. But more rehearsal time was needed to discover the play's two levels, its barely-indicated, shrugged-off implications below its frivolity.

When the play reached Oxford, the *Observer* critic wrote: "I cannot bring myself to write temperately." And: "It obviously intends to exasperate people like myself beyond speech." (But he is paid for "speech", isn't he?)

He then quoted the "theme" as exactly the opposite of what it is. Mr. Donald Albery, the management, was waiting for comfort. He didn't get it. So the play lay upside down at Oxford like a dog with its paws in the air.

"Art isn't easy," wrote Albee.

And again: "It's indecent to fault a work for being difficult."

ENID BAGNOLD

May 1968

Meadow Players Ltd., by arrangement with Donald Albery for Calabash Productions Ltd., presented *Call Me Jacky* at the Playhouse, Oxford, on 27th February 1968, with the following cast:

MRS. BASIL	Sybil Thorndike
ESTATE AGENT	Greville Hallam
DU BOIS	Heather Chasen
NIGGIE	Edward Fox
SHATOV	Sheila Burrell
HERBERT	Paul Eddington
ELIZABETH	Georgina Ward
TOM	Raymond Platt

Directed by FRANK HAUSER
Designed by SAM KIRKPATRICK

CHARACTERS

MRS. BASIL
AN ESTATE AGENT (Charlie)
DU BOIS
NIGGIE
SHATOV
HERBERT
ELIZABETH
TOM

ACT I

Time: An afternoon in summer.

Place: A country house.

Downstage is divided into two parts.

(1) An alcove stage-right, temporarily shielded from the depths of upstage by two large screens. In the alcove are a papier mâché armchair and a small love seat.

(2) A door leads through to (stage-left) the half of a kitchen. In the kitchen all that is necessary are a kitchen table (or half of one), a chair, a sink, and a plastic bin beneath it.

When the screens are removed early in Act One the rest of the drawing-room is seen, with a corridor or hallway running upstage. Part of the drawing-room (and the corridor) is lighted by round port-hole windows looking out on the garden. The drive to the front door runs past the windows.

A spotlight (Act One only) travels from the alcove to the kitchen and back as it is needed.

When the curtain rises, MRS. BASIL, *wearing a muslin summer dress on the grey side of white, sits on the love-seat. She is a grandmother as young as a grandmother can mathematically be.*

The ESTATE AGENT—*hair dyed like a daffodil—stands by the papier mâché chair.*

MRS. BASIL's *distinguished astonishment at the colour of his hair produces a prolonged silence.*

MRS. BASIL (*eventually*): Are you the head of your firm?

ESTATE AGENT: The senior partner is on holiday.

MRS. BASIL: Do sit down. (*Sharply.*) Be careful with that chair!

ESTATE AGENT: A charming period.

MRS. BASIL: No. It's a period I despise. How did the rumour get round that I might be selling the house?

ESTATE AGENT: A gentleman rang me.

MRS. BASIL (*on a separate wave-length*): Ah.

ESTATE AGENT (*nervous—determined*): The back I gather has worm and beetle.

MRS. BASIL: I live in the front.

ESTATE AGENT: The property is very valuable.

MRS. BASIL (*neutral*): How much would I get for it?

ESTATE AGENT: Including the fields by the sea . . .

MRS. BASIL: *Ex*cluding them.

ESTATE AGENT: For the house and garden, at a rough guess, forty thousand pounds. *Site value.*

MRS. BASIL: What would you do with the house?

ESTATE AGENT: Pull it down.

MRS. BASIL (*indifferent*): Where would I live?

ESTATE AGENT: Facing the road one could get permission for five small houses of decorative charm. Three more in the garden. Rustic type. You could live in one of those.

   No reply.

(*Persuasive.*) In that way, if you wished, you could also have a flat in London.

MRS. BASIL: I don't really care about London. It is so up to date about nothing.

ESTATE AGENT: Wouldn't you be happier in a smaller house? (*He has lost her attention. He repeats the question.*)

MRS. BASIL (*into the air—artificially*): What is happiness . . .

ESTATE AGENT (*cautious*): One likes to travel.

MRS. BASIL: Every time I travel I come back to an empty house. I can only keep a cook here—that is to say any living body—by the hourly use of my personality.

ESTATE AGENT (*at sea*): Is that so.

MRS. BASIL (*absently*): I have one now who seems to be a lesbian. I am not a lesbian myself but the wear and tear is much the same. (*Returning to the subject thoughtfully.*) Forty thousand pounds . . .

ESTATE AGENT: It will add to your income.

MRS. BASIL: By investment. More letters more trouble. And once you put it in you never take it out. It's a pipe-dream. You must go now. I have a weekend party.

ESTATE AGENT (*rising*): If you think more of it give me a tinkle.

MRS. BASIL: A tinkle if I think more of what?

ESTATE AGENT: Putting the property into my hands.

MRS. BASIL: I wouldn't dream of it.

ESTATE AGENT: But I thought . . .

MRS. BASIL: It was your thought. You made the running. With forty thousand pounds this is the house I should buy again. (*Dismissingly.*) I have guests soon.

As he goes.

Drop the latch on the front door.

The room blacks out. The kitchen lights up. DU BOIS, *masculine type, coat and skirt, rough, short hair, gloomy, sits with her feet on another chair—a bottle and a wine glass on the table.*

NIGGIE (*balanced on the corner of the table*): What's the first course going to be?

DU BOIS (*mumbling*): Melon.

NIGGIE: Anybody can have melon! (*As she refills her glass.*) How early in the morning do you start drinking?

DU BOIS: At eight. After I've come down for the newspaper. I wake early.

NIGGIE: Why?

DU BOIS: I have a tortured inner life and all about nothing. I doubt myself.

NIGGIE: What about?

DU BOIS: About what is right and wrong. I read and I think

and I drink. And after a couple of bottles I *know* I was right.

NIGGIE: What's that cold tarragon thing you did last weekend? What does it need?

DU BOIS: Prawns. But the fishmonger hates me.

NIGGIE: I can bicycle down and get them. I have rather particular friends coming.

DU BOIS: Are they your age?

NIGGIE: *Your* age. If they were my age my grandmother wouldn't believe in them. I adore her but ... (*Stops.*)

> DU BOIS *looks up sharply*

... since I've been at Oxford I've realized she's dropped out of the world. I want to put her in again. I want her to know what's going on.

DU BOIS: She *does* know.

NIGGIE: She's forgotten. She needs rekindling, relighting, blowing up. So I've invited a woman like a bomb.

> As DU BOIS *reaches to the floor and gets up a second bottle.* Good God—not another one ...

DU BOIS (*a sob or a choke*): My gloom's coming on.

MRS. BASIL (*entering—carrying a small bunch of herbs*): Chives, parsley, tarragon ... (*Looking at DU BOIS.*) Crying again, Du Bois?

DU BOIS (*thickly*): Won't you call me Jacky?

MRS. BASIL: No.

DU BOIS: I feel so distant.

MRS. BASIL: If we were closer how would I have authority?

DU BOIS: Do you need authority?

MRS. BASIL: *You* need it. And your Christian name is compromising.

DU BOIS (*sniffing*): Some employers love those whom they employ.

MRS. BASIL: Not at the end of three weeks. After three years things may be different. Your cooking is excellent. If you weren't so dirty ...

NIGGIE (*leaning over the refuse bucket*): Maggots on the turkey-carcass.

DU BOIS: The bins are too far up the drive. There ought to be a woman for the rough.

MRS. BASIL: I can't get one.

DU BOIS (to NIGGIE): Will you empty that bucket for me?

NIGGIE: No. It's your job.

DU BOIS: I thought you were Left and Labour.

NIGGIE: Everyone to his own labour. (To MRS. BASIL.) Have you sold the house?

DU BOIS: Sold the house!

NIGGIE: I am speaking to my grandmother.

DU BOIS: Don't call her that!

NIGGIE: She *is* it. Have you sold the house?

MRS. BASIL: Did *you* ring him?

NIGGIE: Yes.

MRS. BASIL: Why?

NIGGIE: You said you wanted to be rid of all possessions. You said so last night.

MRS. BASIL: I often say it. I don't mean it. I get tired at the end of the day.

NIGGIE: Thirty bedrooms—six bathrooms—and Du Bois. Makes you think.

MRS. BASIL: But not act.

NIGGIE: It's provocative unco-operative uneconomical and anti-social!

MRS. BASIL: You talk too fast. They always did at Oxford. You know that I shall leave the house to you.

NIGGIE: You know that I don't want it. When I leave Oxford I'm going to live at Oxford.

MRS. BASIL: You'll marry.

NIGGIE: I'm donnish. I like my bed alone. Why are you so obstinate?

MRS. BASIL (a sigh): A sense of continuity.

NIGGIE: What did he say it was worth?

MRS. BASIL: Forty thousand.

NIGGIE: Fifty. I've taken another firm's opinion. Think what you could do with the money!

MRS. BASIL: Do you want it?

NIGGIE: No. I've enough.

MRS. BASIL: Do you call what I let you have at Oxford enough?

NIGGIE: When I say I don't want possessions I mean it. If I had them I'd give them to the poor.

MRS. BASIL: If I give to the poor the poor aren't poor but I am. It doesn't make sense.

NIGGIE: There are modern ways of giving. You don't need to sit here holding the lot.

MRS. BASIL: The cost of the upkeep of this house and garden plus living expenses plus the spirits bill plus Du Bois's wages . . .

DU BOIS: Salary.

MRS. BASIL: Wages . . . balances what I've got.

NIGGIE: The spirits bill?

MRS. BASIL: I have a sherry every evening and you and your friends have the gin. I don't drink vin rosé in the morning!

DU BOIS: *I* pay for that! (*Which reminds her to refill her glass.*)

MRS. BASIL: No, *I* pay. I only get half a cook.

NIGGIE: How much do you get, Du Bois?

MRS. BASIL: Don't tell him! He'll say it's extravagance! She has enough to buy her vin rosé which I deplore. But what is frightful is that she is the same class as me!

NIGGIE: As *I am*. I agree.

DU BOIS: I thought you didn't think in classes.

NIGGIE: I have to. They're still there. When I said I agreed I meant that you give my grandmother a sense of guilt.

DU BOIS: If you don't empty that bucket for me—she will.

NIGGIE (*grinning at her*): You're just *blown* together—you and my grandmother!

DU BOIS: Blown!

NIGGIE: Like a gale at sea. She drops a lifeline and *you* come up. (*Stooping to pick up the bucket.*) All right. I'll empty the bloody thing for you. (*Goes out—offstage through a wing.*)

DU BOIS: Do you love him?

MRS. BASIL (*absently*): Too much.

DU BOIS: Oh if I could be loved by someone.

MRS. BASIL: How many beds did we make up yesterday for the guests?

DU BOIS: It's so many years since I was loved by someone. Three.

As NIGGIE *returns without the bucket.*

MRS. BASIL: What time are your three friends coming?

NIGGIE: Four.

MRS. BASIL (*looking at her wrist watch*): O'clock?

NIGGIE: Friends. I've asked that political woman. The brilliant one.

DU BOIS (*laying her head on the table*): Is she Left and Labour?

NIGGIE: Of course. (*To* MRS. BASIL.) Can she have the yellow room?

MRS. BASIL: A bit of the ceiling's down.

DU BOIS (*sleepily*): That will reassure her.

NIGGIE (*pointing to the now sleeping Du Bois*): Do you allow this?

MRS. BASIL: Me? I allow anything! If you make me look for another cook I shall go insane . . .

    MRS. BASIL *goes through. The light moves back into the alcove. But now that the screens have been taken away it is no longer an alcove but the stage in depth. The rest of the drawing-room now shows, also the exit down a corridor to the front door (or to the garden).*

    Upstage, casual on a table, is a smallish silver tray with handles, like a coffee tray. On this are four silver candlesticks with candles, two small silver fighting cocks, silver mustard pot, salt and pepper. No knives and forks. No napkins.

    This is done to indicate at a point in Act Two—the expectation of dinner. There will be no "laying table" or that sort of clutter. MRS. BASIL *will merely move the silver tray to another table and set out the candlesticks and other little objects, to create the impression that they will dine in that same room later.*

NIGGIE: Is she the best you can do?

MRS. BASIL: She cooks well.

NIGGIE: What else does she do?

MRS. BASIL: Nothing.

NIGGIE: What do you pay her to do?

MRS. BASIL: Everything. I wonder if I should advertise again ... I have a gift for wording an advertisement.

NIGGIE: You have a gift for fishing in the Sea of the Daft.

MRS. BASIL: Only the Daft will serve me. I *must* have a cook! You love bringing your friends, don't you!

NIGGIE: I bring them because you are lonely.

MRS. BASIL: When did I say that!

NIGGIE: You said you were out of touch.

MRS. BASIL: Oh dear how you quote me!

NIGGIE: And you don't know young people.

MRS. BASIL: I know you.

NIGGIE (*struggling with his thoughts*): What I mean is ...

MRS. BASIL: Go on.

NIGGIE: Up at Oxford—we don't laugh at people—as you do. As you make me do. One cares so much more ...

MRS. BASIL: It never strikes you ... (*Stops a moment.*) ... that I laugh ... (*Pause.*) because I don't know what else to do.
He is silent.
When you come here you wouldn't want me to be pouring out ... (*Hesitates.*) ... *my* little vexations. On the other hand I don't want to talk to you of love. I don't force your confidence. It's too like indecency, or ... undelicacy, or ... We're too close, you couldn't bear it. So I use this meeting-ground. A sort of ridiculous ... perhaps eighteenth-century ... debunking of what goes on.

NIGGIE: Yes, but ... don't laugh too much when they come. They're serious people. Watch your language, darling.

MRS. BASIL: I thought my language was special.

NIGGIE: It is. But it's tainted with the past. Your kind of wit might make you seem upper class and old-fashioned.

MRS. BASIL: I'm not!

NIGGIE: Wit's so period. They use something different now.

(*Suddenly remembering*.) And don't put flowers in her bedroom!

MRS. BASIL (*thrown*): Whose . . .

NIGGIE: Shatov. The political woman.

MRS. BASIL: Why not?

NIGGIE: She'll think it frivolous.

MRS. BASIL: She can't say so. She'll be my guest.

NIGGIE: That's old-fashioned too! And don't take her round the house as though you thought it was beautiful!

MRS. BASIL: It is.

NIGGIE: One has no right to beauty.

MRS. BASIL: Are you quoting?

NIGGIE: I must be!

MRS. BASIL: Or else it's the silliest thing I've ever heard you say!

NIGGIE: It means something. Think it over. I'm upset by the state of the world.

MRS. BASIL: The state of the world depends on one's newspaper.

NIGGIE: And whatever you do don't crack back! Don't be shallow! They'll spot that at once!

MRS. BASIL: Are you nervous about me?

NIGGIE: I'm nervous about your ideals.

MRS. BASIL: What are they?

NIGGIE: You like to keep what you've got.

MRS. BASIL (*her mind flickering*): . . . I shall have out the dark blue Bristol finger bowls . . . Is she pretty?

NIGGIE: She's harsh. (*Getting up*.) They might be here any minute! I told her to drive down with Herbert. I wish he was younger.

MRS. BASIL: For my sake? Or yours? Or hers?

NIGGIE: For mine. I can't really talk to him. He's old-time Left, and they have such ridiculous answers! He's indulgent. That's so frightfully undercutting! It puts a damper on things.

MRS. BASIL: And the others?

NIGGIE (*off-hand*): His boy. And her girl.

MRS. BASIL: Heavens.

NIGGIE: What *do* you mean!

MRS. BASIL: It was an expression of surprise. Do I accept these relationships? And how do the beds work? You should have told me before!

NIGGIE: Oh they'll arrange themselves!

MRS. BASIL: D'you mean they'll drag the beds about?

NIGGIE: No. Just leave it. Everything will seem quite normal.

MRS. BASIL: You make me nervous.

NIGGIE: Why?

MRS. BASIL: I'm afraid of doing the wrong thing.

NIGGIE: You won't. You always put your foot in too hard. You have an innocent, violent way that works.

MRS. BASIL: I hope I can work it.

NIGGIE: There they are! Tyres on the gravel—I can hear how badly he puts on the brakes!

MRS. BASIL (*as he goes*): No one would think anyone had driven before . . .

NIGGIE (*an afterthought—returning*): Stay with them, won't you! I mean don't keep escaping . . . (*Goes.*)

    MRS. BASIL *walks to the window to see if the car is passing on the drive—but almost at once* NIGGIE *is bringing them in up the corridor.* SHATOV *and* HERBERT *follow him. Her girl and his boy are not with them.*

NIGGIE: This is my grandmother—Miss Shatov.

SHATOV: Just Shatov.

NIGGIE: And just Herbert.

HERBERT: No I have a name. Bostal. (*Gracefully—to* MRS. BASIL.) How is it done—mathematically—to be a grandmother?

MRS. BASIL (*smiling; provocatively, glancing at* SHATOV): I'm rich. And have no cares!

    SHATOV *giggles nervously, not knowing how to take it.* NIGGIE *looks annoyed.*

Did you lunch on the way down?

SHATOV: No.

MRS. BASIL (*a tremor*): Haven't you lunched?

SHATOV: No.

MRS. BASIL: Oh dear.

> *Silence.*

SHATOV (*unable to bear the silence*): Don't bother.

HERBERT: Are you losing your nerve? You said you would tell her we're starving.

MRS. BASIL: It's four o'clock.

HERBERT: Tea time.

MRS. BASIL: I don't have tea any more.

HERBERT: Is there food?

MRS. BASIL: Only raw.

HERBERT: Cheese?

MRS. BASIL: Oh on those lines! Oh yes. Niggie—fetch cheese and biscuits and butter and knives and plates. Do sit down.

> *They sit. And are blotted out. Spotlight goes with* NIGGIE *into the kitchen.* DU BOIS, *heavily asleep, groans.*

NIGGIE: *Wake.* They've come. They want food.

DU BOIS (*dreaming aloud*): Goodbye. It's finished now. I knew I was right.

NIGGIE: Du Bois!

DU BOIS (*dreaming away*): People tell me I decide wrong! (*Stirs in her sleep.*) I do what I think best.

> NIGGIE *goes round hunting for a tin of biscuits.*

(*Dreaming voice.*) Just look at her face! That's peace. (*Pause.*) Mustn't one hold on to what one thinks is right?

NIGGIE: Where are the biscuits. I can't find the biscuits ...

DU BOIS: When the hour comes and she needs me.

> *He turns and stares at her.*

If *once* she called me Jacky ... I'd do it for her ...

NIGGIE (*shaking her shoulders*): What are you muttering about!

DU BOIS (*suddenly awake—dignified*): I have romantic dreams. (*Gets up—breathes deeply; then—normally.*) The biscuits are in that tin. I'll get the butter.

NIGGIE (*surprised*): You were fast asleep!

DU BOIS: I hear on two levels. The plates are on that shelf.

NIGGIE: How is that done?

DU BOIS: What?

NIGGIE: Total recovery.

DU BOIS: Routine. (*Goes to a wall mirror—combs her short hair. Picks up a dirty plate and scrapes the food on to the floor where the bin had stood.*)

NIGGIE (*having collected his tray*): I see it's not total.

As she looks up.

I left the bucket outside! (*Goes through door: spotlight follows him. Now back in the drawing-room.*) Here we are! (*Puts tray down on a stool in front of* SHATOV. *Looks round—annoyed.*) Where's my grandmother?

SHATOV (*prim*): She disappeared without reason.

HERBERT: She walked to the door talking and went through.

NIGGIE: That needs more practice than you'd think! (*Looks up at ceiling.*) What's that . . .

HERBERT: Was it thunder?

NIGGIE (*hurrying*): No it's beds. (*Goes.*)

SHATOV (*now alone with* HERBERT): I hope I shall be happy here. I doubt it.

HERBERT: You're here on a mission.

SHATOV: She confuses me. I'm happier on a platform!

HERBERT: She doesn't confuse me at all. She has the manners of her class.

SHATOV: She's complacent.

HERBERT: Point it out to her.

SHATOV: She doesn't look open to pointing.

HERBERT: Well, don't bring me into it. I like it here. It's High Tory, I remember the atmosphere.

SHATOV (*shocked*): Herbert!

HERBERT: Well a fact is a fact, isn't it.

NIGGIE (*returning*): I was in time to stop her.—I thought you were bringing two friends with you?

SHATOV: They're outside by the car.

NIGGIE: Can't they come in?

SHATOV: They're quarrelling. How long have you lived here?

NIGGIE: I was born here. Though not really there at the moment. My grandmother will tell you we're an old county family.

SHATOV: And are you?

NIGGIE: You can have it out with her.

MRS. BASIL *enters.*

SHATOV (*stammering*): Your house ... I was ser ... I was ser ... say ...

MRS. BASIL: Take a breath.

SHATOV (*taking one*): I was saying—your house ...

MRS. BASIL: Immense. Isn't it. (*Vaguely.*) There's a weakness in the rooftree.

NIGGIE: She resists warnings!

MRS. BASIL: I noticed long ago with so-called inanimate objects that they are not inanimate at all. They're bluffing! They cry for attention! You must ignore them— Cars— for instance!

NIGGIE: Dear grandmother, what can you know about cars!

MRS. BASIL (*airy panache*): Me? I drove in extraordinary days! but the composition of the things was the same! Just as you have a heart, lungs, kidneys, like early man—so there are still carburettors and transmissions and crown wheels. Have you ever heard a crown wheel come to its end through lack of oil? It's like the grinders of a gorilla. (*Immediately and politely to* SHATOV.) Have you noticed how beautiful this room is?

SHATOV: Ner no. (*Looks round hurriedly.*) Yes, it is isn't it.

NIGGIE: But my grandmother has no right to beauty! You're caving in at once! You've come here to get her up to date with what we're all thinking! Don't let her off! Give her the works—as you give it to us at Oxford!

SHATOV (*mumbling*): I shall say what I think presently.

MRS. BASIL: I *hope* to *me*. I mean I shall be so interested.

Niggie is so worried about my way of life. I'm so rich. It's like having cancer.

NIGGIE: Shatov *has* cancer.

Ghastly silence.

SHATOV (*heavily*): I was diagnosed in New York.

MRS. BASIL: Oh, but I really think you might get off scot-free over here! I mean they have a different standard. I mean it's a sort of universal heading with them—covering and including all sorts of small spots. Would you like coffee?

SHATOV: Yes.

MRS. BASIL (*low*): Niggie.

NIGGIE (*low*): Am I a maid of all work?

MRS. BASIL (*low*): Nescafé.

SHATOV (*who has heard*): No. It gives me heartburn.

MRS. BASIL: Good. (*To* NIGGIE.) Don't bother.

SHATOV: This house must need a lot of servants.

MRS. BASIL: Yes it does.

SHATOV: How many have you?

MRS. BASIL: One.

SHATOV: One!

MRS. BASIL: I couldn't bear two. There's a sort of lunatic fringe or Vale of Shadows from which I get them. By advertising.

SHATOV (*uncertain*): Do you make fun of them . . .

MRS. BASIL: It's all the fun I get. I had one who sat still in the kitchen chair all day.

SHATOV: Who cooked the dinner?

MRS. BASIL: I cooked around her. Another sat down every time I came into the room.

SHATOV: Would you expect the reverse?

MRS. BASIL: Yes. I stand up for every human creature. It's a welcoming gesture. Have you noticed that there is a sad class of person now who can't shut doors?

SHATOV: It seems a trivial failing.

MRS. BASIL: No it's a deep one. It's the unfinished gesture

that indicates everything. I am sure you manage better. Do
you cook for yourself?

SHATOV: My old Nannie comes in. I can't boil an egg.

MRS. BASIL (*politely agreeing*): Yes, why should one use one's
hands when one can use one's brain ... Don't your two
friends want cheese?

SHATOV: Have you seen them?

MRS. BASIL: From the window. Won't they come in?

SHATOV: When they want food they'll come.

MRS. BASIL: But then we'll have to get clean plates again ...
A red-haired, blooming tropical girl runs on.

GIRL: He's bitten me, the brute!

HERBERT (*horrified*): *Tom* has!

GIRL (*to* MRS. BASIL): No—your dog.

MRS. BASIL: My *dog*! My *dear*! Let me *look*!
The GIRL *holds out her thumb.*

Not a drop of blood!

GIRL: The white outer skin has been removed.

MRS. BASIL: That's nothing!

GIRL: How can you say it's nothing! Rabiemyelitis can enter
through the second skin.

MRS. BASIL: Nonsense! Where do you come from?

GIRL: Trinidad.

MRS. BASIL: There's no rabies in England. Just wash your
hands. And what's your name?

GIRL: Elizabeth.

NIGGIE: Eat some cheese and forget about it. Where's Tom?

ELIZABETH: Gone.

HERBERT: What do you mean *gone*?

ELIZABETH: One of his moods came on.

HERBERT: Has he forgotten that he has to ring his analyst?
Have you a neurosis, Mrs. Basil?

MRS. BASIL: What does it mean?

HERBERT: It's where you can't adjust to life. Some deviation
from the normal. Some unknown factor that makes you
different.

MRS. BASIL: We used to call it originality. We must have been wrong.

HERBERT (*to* ELIZABETH): Has he taken the car?

ELIZABETH: Yes.

HERBERT: I should never have left him alone after the row at breakfast!

ELIZABETH: Row?

HERBERT: About what he was to wear. He's never been a gentleman. That infuriates him. Naturally I remember things like country houses and tipping. And what to wear in them.

ELIZABETH: He says it's just those things that you keep knowing that are the root of all his anxieties.

HERBERT: Oh, I know where that leads to!

MRS. BASIL: Where does it lead to?

HERBERT: Suicide.

MRS. BASIL: Good heavens!

HERBERT: But not quite.

MRS. BASIL: Not quite what?

HERBERT: Not—quite—suicide. Or how would he relish my distress?

MRS. BASIL: How can you joke about it?

HERBERT: It's best to joke about what you have lived through. Will he come back, Elizabeth?

ELIZABETH: I couldn't care less but he will.

SHATOV (*with disapproval*): An upper class and dated expression.

ELIZABETH: Leave my choice of words alone! (*To* MRS. BASIL.) Are you sure I shan't develop anything?

MRS. BASIL: Quite sure. What were you doing to the dog?

ELIZABETH: Scraping the tobacco stains off his teeth with my nail file.

MRS. BASIL: He doesn't smoke. Shall I show you to your rooms?

ELIZABETH: Am I sleeping in Shatov's room?

MRS. BASIL: If someone can push a bed for me I can arrange it.

ELIZABETH: I don't want to. I like a room alone.

MRS. BASIL: Well, you have one.

SHATOV: Do you flout me?

ELIZABETH: Every time I possibly can.

SHATOV (*jumping up*): Then I wish I hadn't brought you! And I wish I hadn't ... c ... c ... c ... (*Stuck—changing form of sentence. To* MRS. BASIL.) I came because of Niggie! But I really care nothing for a house enclosed by a lot of land!

MRS. BASIL: Don't you like to be private?

SHATOV: No! I am ravaged by the passion to be up and doing! I'm a sort of political doctor—for misery!

MRS. BASIL: Do you think the rich suffer?

SHATOV: Only spiritually. About some intricacy. It's not direct suffering!

MRS. BASIL (*absent—perambulating*): You put spiritual suffering on a low level?

SHATOV: Lower than hunger.

    MRS. BASIL *edges towards the corridor.*

NIGGIE (*to* HERBERT): Head her off! She's slipping out ...

MRS. BASIL (*caught*): Nonsense! (*To* SHATOV.) Would you like to see round the house?

ELIZABETH: She'd hate it!

SHATOV: I wish you wouldn't edit me!

ELIZABETH (*quoting*): "The things that men have built with their hands ..."

SHATOV: I didn't say that! I said that when people are hungry art should be sold for food!

ELIZABETH: Would you sell a picture to feed people who couldn't paint a picture?

SHATOV (*goaded*): Yes I would.

ELIZABETH (*to* MRS. BASIL): Is that a good answer?

MRS. BASIL: I was thinking ... perhaps irrelevant ... Millions have died like grains of sand. But the drawings in the caves remain.

SHATOV: That's a leisured ellipticality!

ELIZABETH: Bravo, Shatov! You're getting the language!

SHATOV: What do you mean?

ELIZABETH: Up till now you've been pushed about by gossamer—and haven't known it! There is so much you don't take into account! Art—for instance! And human nature! A total blank! In fact your politics are probably compensatory! All you can do is shout brilliantly on one side!

SHATOV: It's easy to make fools of passionate people! Why have you chosen today to be odious to me!

ELIZABETH: Because since I've been here I see what I've missed by being labelled by you!

MRS. BASIL: All the same you're not kind.

ELIZABETH: Do you know about these things? I mean—between women?

MRS. BASIL: Not much.

ELIZABETH: Neither do I! Nor care! But she chains me with this label! Perhaps she has no other chain!

MRS. BASIL: You really go for her with a dagger in your hand! (*Looks at* ELIZABETH.) And then . . . (*Stops.*)

ELIZABETH: "And then" . . . I'm younger and better looking and perhaps even cleverer. Yes. I'm a swine.

MRS. BASIL (*murmuring*): Why say . . . everything?

ELIZABETH: I suppose it's my line. (*Pause.*) I talk too much?

MRS. BASIL: We have that in common.

ELIZABETH: I arrive over here from a far island and don't know anybody and feel out of it. Well, then she puts me in it. But I hate being grateful.

SHATOV: Who would you know—ignorant girl—if it wasn't for me?

ELIZABETH: I ought to have come here with introductions.

SHATOV: Who to?

ELIZABETH: Conservatives! (*To* MRS. BASIL.) I adored England until I met Shatov!

SHATOV: But you met me at once!

ELIZABETH: I mean I adored the thought of it.

MRS. BASIL: How did you see it?

ELIZABETH: Smooth lawns and very eccentric. People like you and houses like this. We had Trollope in the Public Library. But I shall adapt myself! Don't rest your eyes on me, Shatov! *You're* not going to teach me! Wherever you lived you'd be pulling down the temples! I shall have to cut your hair!

SHATOV: It's uncuttable! And you are totally uneducated politically! You don't know Right from Left!

ELIZABETH: I know Right from Wrong. I don't believe God made you!

SHATOV: Who?

ELIZABETH: God. A gentleman I was brought up with.

SHATOV: Then who made me?

ELIZABETH: Oh—the other man! But he didn't even make you wicked! He made you boring. Nor black. He made you dun-coloured.

NIGGIE (*to* SHATOV): Why do you stand for it?

SHATOV (*near tears*): I love her.

ELIZABETH: And God knows why. All right. Give over. I just wanted to make sure I didn't sleep in your room. Don't start crying.

SHATOV (*sniffing*): You know it's a weakness . . .

MRS. BASIL: May I call you Elizabeth?

ELIZABETH: Please do.

MRS. BASIL: If I may venture upon your relationship—does she love you? I have been accustomed to love.

ELIZABETH: From a woman?

MRS. BASIL: No But all love has rights.

HERBERT: Very gravely said. Said with authority. I applaud it. I'm worried about Tom. (*Pause.*) I hope we shan't annoy you. Living with Tom is like living with a stinging nettle. Fraught with discomforts. You never know what upsets us. Intimate allusions to past rows like whiplashes. And so many of them! Makes us touchy!

MRS. BASIL: "Us"?

HERBERT: Me, yes. And Tom. Are you up in these things, Mrs. Basil?

MRS. BASIL (*taking a slight breath*): If we are going to talk about men who love men . . . (*Stops—to be sure.*) Is that what you mean?

NIGGIE: Very nicely put.

MRS. BASIL: I once read Proust. Sodom and Gomorrah . . .

HERBERT: We are descendants, yes. Spared by the Fire of Heaven.

MRS. BASIL: The Cities of the Plain. I recollect a vast concourse of men. Curiously described—like sea shells. It made me think of all the shores of the world. I couldn't begin to remember the infinite varieties. I saw how little I knew. I couldn't classify anyone. The heart beats. That's all. And it beats *for* someone.

ELIZABETH: Oh what good manners you have!

MRS. BASIL: I am ashamed of being ignorant.

SHATOV: Have you been very sheltered?

MRS. BASIL: Well it's difficult to get on terms.

SHATOV: We talk of nothing else.

MRS. BASIL: "We"?

ELIZABETH: She means intellectuals.

MRS. BASIL: I never know what that means.

SHATOV (*angrily*): Nor I either!

ELIZABETH: It means people intellectually adjusted . . .

SHATOV: Be quiet!

ELIZABETH: . . . to each other!

SHATOV: For God's sake . . .

ELIZABETH: Not even for God! I have the Gift of Tongues! It means a gang who exchange monkey-signs with each other and keep everyone else in the dark! And they have one underlying principle! "Never admire"! To admire gives you away! It pins you to a form of art that may alter on a Tuesday. And if it does, and it's certain to, you are left in the lurch! And the greatest luck that ever happened to them was the Atom Bomb. Or the Hydrogen Bomb. They can

lift any argument right out of focus by mentioning it! And
if anyone dares to say they are happy—that's when they
mention it! It's like being told to stop talking in church!

NIGGIE: Good God.

HERBERT: Just that!

ELIZABETH: Who wants to enter me as a Member of
Parliament?

SHATOV: A what!

ELIZABETH (*ironically*): Can you beat it! I respect your
institutions!

NIGGIE: Ask Shatov to get your rhetoric toned down!

ELIZABETH (*disregarding him*): And I want to say something!
I've been trying to say something! This is a most beautiful
house! And a beautiful garden!

MRS. BASIL: I have fought with it for forty years. That has a
kind of beauty. (*To* SHATOV—*polite.*) Do you like gardens?

ELIZABETH: Don't give her the chance! (*Eager.*) . . . and the
waving things that grow round the pool—and the yew
hedge with the gentians—and that sheet of grass that isn't
grass . . .

MRS. BASIL: My camomile lawn.

NIGGIE: And all for one not so young woman!

MRS. BASIL: Whose side are you on?

NIGGIE (*to* SHATOV): Is it fair that she should have all this for
herself!

SHATOV (*uncomfortably*): I'm a guest.

NIGGIE: My grandmother doesn't mind.

MRS. BASIL: I mind terribly. I inherited this house from my
grandmother. I believe in family and tradition and the Past.

NIGGIE: Darling—*be* modern.

MRS. BASIL: I've been modern. I got tired of it. (*Switching.*)
. . . I mustn't forget the finger bowls at dinner . . .

ELIZABETH: Mustn't forget what?

MRS. BASIL: Bowls to wash your fingers in after the peaches.

ELIZABETH: Like in China!

MRS. BASIL: Like in England. My family has lived here for

two hundred years. I have forgotten many of their customs. I wish I hadn't. In the house they had servants. But in the garden they were in the earth up to their elbows. I know from their diaries. My grandmother planted a mulberry tree on the day she knew she was going to die. The crate came in the morning and she said nobody else could plant it. It comforts me to feel my line running back. Not out of pride but because it binds me to eternity. We have been well-to-do county people ... Did you speak?

NIGGIE: The word upset Shatov.

MRS. BASIL: County people are humdrum. They certainly have their prejudices. But they were not despised in their day and I understand them. They weren't in gay society and they would like to have been and grumbled about it. But they put up with the country. They must have had a lot of thoughts—bending over flowers. If I said I was descended from the Queens of Egypt would you think me romantic or a snob?

ELIZABETH: Romantic.

MRS. BASIL: Yes. Well—I think it's a snobbery and a sort of outrage to despise people for the way they were born. And I mind death just a little less because I shall die where those people died who never knew they would have me.

NIGGIE: And the argument against all this is that she runs it with the greatest difficulty and won't give up so much as a gardener's shed.

MRS. BASIL: There's no argument. I shall live here and die here and leave it to Niggie.

NIGGIE (softly): Who doesn't want it.

ELIZABETH turns her head to stare incredulously.

MRS. BASIL (as though she hadn't heard): And if he does what I think he won't do I shall turn in my grave. (To HERBERT.) Or do you think one should be more indulgent?

HERBERT: I'd stop short of death.

MRS. BASIL: Perhaps you are right. Do as you like then, Niggie.

SHATOV: You talk as though things were perpetual! (*Deeply.*) Changes will come, Mrs. Basil.

MRS. BASIL: They have! They have built a painful lamp-post in the village.

SHATOV: A lamp-post won't cover what I mean.

MRS. BASIL: I had not mislaid your meaning. I know that opposing change is like a fly sticking to something sticky! It's madness to oppose it! But I still have to learn how it's done!

SHATOV: What would you prefer?

MRS. BASIL (*with her teasing smile*): Horses, wheels, and gentry —and not too many of them! And somebody to light the candles in the evening ...

A young man comes in from the corridor. His head is shaven to the skull. He wears a bright pink polo-necked pullover and checked riding breeches.

YOUNG MAN: I am Tom.

MRS. BASIL (*rising—hand outstretched*): You are all so easy to know! How do you do.

TOM: Not well.

MRS. BASIL: I wasn't asking a question. Come and sit down.

HERBERT: This is our hostess—Mrs. Basil.

TOM: I want to be alone.

MRS. BASIL: Then why did you come in?

TOM: I wanted to tell you that I wanted to be alone.

HERBERT: He likes you to see his pain.

MRS. BASIL: Take him into the garden, Niggie. You seem the same age.

NIGGIE: I can't spare the time from Elizabeth. She might say something extraordinary while I'm gone.

ELIZABETH: I'm going to say something extraordinary—I rather fancy Herbert.

HERBERT (*startled*): As what?

ELIZABETH: As my first husband.

NIGGIE: Don't be a goose! He's not that kind!

ELIZABETH: It may be a bluff—owing to his extreme shyness. (*Suddenly—to* TOM.) And why are you laughing like a hyena?

TOM: He's not shy at all . . .

ELIZABETH (*lower*): And why are your hands shaking?

TOM: Shut up! (*Sticking his hands into his pockets.*) And I wouldn't go nap that he's the kind you think!

HERBERT: And why a first husband?

ELIZABETH: I'm not ready yet for a total male. Sex is all right if you like that kind of thing . . .

NIGGIE: Don't you?

ELIZABETH: It's two a penny where I come from! (*To* HERBERT.) Are you married?

HERBERT: Only to that hideous Tom.

TOM: I'm not hideous.

HERBERT: No, but your pullover is.

TOM: I thought that was finished at breakfast.

HERBERT: It's never finished! It's fundamental. You look like cubbing on Boxing Day.

ELIZABETH: How long have you had him in tow?

HERBERT: Since before he came out of prison.

ELIZABETH: Is that why his head is shaved?

HERBERT: He had it shaved when he came out to show he'd been in.

ELIZABETH (*to* TOM): What did you do?

TOM: I took stuff.

ELIZABETH (*low*): Is that why your hands were shaking?

HERBERT: I've cured him.

TOM (*muttering*): You think you have . . .

MRS. BASIL (*apologetically*): I'm so sorry to be so out of touch.

ELIZABETH: Tom took drugs, Mrs. Basil.

MRS. BASIL: Is that . . . I mean—mustn't you?

ELIZABETH: No.

TOM (*boastfully*): I took enough to kill me. They pumped it out.

MRS. BASIL: But what about freewill? I do think people

ought to be allowed to ... kill themselves and so on if they want to.

TOM (*indignant*): Then I should have been dead, shouldn't I!

MRS. BASIL: Didn't you want to be?

HERBERT: That's what I meant by not-quite.

TOM (*furiously*): What have you been saying about me?

HERBERT: What is there to say!

TOM: He can't keep his hands off talk! I hate it!

ELIZABETH: Poor Tom.

HERBERT: You react angelically!

ELIZABETH: You say that savagely!

HERBERT: "Poor Herbert" would have been nearer the mark! You have curious visitors, Mrs. Basil.

MRS. BASIL: Well this weekend is to be my education. People don't generally say so much so soon. Niggie thought I was lonely.

HERBERT: And are you?

MRS. BASIL: Yes—as the day goes down. One is not always sufficient for oneself. It takes doing.

NIGGIE: That's why you should sell this house and live in London.

ELIZABETH: Sell this house! This romantic house! I wish I could be in love in this house! Fancy owning a house like this to be in love *in*!

MRS. BASIL: I did. I was.

ELIZABETH: With your husband?

MRS. BASIL: Yes.

ELIZABETH: What was he like?

MRS. BASIL: Like Niggie. (*Smiling.*) Less silly. He thought I was the queen of the earth.

ELIZABETH: How long did that go on?

MRS. BASIL: For years. And years and years.

ELIZABETH: How can you bear it without him?

MRS. BASIL: One gets accustomed to everything.

ELIZABETH: How old are you, Herbert?

HERBERT: Fifty.

ELIZABETH: Well don't waste time. There's me.

SHATOV: D'you think that's funny!

ELIZABETH: It wasn't meant to be. I didn't know till I saw him here that Herbert was a gentleman.

SHATOV: One doesn't use that word.

ELIZABETH: Why not? It's in the dictionary. And I was going to say "indulgent" if you'd let me go on! I *need* a man of fifty! I'm dynamite! I haven't learnt anything yet! I haven't learnt how to be kind! I'd sooner be clever than kind! I've been looking everywhere for a queer like Herbert . . .

MRS. BASIL (*rising*): Does anyone here play billiards?

HERBERT: D'you mean you've got a billiard table?

MRS. BASIL: Full size.

TOM (*eyes alight*): *I* play.

SHATOV: *I* play.

MRS. BASIL: How unexpected!

HERBERT (*with pride*): Tom won the Open Amateur Championship. Tom's a swell.

MRS. BASIL: Take them, Niggie. The cover's off. Don't let them drop ash on the table.

ELIZABETH (*watching them go*): I went too far?

HERBERT: You did.

ELIZABETH: I thought one could say anything!

HERBERT: No.

ELIZABETH: What are the rules then?

HERBERT: You make them up as you go. And when you call me a queer—remember our hostess said the heart beats. Mine beats for Tom.

ELIZABETH (*incredulous*): You love him?

HERBERT: He makes me suffer. That's as near as I can get to love. He's objectionable and makes himself more so. He's a cad and in despair. He's the only thing in the world that fills me with pity till I could explode! (*To* MRS. BASIL.) By what magic did you know that billiards would make him happy?

MRS. BASIL: It was accidental.

HERBERT: It's the one thing he can do better than other people. I thought of it years ago. I had him trained. It took doing. He was clumsy at first but he got over it. When he won that championship I thought I had pulled it off.

ELIZABETH: And hadn't you?

HERBERT: No. The drugs started. His hands shook.

ELIZABETH: Why do you care?

HERBERT: I'm not much use to myself—I thought I could be useful to him. One's got to care for somebody. It's bad luck it should be Tom.

An exclamation—or cry—is heard. Up the corridor comes SHATOV. *She is followed by* TOM *who carries a billiard cue.*

SHATOV: First go off—can you beat it—he cut the cloth!

HERBERT: Good . . . God.

TOM stands speechless, holding the cue.

SHATOV (*looking at him*): You're sweating! And look at your hands.

The cue falls to the floor. NIGGIE *comes up from the corridor.*

HERBERT (*picking up the cue—feeling the tip*): There's a slight irregularity . . .

TOM (*hoarse*): No there isn't.

NIGGIE: The thing curled up like a snake!

TOM's knees give way.

SHATOV: Look out . . . he's going to faint.

They catch him, push him into a chair and make him lean over with his head down.

NIGGIE: Keep your head down! *Lower!*

TOM (*struggling back into the chair*): Let go! (*He sits, his face buried in his hands.*)

HERBERT (*to* MRS. BASIL): Could he drink something?

MRS. BASIL: Of course! Niggie—get ice!

NIGGIE goes into the kitchen.

HERBERT (*pouring*): Never mind the ice. (*Holds glass to* TOM.) Tom!

TOM waves it away.

Drink it!

TOM *covers his face as before.*

I'll drink it then. (*To* MRS. BASIL.) I'm so sorry . . .

MRS. BASIL: It's because the cloth's so old. Like everything here. Perhaps it would have gone whoever had played on it. No one has touched it for years. The weight of a ball must have astonished it—like the weight of a feather on the heart . . . oh *dear.*

ELIZABETH: Was it his?

MRS. BASIL: Yes.

The door opens. DU BOIS *enters—carrying ice in a bowl.*

DU BOIS (*sober*): I'm just as you see me!

NIGGIE (*following*): I told her not to wash.

She goes to the drinks table and puts down the bowl.

MRS. BASIL: Miss Du Bois—Mr. Bostal—Elizabeth . . . S . . . S. (*Makes an uncertain hiss.*) . . . Shatov. And . . . And Tom.

DU BOIS: Is he ill?

TOM (*through his hands*): I wish I was dead.

DU BOIS: You have only to ask. Shall I deal out the drinks, Mrs. Basil?

MRS. BASIL: Do.

DU BOIS: What shall I bring you?

MRS. BASIL: Not yet.

DU BOIS (*looking round the guests, seeing that* HERBERT *has his drink, takes a look at* SHATOV, *opens the bottle of gin*): Gin— Dulcie?

Silence.

(*Smiling at her.*) How much?

SHATOV: Who do you think I am?

DU BOIS (*pouring*): I know. (*Snapping the top off the tonic water.*) I was at school with you. (*Pours tonic.*) Behind Whiteleys. I was called Jacqueline. (*Holding out the glass.*) Like that?

SHATOV *as though hypnotized—comes and takes the glass.*

(*Crossing to* TOM. *Waits a moment.*) Jump up, lad—when a lady asks you what you'll drink!

TOM (*from his buried face*): I couldn't . . . I can't . . . I couldn't touch it!

DU BOIS (*contemplating him—suddenly stoops and removes his hands—tilts his twitching face up. Sharply*): Who's looking after you!

HERBERT (*anxious—startled*): I am.

DU BOIS: Well—*watch out!* (*With a deft movement she sweeps* TOM'*s loosely-knitted pullover up his arm—baring it.*)

TOM (*on his feet*): Hell! Keep off! (*Drags his sleeve down.*)

DU BOIS: It's written all over you—up and down your arm!

TOM: Who the devil are you!

DU BOIS: The cook.

TOM (*turning sharply*): I'm going out!

DU BOIS (*immediately pinning his arms behind him*): Not you— you aren't. (*Dives one hand swiftly down into his trouser pocket and pulls out a syringe. Holding it up.*) You didn't want to be dead! You wanted a fix!

TOM (*pulling his hands free*): Are you a bloody nurse!

DU BOIS: I was.

TOM: Then why have you come down to cooking!

DU BOIS: They wouldn't let me nurse any more. (*Propels him towards the kitchen door.*)

   NIGGIE *holds it open.*

TOM (*resisting*): Why not?

DU BOIS (*he is as soft soap in her hands*): A point of professional honour!

SHATOV (*trying it over*): . . . Du Bois . . . Jacqueline . . .

DU BOIS (*mocking*): Try the other way round!

TOM: Let go! You hurt! I'm going to be sick . . .

DU BOIS: Be sick in the kitchen, boy, with me.
   They go through.

ELIZABETH (*immediately—to* SHATOV): *Do* you remember her at school?

SHATOV (*puzzled*): What I remember better is her grown-up face . . .

   As MRS. BASIL *collects her garden basket and scissors.*

FP–K*

It'll come back to me. Things do. (*Suddenly—to* MRS. BASIL.) Where did you get her? Where did she come from?

MRS. BASIL (*frivolously—picking up a ball of raffia*): China! (*She goes to the door leading into the garden. To* HERBERT.) Aren't you going **in**?

HERBERT: If I did he'd act up.

   She goes.

NIGGIE (*taking* HERBERT *by the arm*): Do you like gardens?

HERBERT: No.

NIGGIE: Well go into the garden all the same!

   HERBERT, *after a faintly astonished look—goes.*

SHATOV (*jumping to it, sarcastic*): Am I in the way?

NIGGIE (*returning to* ELIZABETH): Of course you are! But I need you ... (*Picking up* ELIZABETH'S *hand.*) I need a chaperon! (*Kisses the hand.*) One makes love better with two!

CURTAIN

ACT II

The same scene—continuous. NIGGIE, ELIZABETH, SHATOV.

NIGGIE (*to* SHATOV): Go over to the window. Look out of it. So that my grandmother remembers perfectly you're here. That we're not alone. Me, I mean. And Elizabeth.

SHATOV (*crossing to window*): Would she be jealous?

NIGGIE: No. She'd be entranced and want to overhear. (*To* ELIZABETH.) I'm in a hurry because I want to speak seriously. If my grandmother heard me speak seriously— even I would know it was bad form! I'm interested in Elizabeth, but I have to pursue it secretly.

SHATOV: Are you in love with her?

NIGGIE: I'm fascinated. But I wouldn't marry her!

ELIZABETH: Why should you think I would?

NIGGIE: I've no idea but the idea occurs to me. Or it might occur to my grandmother!

ELIZABETH: She doesn't like me.

NIGGIE: One can never be sure. My grandmother brought me up. She taught me to laugh in all circumstances. It's a trick too easily learnt. I'm often in love. I'm very subject to love—like a man who gets colds . . . (*Breaks off.*) There you are. (*Annoyed.*) When I most want to be grave I'm *corroded* with these little jokes. (*Pause.*) Are you passionate, Elizabeth? (*Waits.*) Why don't you answer?

ELIZABETH: I should like to answer but I have the wrong manner.

NIGGIE: Don't copy mine. Mine doesn't weigh heavily. (*Pause —awkwardly.*) What is your sexual attitude towards men?

ELIZABETH *looks startled.*

289

Don't laugh at me. I have to ask across a great distance. I have to ask the foe.

ELIZABETH: Are you serious?

NIGGIE: I'm trying to be, but fear makes me witty. It's my cover-up when I'm stung. (*Another effort.*) Have you slept with someone?

ELIZABETH: No. I'm a virgin.

SHATOV: You shouldn't ask her! It puts her in a bad position. Either way she's committed. She has to choose between being cold or a loose woman.

ELIZABETH: It's my choice! *I* made it!

SHATOV: I'm defending you!

ELIZABETH: I don't need it! Sex is just an old carrot used by God to get children! Life is long and it doesn't consist of sleeping! Besides—it's been done!

NIGGIE: Done what?

ELIZABETH: Done for so long.

NIGGIE: You talk as though it wasn't important.

ELIZABETH: Of course it isn't!

NIGGIE: But so much stress is laid on it.

ELIZABETH: By whom?

NIGGIE: By all the men at Oxford. The goings-on at night . . .

ELIZABETH: They're bragging! What else do they do for a living?

NIGGIE: But men at Oxford don't . . . I mean they're studying. Life has begun and yet it hasn't. They talk all night long . . .

ELIZABETH: They don't where I come from. They fill the bushes with tumbling children. Do you like women?

NIGGIE: Yes. But I sweat at night in bed for fear of them.

SHATOV: Be careful of Elizabeth! She hurts.

NIGGIE: It's time I was hurt. I've been idle about pain . . .

ELIZABETH (*interrupting*): How old are you?

NIGGIE: Nineteen. But highly defended and brilliantly sophisticated . . .

ELIZABETH (*another interruption*): Are *you* a virgin?

NIGGIE: You don't suppose I'm going to tell you in a moment of expansion ...

ELIZABETH: *I* did!

NIGGIE: That's different! I have to cut ice with my desperate generation! Oh ... I *knew* this moment would come—so riskily casual! Like a gun that gets you by mistake out shooting! And I don't know a thing about you and I haven't a minute to learn ...

ELIZABETH: If you mean sexually it's perfectly idiotic! The thing works by itself if you leave it alone.

NIGGIE: How do you know?

ELIZABETH: I'm twenty. I've lived twenty years in a hot country. Much better ask if I've a hot temper. If I'm mean. If I'm narrow-minded and a nagger. If I'm ... Don't let's go on! Worse things are wrong with me than sex.

NIGGIE (*eager*): What for instance? What do you mean ... I have to hear before my grandmother ... Shatov, *quick*! Do you see her? Is she coming in?

SHATOV: She's there on the lawn with Herbert looking from right to left pointing.

NIGGIE: She is pointing out what belongs to her.

SHATOV: That's what it looks like. But why say it with pride?

NIGGIE: Just for the moment I see it with Elizabeth's eyes. (*To* ELIZABETH.) Do you think it right and good and marvellous to have what my grandmother has?

ELIZABETH: Of course I do.

NIGGIE: Shouldn't she give it away?

ELIZABETH: Why should she? It's nice to have things. How can anyone think differently?

SHATOV: *I* do.

ELIZABETH: But you've nothing to give. So you can't know —can you! I like people with so much money they don't want money.

NIGGIE: And what about inheritance? And pride in an old family? No shame attached to it?

ELIZABETH: Only envy.

NIGGIE (*mocking—light*): This *must* be love! I'm in a panic and a fury! Every time before I've wriggled out of it!

SHATOV: You never talk like that at Oxford!

NIGGIE: I fall in love at Oxford. But I always decide when I get here that my grandmother is the more fascinating of the two!

SHATOV (*grim*): Perhaps I don't understand humour.

NIGGIE: It may be.

SHATOV (*irritated*): Your grandmother infuriates me!

NIGGIE: Why should she?

SHATOV: By her air of authority! Over nothing.

NIGGIE: It's worn naturally. She doesn't know it.

SHATOV: By her total command of a situation! By her *Owner-ship*! By the way she walks in it!

NIGGIE: Are you going to tell her so?

SHATOV: Leave it to me.

NIGGIE (*warning*): After she has passed the wistaria—the door is *nearer than you think*!

MRS. BASIL *enters.*

We're discussing you.

She smiles—sits down—draws up a small table with a board and cards for patience.

Don't you want to hear it?

MRS. BASIL (*still smiling—picking up the pack*): No.

NIGGIE: Where's Herbert?

MRS. BASIL (*laying out the cards*): He has gone to sleep under a tree.

NIGGIE: I don't believe it! Shatov has something to say to you.

SHATOV *looks up, alarmed.*

MRS. BASIL: I expected she would.

SHATOV (*funking it*): I'm preoccupied . . .

NIGGIE: She's indignant!

SHATOV: I'm trying to remember where I saw that woman . . .

NIGGIE (*teasing*): She's bursting to tell you . . . (*Stops—lets her off the hook.*) . . . I made love to Elizabeth!

MRS. BASIL (*lightly*): I feared there being three of you!

NIGGIE: I knew you did.

MRS. BASIL (*to* ELIZABETH): Didn't it embarrass you?

ELIZABETH: No. But it does now.

MRS. BASIL (*occupied with her game*): Tell me about her, Niggie, since you are making love to her in public. (*Polite —glancing at* ELIZABETH.) Do you mind?

ELIZABETH: He doesn't know me.

MRS. BASIL: Aren't you in his set at Oxford?

ELIZABETH: No.

NIGGIE (*to* SHATOV): Will she mind?

SHATOV: Ask her.

ELIZABETH: I don't like to be asked questions. I hate to be investigated.

NIGGIE: Don't you like to be admired?

ELIZABETH (*gravely*): Only by the best people.

SHATOV: What an expression . . .

ELIZABETH (*ignoring—addressing herself to* MRS. BASIL): In this house. At your level. I like people to be unquestionable.

MRS. BASIL: You don't know me.

ELIZABETH: I've read about you.

MRS. BASIL: In Trollope?

ELIZABETH: In Henry James.

MRS. BASIL (*faintly ruffled*): Oh . . . But I don't know how your mind works! Or *which* Henry James! Or *which* woman!

NIGGIE: She's wriggling! She doesn't like being pinned down!

MRS. BASIL (*a little laugh*): Well one is unique! I may be the last person to want to be! Personality is at a discount. People don't like being built up. They like being broken down. Broken back to elements . . . (*Suddenly smiling at* NIGGIE.) She's *your* guest! Stop me talking!

NIGGIE: You didn't know my grandmother was a talker? She exerts enormous power to stop it. But one has to help her . . . *Now* Elizabeth . . .

ELIZABETH: I'm out of my depths.

SHATOV: Don't be taken in! Elizabeth is a talker whatever depths she is in.

ELIZABETH: But frogs jump out of my mouth as well as words! I have to watch them.

NIGGIE: You don't watch well enough.

ELIZABETH: Why what have I said!

NIGGIE: Nothing yet. Sit in the middle of the room—on that chair. You're in the dock. You're not the sort of girl I usually meet . . .

ELIZABETH: Socially?

NIGGIE: Politically. You're a throw-back, a property-lover, and out of date. Did I say you were pretty? Or did I forget? You're witty. But you have so little ear it's like a want of taste—or the other way round! You're uneducated. And brilliant. Like an intermittently—careful savage . . .

ELIZABETH (*disconcerted*): Savage . . . (*Recovering.*) What's the net result?

NIGGIE: Magic—in short. Did you mind the bad things?

ELIZABETH: Yes I did.

MRS. BASIL: Niggie talks a lot of nonsense.

ELIZABETH: I wish he'd stop!

NIGGIE (*mock surprise*): Don't I talk like a lover?

ELIZABETH: No.

NIGGIE: That's because my grandmother is here. I get detached.

MRS. BASIL: Is he different without me?

ELIZABETH: He tries to be.

MRS. BASIL (*thoughtfully*): I never knew that.

SHATOV (*suddenly—cutting across everything*): Mrs. Basil . . .
　　They look up.
　　Her *face*! It's come back to me! In the *newspapers*!
　　As the door opens behind her.
　　I know what she did!

DU BOIS (*dishevelled—a wineglass of red wine in her hand, truculent*): People tell me I decide wrong. But I do what I think best. (*To* MRS. BASIL.) What time do you want dinner?

MRS. BASIL: What time is it now? (*She crosses to silver tray.*)

DU BOIS: The clock fell down on the dresser.

MRS. BASIL (*moving the tray to another small table*): Shall we dine in here?

DU BOIS (*drawing a chair up against the kitchen door, truculently*): Where else could you dine?

MRS. BASIL (*standing the four candlesticks and fighting cocks on the table, mustard etc.*): True. (*Forgetting to remove the tray now that she has seen that* DU BOIS *has sat down. In surprise. Walks over to her.*) What do you want, Du Bois?

DU BOIS: Company. Am I not as good as anyone?

MRS. BASIL (*severe*): No I don't think you are.

DU BOIS: Morally? Or because you buy me?

MRS. BASIL (*deliberate*): Both. (*To* NIGGIE—*low.*) Pay no attention. Or if you pay it pay it *sharp.*

NIGGIE: What's the matter, Du Bois?

MRS. BASIL (*impatient with him*): You know what's the matter!

DU BOIS: My mind. (*Draws up a small table and puts her wine on it.*)

NIGGIE: What's up with it?

MRS. BASIL (*returning to her cards*): The bottle.

DU BOIS: It ticks between right and wrong.

MRS. BASIL (*having had enough of it*): Have you chilled the melon?

DU BOIS (*panicked*): *I can't be alone in the kitchen!*
  They look at her.
  You ought to ring up . . . I ought to go back . . .

MRS. BASIL (*knowing the answer—daring her*): Where?

DU BOIS (*quelled—sullen*): Where you got me from.

MRS. BASIL (*off-hand*): You said you had a neurosis—I didn't believe you. I may have been wrong.

DU BOIS (*playing with something in her lap*): I am moving into action . . . and it may be the wrong one . . . *Mrs. Basil!* Everyone in this room *needs help!*

MRS. BASIL: Why?

DU BOIS: Because I am a strong woman . . . (*Takes a large kitchen knife from her lap and holds it up.*) . . . and I have a knife here. (*Lays it on the table near her, irritably, as* SHATOV *jumps back.*) Could you keep still, Dulcie! Movement confuses me! I am trying to help all of us and myself as well! (*Leaning forward and asking earnestly. To* MRS. BASIL.) Is it *wrong* to take away the life of a person?

MRS. BASIL (*seeing* HERBERT *come in, making light of it*): Here's Herbert! He has a neurosis. You can ask him.

HERBERT (*looking round*): Where's Tom?

DU BOIS (*casual—still thinking of her question*): His throat is cut with a kitchen knife.

HERBERT: *Dead!*

DU BOIS: Quite.

HERBERT: Beyond anything I can *do*? *Over*?

DU BOIS (*a trifle smug*): It's finished now.

HERBERT (*collapsing into a chair*): Oh what a miracle what a miracle—*safe*.

NIGGIE: Good *God*.

HERBERT (*exhausted voice*): I've done it twice. I couldn't do it again. Crawled back with him in my arms—my inefficient arms—back through the long recovery. But they never recover! They have the whip hand after that for ever! You know why he did it?

DU BOIS: Of course. He cut the cloth.

HERBERT: It crossed my mind. It *always* crosses my mind! One can't watch all the time! The egotism of someone who has once tried to kill himself is too great to be borne!

DU BOIS: It comforts you?

He nods.

(*Complacent.*) Then I must have been right. People kill themselves for a last straw. I saw it in his eyes.

SHATOV (*outraged*): Couldn't you have stopped him!

DU BOIS: I didn't try. I'm irresponsible about death. I thought you knew. You shouted out something! You always shouted when you stammered!

SHATOV (*immediately stammering*): Y . . . Y . . . you . . . you . . .

DU BOIS: That's more like it! Could someone ring up . . .

MRS. BASIL (*diverting*): . . . the police.

DU BOIS: *No!*

MRS. BASIL (*fixing her with her eyes*): Why not? Someone has died. They must arrest someone. (*To* HERBERT—*diversion.*) What were *you* doing in the garden?

HERBERT (*aghast*): *Me!*

MRS. BASIL: There is naturally a back door to the kitchen. It will be *you*, dear Herbert. They always arrest the loved one.

HERBERT (*stiff*): I am not prepared to die for Miss Du Bois.

MRS. BASIL: You keep saying you are useless to yourself.

HERBERT: Faced with death I find myself more valuable. I shall certainly ring up . . .

MRS. BASIL (*inserting softly*): . . . the police.

DU BOIS (*a shout*): The ASYLUM!

   As they react.

(*Frowning.*) They didn't call it that but I've forgotten . . .

NIGGIE: Did you run away?

DU BOIS: No I was discharged. Cured.

   As HERBERT *gets up.*

The janitor will put you through to the doctor on duty. Tell him I'm listed under D. Du Bois. Jacqueline. (*Thinks.*) No. Du Bois. *J.* I think it will be. The number is by the telephone in the hall.

SHATOV: *Why should it be!*

DU BOIS (*a wink*): She had to have someone! (*Mischievously.*) And then she is on the Board.

SHATOV (*exploding but racing against the coming stammer*): I never cease to be astonished by the unutterable . . . intoler-able . . . (*She is stuck.*)

DU BOIS: She always got out the big ones!

SHATOV (*fighting on*): . . . lev . . . lev . . . lev . . .

MRS. BASIL: Take a breath.

SHATOV (*taking one*): . . . levity of your class!

MRS. BASIL: What's unutterable and intolerable is to have no servants! (*Which reminds her to walk over to the tray she has left behind and remove it to where it formerly was. Glancing at* DU BOIS.) And to be losing the one I've got! Did you kill him?

DU BOIS (*off-hand*): No. I didn't have to. Not this time. (*Calling to* HERBERT.) Tell them I'm dangerous again and to send the ambulance!

   He goes. Silence.

MRS. BASIL (*low*): You weren't as dangerous as you thought.

DU BOIS (*looking at her—outraged. Slowly turning her head to* SHATOV): Tell them.

   SHATOV *looks up—alarmed.*

Were you in court? Finish what you were going to say.

SHATOV: Nothing . . .

DU BOIS: Nonsense! You hadn't time to! *I* came in.

SHATOV (*unwillingly*): You nursed in a . . . (*Stops.*)

DU BOIS (*clearly*): Home for the Dying. They needed help—poor creatures! *I helped them.*

   Silence.

Could we keep on talking?

   No one says a word.

(*To* NIGGIE.) *Say* something!

NIGGIE: I can't.

DU BOIS: You *must.*

NIGGIE: What about?

DU BOIS: *You.* Not me. I am keeping down things like fish rising! Don't you understand! This is the last time anything will happen! Talk! You have no idea how frightfully boring it is to be mad! Everyone halted dead in their tracks! No giving in marriage—no marrying. No birth! Or if anyone dies—screens, screens . . . and the locked doors in every direction . . . (*To* NIGGIE *violently.*) *Talk!*

NIGGIE: Drink up your wine while I think of something.

DU BOIS: This isn't wine. It's carbolic. I should be dead in five minutes if I drank it. (*Lifts the glass to her lips. Over the rim—slyly.*) I still have the choice, of course! Which would you do, Dulcie?

SHATOV (*unwilling*): What . . .

DU BOIS: Die? ... Or live? But you never had an opinion!
(*Seeing* HERBERT *return. With panic.*) Are they coming?

HERBERT: In a quarter of an hour.

DU BOIS (*strangled*): A quarter of an hour left—before I go
in ... (*To* NIGGIE—*piteously.*) Talk—for dear life or dear
death! (*Sudden switch to irritation.*) Is it the knife that stops
you talking! I'd throw it away but I know I mustn't.

NIGGIE: Why?

DU BOIS: I don't know. Don't ask me questions! Tell me
about love. I've been ugly all my life. I've been so frightened
of men. Talk to me of love—you're always in love!

NIGGIE (*keeping it light*): But it always blows over. And then
I think "How marvellous to be without her!" To eat my
breakfast off a crumby table. To prop a book ... To order
a boat ...

DU BOIS (*surly*): That's frivolous love.

NIGGIE: It's all I have time for.

DU BOIS (*brooding*): I don't know how it's *done*. Living with
a man. To me when it comes it's like a long illness. I wonder
if I'll live. There must be something easier than these
terrible adorations ... (*Darkly.*) Do you know what it is
to idolize someone?

MRS. BASIL (*low*): Don't answer.

DU BOIS: Don't *whisper*! (*Leaning forward—excited—hoarse.*)
If we got rid of him you and I could be together!

MRS. BASIL (*outraged*): *Du Bois!*

DU BOIS: *Call me Jacky!*

MRS. BASIL (*pacifying*): Later on.

DU BOIS (*ominous*): *Call me Jacky pretty soon!* (*Pause.*) Those
we love might be better dead and then it would be over.
(*To* NIGGIE.) I see you looking at that girl ...

NIGGIE: Well that's not love!

DU BOIS: It might be.

NIGGIE: She irritates me violently! Would that be love?

DU BOIS: It could be.

NIGGIE (*a change: an alteration*): Not at all. It's merely ...

(*Pause.*) . . . that when I look at her I have a high sense of drama. (*Stops. Soberly.*) And that's not love.

DU BOIS: Yes it is!

NIGGIE: Are you an expert?

DU BOIS (*passionately*): God knows I'm an expert!

NIGGIE: All right. (*To* ELIZABETH.) I love you.

ELIZABETH: Is that a joke?

NIGGIE: No.

ELIZABETH: Then why do you say it publicly?

NIGGIE: I want to be pinned down.

ELIZABETH: I should like to live here. (*Looking round the room—then to* MRS. BASIL.) Do you know what girls want?

MRS. BASIL: In my day love.

ELIZABETH: In my day security. I've never been in love. Jewels, cosmetics. To spend, to attract . . . Social position . . .

DU BOIS: Or that your difficult hair could be seen to every day!

ELIZABETH: Why do you say those things to me?

DU BOIS: To cook your goose—if there is one!

ELIZABETH (*fiercely*): Well I love this house. I love what is here! And I wish to God it was mine! (*Pause. To* MRS. BASIL.) Ought I not to have said that?

MRS. BASIL: It depends why you said it.

ELIZABETH: I'm half educated. I avoided school and took up reading. I read and read . . . about this sort of England. I loved what I read. I loved the affluence and the graces. The slowness and the horses . . .

SHATOV (*who is standing near* DU BOIS): You are sucking up to his grandmother!

ELIZABETH (*turning on her, therefore face to face with* DU BOIS): You're sucking up to the age you live in! I read the Elizabethans! I admire—I adore the English! I suffer that they cut no ice! . . . I'm a Colonial . . .

DU BOIS: You're *coloured*!

Sudden total silence.

(*Muttering.*) I have known so many coloured nurses in

hospital. The sun gives you away. You burn wrong ...

ELIZABETH (*deliberate—to* MRS. BASIL): Did you hear him propose, Mrs. Basil?

MRS. BASIL (*inscrutable*): Elliptically.

ELIZABETH: Did you like what you heard?

MRS. BASIL: I reserve my opinion.

There is a sudden, blood-curdling shriek from DU BOIS. TOM *stands in the hallway.*

DU BOIS (*crossing herself*): The Dead!

HERBERT: Not—quite.

TOM (*mopping a small cut on his chin*): It's usual to say "Thank God". (*Comes forward with a final mop: puts his handkerchief away.*) The Dead Awaken—Lazarus Laughed—Bom Bom! Don't imagine I've read 'em. I've only read the titles. (*To* HERBERT.) Getting me back is a poke in the eye—isn't it? (*Turning on* DU BOIS. *Viciously.*) You Great Lunatic Cow— I heard you through the door!

HERBERT (*quietly*): Did you hear *me*?

TOM: You spoke too low. As usual. So cultivated! But I can guess. If I'd gone flipping off to God by my own hand you'd have got out of a mess! Isn't that true?

HERBERT: Something like that—yes.

TOM: Aren't you ashamed? Aren't you inhuman?

HERBERT: No. I'm sick and tired of you. You're making me old.

TOM: I've noticed it! I hate an ageing face!

MRS. BASIL: Do you hate mine?

TOM: No. I can stand age in a woman.

HERBERT: If it had been your wish—all right. We've talked it out. You'd have gone. Yes. I should have been ... (*Hesitates.*)

DU BOIS: Comforted.

TOM: Shut up!

DU BOIS: It was *my* word.

HERBERT: "Comforted" will do. Even a path of agony can't be walked three times. The shoe leather wears. If you'd been murdered that's another thing. We didn't know.

TOM: By Mrs. Cow there—with the strength of ten! (*To* DU BOIS.) And what are you doing with that knife—you cut me once!

ELIZABETH: What did she do?

TOM: Made a pass at me. Or I thought she did. I hit her. She picked up the knife and jabbed. (*Pulls out his handkerchief again and mops.*)

HERBERT: Why didn't you come back before?

TOM (*jeering*): I was washing the blood off me pullover, m'lord! So—all right, Herbert. I've taken it in. You thought I was dead. For twenty minutes you thought I was dead and you were glad.

HERBERT: It's more complicated than that.

TOM: I bet it is! *Pick* among your words! Find the right bloody one! With the special meaning that lets you out. The truth is ... the truth is ... (*Almost crying.*) ... that when you're dead you're not wanted back! (*Shouting.*) Put that in your pipe! The dead aren't wanted back!

HERBERT: Tom ...

TOM (*head up—staring at the ceiling*): I ought to know! I've had it before! I had a brother who went to the war and died and came back. I cried. Mother cried. I was fourteen. I *suffered* his dying. I suffered through nights and nights. Partly for him and partly for me. It was the first time I knew the world would go on without me. I suffered I tell you because Arty died. And when he came back we had *mended*. We'd divided his things. We'd taken over his room. There wasn't *room* for him.

HERBERT: Oh Tom ...

TOM (*bringing his eyes down*): Don't "oh Tom". You've rubbed it in.

HERBERT (*reflecting*): One can *want* them back. It isn't that. But *when* they come ... *If* they come ... the cicatrix has begun to mend.

TOM (*yelling*): Cicatrix—cocatrix—cock*atoo*! You literary—

excuse me, lady—I said it under me breath! You make me
sick. Your cultivated heart! Mine aches *direct*. Smack! Give
me some money! I'm off.

　　As HERBERT *takes out his wallet and peels off something.*
　　... *more* than that!

HERBERT (*throwing the wallet at him*): Take the lot! And don't
come back!

TOM: To all that *talk*. No fear! (*To* MRS. BASIL.) So long.
Cheerio!

MRS. BASIL: You'd much better stay here and swallow his
talk.

TOM (*jaunty*): I'm for feelings! I can feel and stay dumb!

MRS. BASIL: Not for long.

TOM (*gaily—putting the wallet in his pocket*): I suffer like the
animals!

MRS. BASIL: But they forget! You can only hold life down
with words. Why are you so stupid? Stay here. I want a
boy for the rough.

TOM (*leering*): D'you want a walk-out too?

MRS. BASIL (*flaming*): Don't you understand *any* other relationship! Do you think you're fascinating in those terrible
clothes?

TOM (*laughing*): To some I am! (*Goes.*)

MRS. BASIL (*watching him go; to* HERBERT): There must be
more in your neurosis than I thought! (*With sarcasm.*) ...
Those analysts of yours ... Do they examine the mind!

HERBERT (*annoyed*): They take it to pieces.

MRS. BASIL (*a shrug*): Do they put it together again? *Why*
must you have such dreadful loves!

HERBERT (*hostile*): There is something in my spinsterhood
that needs them.

MRS. BASIL (*still indignant*): Why ... then ... one can love
anything! A stick or a stone or the public hangman!!

ELIZABETH (*low*): Or me.

MRS. BASIL (*gravely*): Or you. (*Considering.*) Niggie? You say
nothing?

NIGGIE: What do you want me to say?

MRS. BASIL: You told Elizabeth you loved her. Something must be done about that.

DU BOIS: Aren't you going to marry her?

NIGGIE: Will people say, do you suppose, that I married a black?

DU BOIS: I am chairman. I don't answer.

NIGGIE: But you should. It's your hold-up. Elizabeth says the word "gentleman" is in the dictionary. So is the word "black". If it's for keeps—as I like to think marriage would be—I want the picture of what I might do painted like that! My wife has a ... (*Breaks off.*) Is it your mother who is black?

ELIZABETH (*but she says it with pride*): My father.

NIGGIE: My children may be black. I hate this backing-out from words that have been used for centuries! (*Looking round them.*) Give me the weight of your prejudices! (*Looking at his grandmother.*) What will be the effect of my marrying Elizabeth—if the chairman won't answer!

ELIZABETH: Don't ask her! Don't ask your grandmother!

NIGGIE: Why not?

ELIZABETH: She doesn't like me!

MRS. BASIL (*inscrutably*): I may have been wrong.

NIGGIE: Herbert?

HERBERT: I don't think you—being what you are—could support it in the end.

NIGGIE: Could you?

HERBERT (*wryly*): Being what I am—don't ask me.

NIGGIE: Shatov?

SHATOV (*sullenly*): Elizabeth knows what I would say on a platform.

NIGGIE: What would you say if you were alone?

SHATOV (*looking away from* ELIZABETH): I should be sorry for the child that she might have.

NIGGIE: So the opinion of modern people in this room is that it's bad!—I'm going to do it.

ELIZABETH (*her voice mounting in a panic*): You haven't asked *me*!

MRS. BASIL: I thought you took it that he had.

ELIZABETH: I'd *never* have a child! I don't like people enough to want to make more of them! That's why I thought of Herbert—I thought I wouldn't have a child.

No one comments.

Do they come any *better* as they are continually being born . . .

MRS. BASIL: Nor any wiser. Nor more beautiful. I'm for depopulating the earth and trying harder.

ELIZABETH (*startled*): With what?

MRS. BASIL: With fewer.

NIGGIE (*observing*): But geniuses are born.

MRS. BASIL: Accidentally . . . we have no control . . . look at Beethoven . . . (*Thoughtfully.*) Or who could have supposed —that from Corsica, or a stable . . . such men would come? (*Pause.*) Why do I meddle with destiny? Perhaps I am wrong.

ELIZABETH: That's twice you've said it!

MRS. BASIL: The older I get the more I think I may be. The conundrums get richer and the complications more enchanting! Genes, factors, reasons, stray winds that blow a man and girl together . . . (*Smiling at* ELIZABETH.) *Yours* might be the combination!

ELIZABETH: Of what?

MRS. BASIL: Of gifts—and their frustration! One must be tossed about by accident!

SHATOV: D . . . d . . . d . . . Don't be taken in!

ELIZABETH (*in surprise*): You're crying.

SHATOV (*furious—but chiefly with herself*): It's these damn tears! They fall without my noticing! She's building airy castles out of nothing! She'll never let you have that boy! She's fooling you! She's in love with her own liberality! If you want to marry him—stick to it. But I don't think *he* will. It's the show-off tolerance of the educated rich!

MRS. BASIL: Must one be poor to be believed?

SHATOV: I almost think so!

MRS. BASIL: Have you never had money?

SHATOV: Do I look it? (*Holding both her arms out awkwardly from her poor and unattractive dress, and indeed she doesn't.*) I have never had more than I have now.

DU BOIS: Have you forgotten that you asked me home to tea?

SHATOV (*turning—stammering*): T . . . t . . . te . . .

DU BOIS (*mocking*): *Tea.*

SHATOV: I never asked anyone . . . h . . . home.

DU BOIS (*comically—pointing to her breast*): *Me.*

SHATOV: When!

DU BOIS: When we were at school together. You came in a Rolls-Royce every morning. And it fetched you. I was the only girl that you took home. To that house like a trifle in Millionaire's Row. The Bayswater end. That's where you learnt to play billiards. You showed me.

> SHATOV's *tears fall.*

I remember the shine on the silver when your father came in to tea. Is he dead?

> *A sob.*

Did you get the money? (*Taking it for granted.*) Lucky you! You can give me a fiver . . . (*Suddenly looking up at the clock.*) . . . when they come . . .

MRS. BASIL (*rising—to the weeping* SHATOV): Don't be upset . . .

DU BOIS (*sharp*): Look at the *clock*—the *time*!

MRS. BASIL (*paying no attention—moving across to* SHATOV): . . . as a matter of fact I prefer you . . . (*Lays a hand on her shoulder.*) . . . a little humbled.

DU BOIS: Keep the talk on love!

MRS. BASIL: I chose my own subject.

DU BOIS: Dulcie is a dull subject!

MRS. BASIL (*to* SHATOV): Niggie said you were to put me in touch. (*Leisured.*) But I often ask myself *why* . . . when one devotes—*now* ... *all* one's time to thought ...

DU BOIS: For God's sake *get on!*

MRS. BASIL (*becoming purposely more leisured*): You have broken the sequence. I shall start again. (*Deliberate.*) ... when one devotes *now*—*all* one's time to thought ... (*Holding* DU BOIS *with her eyes.*) ... one should be called more out of touch than when one had time for *none.* (*Sitting down by* SHATOV.) Would I be very tactless ... I so love reasons. Was your father very rich?

DU BOIS (*picking up the kitchen knife; to* SHATOV): Cough up! Come on!

SHATOV (*her eyes on* DU BOIS, *with surprising pride*): Very. (*Defiant.*) And I'm very rich, too.

MRS. BASIL (*fascinated*): Against your principles?

SHATOV: I hadn't any.

MRS. BASIL: The only thing we never expect is the truth.

DU BOIS (*exasperated*): No generalizations!

MRS. BASIL: I have my own way of talking.

DU BOIS: Cut out the frills!

MRS. BASIL (*rising*): How dare you interfere with the exactitude of words chosen!

DU BOIS, *astonished, goes back a step.*

Do you think a *knife* is going to alter my way of speaking!

DU BOIS *goes back another step.*

(*She advances.*) I say what I like in this house! And in my own manner! I am a *mannered* person. Give me that knife.

DU BOIS (*unsteadily*): No ...

MRS. BASIL: Give it to me at once! I am tired of you.

DU BOIS (*distractedly*): Anything may happen ...

MRS. BASIL: I have developed a particular attitude to what happens! Put down that knife.

It falls with a clatter to the floor. DU BOIS *retreats behind the table.*

Give me the carbolic, too.

DU BOIS (*now behind the table, snatching up the glass*): No no no no ... (*Holding it high in the air.*) A toast! An end to suffering!

MRS. BASIL: I don't suffer.

DU BOIS (*the glass to her lips, across the rim*): I wasn't thinking of you.

MRS. BASIL: Put down that glass.

DU BOIS: On whose authority?

MRS. BASIL: Mine.

DU BOIS (*her flickering mind changing; holding the glass right across the table*): I offer you death!

MRS. BASIL (*not touching the glass*): I am immortal.

> The white lights of the headlamps of the ambulance pass over her face, the ambulance bell rings.

DU BOIS (*trembling and hoarse; the arm with the glass shudders down to table level—the wine spilling*): Can you be God . . .

MRS. BASIL (*as though struck by this thought—airily*): I may be. But if I were God I would put the world back!

NIGGIE: To where?

MRS. BASIL (*with gaiety*): I don't ask much! Just banish the engine! (*To* DU BOIS.) Where's your coat?

DU BOIS: In the hall. (*Pleading.*) Shall I see you again?

MRS. BASIL (*linking an arm in* SHATOV's): Let's take her to the ambulance. (*Turning.*) Herbert! Come too.

> They go down the hallway leaving NIGGIE *and* ELIZABETH *alone.*

ELIZABETH: You never meant to ask me to marry you.

NIGGIE (*gravely*): I ask you.

ELIZABETH: I refuse you! I let you off. I was trying it on like a shoe.

NIGGIE: It didn't fit?

ELIZABETH: No.

NIGGIE: That's totally inconceivable!

ELIZABETH: Why?

NIGGIE (*encircling her with his arm*): Because I have the sense— don't laugh—of the magic conquest by myself—of another human being.

ELIZABETH (*standing within his arm as though unaware of it*):

You heard what Shatov said about the child.

NIGGIE: You needn't have a child! Why should we remake ourselves? We *are* ourselves! Do you love me?

ELIZABETH (*absorbed in herself*): Yes I should have a child ...

NIGGIE: Do you love me?

ELIZABETH (*now looking at him*): We are promised glories— and filled with children! At home they swarm. They used to jeer because my hair is red. I prayed to be black. I thought it could happen ...

NIGGIE: Answer me, Elizabeth.

ELIZABETH: I am answering myself. Myself is all I have. I can't transfer my passionate interest to anyone! Judged on my colour and never on myself ...

MRS. BASIL (*who, unseen, has returned to the doorway*): What a fuss you make, Elizabeth!

ELIZABETH: Fuss!

MRS. BASIL: About being coloured! This isn't a bad moment in history to be coloured! (*Lightly, coming further into the room.*) Someone's got to be the first coloured woman to enter Parliament!

ELIZABETH: I never know whether you are laughing at me or snubbing me ...

MRS. BASIL (*taking a breath: taking the plunge*): You would know if you married Niggie.

ELIZABETH: Do you mean what you've said?

MRS. BASIL: Yes.

ELIZABETH (*scornfully*): You think he'll be happy with me?

MRS. BASIL: No. What is happiness? This is marriage.

ELIZABETH: Aren't you taking a risk.

MRS. BASIL: I am taking a gamble. There is something in you that might produce what we are looking for.

ELIZABETH (*defiant*): He might be black!

MRS. BASIL: He might be the hope of the world.

ELIZABETH: Why should he be! I wouldn't want another puzzled child like me! Would you give us the house?

NIGGIE: I don't want the damn house!

ELIZABETH: If I marry it will *be* for the house. (*Taking his arm to take the curse off what she says.*) I don't love you, you know.

NIGGIE (*confident*): You will.

ELIZABETH (*to* MRS. BASIL): I would marry him for the house! If this was the last house in England—and about to be blown up—*this* is where I should like to die! Under the mulberry tree—or on the camomile lawn ...

MRS. BASIL (*drawing herself up*): I have booked that for me.

ELIZABETH: I'd be mistress of this house if I married Niggie!

MRS. BASIL (*twice her height*): The compliment to the house is well taken. *But I should have to die first.*

ELIZABETH (*meaning death and not minding saying so*): Then we'll *wait*! (*Turning passionately to* NIGGIE.) If you want me —then come to Jamaica! My uncle grows coffee in Jamaica! We'll wait ... we'll ...

MRS. BASIL (*calm*): I shall live a long time.

ELIZABETH (*blazing*): And you couldn't put up with *me* here! I couldn't be here—though his *wife*. (*Pause—furious.*) You mean no? ... You mean *NO*!

MRS. BASIL (*shaken by "Jamaica"*): I could furnish the house by the gate ...

ELIZABETH (*lost to decency*): *You* could live in the house by the gate!

MRS. BASIL: You say things of an immense unsuitability without winking an eye!

NIGGIE: That's enough Elizabeth! We'll go! You'd have to live inside her world and you *can't*! (*As she is about to retort.*) *Stop*—Elizabeth! She has answers cleverer than any you can make!

MRS. BASIL (*shocked, warned*): I ...

NIGGIE (*a new and bitter Niggie*): The *amused*—the *amusing* grandmother, the woman whom nothing shocks! (*To* ELIZABETH.) Go outside, and wait for me.

ELIZABETH *goes.*

(*To* MRS. BASIL.) It's time you knew how wrong and strong
you are.

MRS. BASIL (*hardly able to believe her ears*): For you? To you?

NIGGIE: Or *right* and strong. Which is worse.

MRS. BASIL: I see. I know. (*With pain.*) I *didn't* know.

NIGGIE: When I leave here I leave your world. For a girl.

MRS. BASIL: Stay here with her. (*Brokenly.*) I can try.

NIGGIE: You aren't made that way.

MRS. BASIL: Am I such an egotist? (*There is no reply.*) You
are my last piece of magic . . .

NIGGIE: I don't want to hear it.

MRS. BASIL: I have so loved . . . (*Stops—with irony against
herself.*) . . . my portrait—in your heart.

NIGGIE (*with cruelty*): You young. I old. (*Goes.*)

MRS. BASIL (*not realizing he has gone*): Both the same age. . .
(*Draws a breath—pause—fired by a new resolve.*) *Next* time
you dine . . . (*Blows out a candle.*) . . . I shall have *changed*
my age . . . (*Another candle.*) for dinner!

CURTAIN

ACT III

The same room. But there must be a leak in the ceiling for in one corner of the room there is a two-handled zinc bath tub.

MRS. BASIL *and* HERBERT *play chess. An open mahogany box for the pieces lies near.*

MRS. BASIL *is strangely made-up. Face white: too white. Eyes blackened: too black. A trifle clownish—as with women who no longer see so well. She wears a frontal hair-piece of moss-green hair (none at the back). She has on a black organza house-dress or dressing gown, of no fashion, which floats.*

HERBERT, *having come down from London, now wears dark city clothes. His hat and document bag lie in view, near the hallway. As they play they are in two different concentrations. She, head tilted up, speaks into the air. He, engrossed with the game, hangs over the board.*

MRS. BASIL: Eight years!
HERBERT (*hand hovering over board*): Since when?
MRS. BASIL: Since I changed my dress that night. (*Moving a piece.*) I had never allowed myself to grow old.—I thought it was better.
HERBERT (*absently*): And is it?
MRS. BASIL: We have yet to see.
HERBERT (*doing so*): I've taken your bishop.
MRS. BASIL: What will he be like?
HERBERT: Don't they write?
MRS. BASIL: But in letters they say nothing.
HERBERT: You'll know tonight.

MRS. BASIL: Married couples are as blank as letters! Why didn't you bring Tom?

HERBERT (*preoccupied*): He cut his throat under the protection of somebody else.

MRS. BASIL (*off-hand*): He was set on doing it!

HERBERT (*reasonable*): He wasn't at all. He just went further than he meant. *Your* move.

MRS. BASIL (*idly*): Have you found another?

HERBERT: Another what?

MRS. BASIL: Boy—wasn't it?

HERBERT: One always does. *Your* move.

MRS. BASIL (*now examining her position*): What do you call him this time?

HERBERT: Charlie.

MRS. BASIL (*moving a piece quickly and carelessly*): Do you love him?

HERBERT (*hand out again, no hovering, the hand has a victor's look*): The same answer. We only have our own capacity.

MRS. BASIL: Oh you are so educated—*bother*. That's what annoyed Tom . . .

HERBERT (*triumphant, looking up*): Check queen.

MRS. BASIL (*delighted, she is sick of the game*): She's done for! (*Rises and puts out a hand to gather up the pieces.*)

HERBERT (*looking up—shocked*): You're not *giving up*!

MRS. BASIL (*putting a few pieces into the box*): I always give up when I lose my queen. (*Walks towards the mirror on the wall. Then stops.*) Eight years . . . (*Listens.*) Was it the bell?

HERBERT: It doesn't ring.

MRS. BASIL (*leaning far over the wide console table in front of the mirror, to examine herself*): I am older . . . (*She is unaware that* NIGGIE *stands just in sight in the hallway. Not satisfied she steps a pace back as one does in front of an Impressionist picture.*) . . . but of course I don't look it! (*Turns—sees him.*) Oh . . . (*Surprise and delight. Goes quickly to him.*) Oh . . . my dear enchanting Niggie . . . (*Before she kisses him she takes both his hands and stares up into his face.*) . . . you are a middle-aged man! (*Then she is in his arms.*)

ELIZABETH *comes up the hallway.*

(*Turning—still holding his hand.*) Elizabeth!

She and NIGGIE *stand together, welded in love, facing the wife.* ELIZABETH *is colder, dryer. That exuberance, that bloom, unEnglish and tropical, has gone.*

ELIZABETH (*a deep sigh—a relief of the bosom; half-closing her eyes*): We are here.

MRS. BASIL: Does it satisfy you?

ELIZABETH: Not yet. (*Looks round.*) The room seems emptier! What has gone?

MRS. BASIL: Are you making an inventory . . . (*Alters her tone —she mustn't begin like this.*) You remember Herbert?

HERBERT *rises:* ELIZABETH *nods.*

He got here before tea. I've arranged the same weekend.

ELIZABETH: You haven't asked *Shatov?*

MRS. BASIL: Yes I have.

As ELIZABETH *moves away.*

But I don't expect her. She never replied.

ELIZABETH *goes to the window, the little porthole, and holds aside the curtain to try and peer out at the garden.*

NIGGIE (*to* MRS. BASIL): You look wonderful.

MRS. BASIL (*patting a chair beside her*): Let us share the illusion!

He sits down.

(*Airy.*) Time left a mark or two, but I removed them. I drew the face again. Things that have annoyed me for years are now corrected. Eyebrows too short and never large enough eyes . . . (*Sudden preoccupation.*) Oh . . . (*Her hand goes to the back of her head.*)

NIGGIE: What!

MRS. BASIL: I forgot my back hair.

HERBERT (*smiling*): You must take it in your stride when one day you forget the front. Moss-green—isn't it? Charming!

MRS. BASIL: I was so sick of the shades of human hair! *Dear* Herbert—you have such a gift for intimacy—may I call you

Herbert?

HERBERT: You have.

MRS. BASIL: You have a marvellous tolerance for the idiocy of my appearance! You accept personality instead!

HERBERT: Of course.

MRS. BASIL: The Male won't! He is adamant. How comforting you are! Come and live here! Bring Tom.

HERBERT (*automatically*): Charlie.

MRS. BASIL: Ah yes. What was that pretentious word everyone used when you were here before? Latin or Greek? I rather think Greek. Homo . . .

HERBERT: Sexual.

MRS. BASIL: Yes. A monstrous invasion of privacy—giving everyone those little tags about their private life! Why should people ask in what manner one fulfils one's poor pleasures! And for such a short time! (*Turning her head to watch* ELIZABETH, *suddenly—different tone.*) Have you children?

ELIZABETH (*without turning her head*): You know we have.

MRS. BASIL (*silky*): But I've forgotten. Is one black?

ELIZABETH: Coal black.

MRS. BASIL: And the other?

ELIZABETH: White.

MRS. BASIL: Nurse-trouble, school-troubles, social-troubles?

ELIZABETH (*indifferently—still staring out of the window*): Yes.

MRS. BASIL: What do you do about it?

ELIZABETH (*still her back to them*): I am consumed about my own life. I have hardly time for theirs . . . (*Goes on looking out.*)

MRS. BASIL (*to* NIGGIE): Do you allow this?

NIGGIE: A man can do nothing against the will of a wife with her children. A man goes out in the morning and says goodnight in the evening.

ELIZABETH (*impatiently*): I can't *see* anything! It's dark!

MRS. BASIL: It's November. You swore you wouldn't have a child. You'd have done better in Parliament!

ELIZABETH (*taking no notice, still peering out*): I adored the garden. Is it as beautiful as it was?

MRS. BASIL (*occupied with putting away the rest of the chess pieces, murmuring*): ... such a long way through the winter and such a short way through the summer ... (*Direct.*) *More* beautiful! (*Artificial.*) I have learnt to *imagine* flowers! (*To* NIGGIE.) Of course I know what should be done at this time of the year to the borders—what should be covered before the frost—what plants should be taken indoors ... (*Breaking off, airy.*) I don't *do* it! That's all!

ELIZABETH (*irritated at her "twists" of mind; returning*): Are the plants there *or not*?

MRS. BASIL (*sphinx smile*): That's as you like to take it! Did we get on? I don't remember.

ELIZABETH: You do remember—and we didn't.

MRS. BASIL: You always said everything! You left no margin for No Man's Land!

ELIZABETH: You hardly knew me!

MRS. BASIL: You whisked him off to Jamaica before I could find out! But I admired you! I hope I shall admire you still. Put rosemary on the fire, Niggie. (*Takes some branches from a vase.*)

ELIZABETH: It's not lighted.

MRS. BASIL (*handing the bunch to* NIGGIE): Put rosemary all the same. I haven't done much about your rooms, Elizabeth.

ELIZABETH: Are the beds aired?

MRS. BASIL: I told the housemaid.

ELIZABETH: *Housemaid!*

MRS. BASIL: She keeps an antique shop and steals.

NIGGIE: From you!

MRS. BASIL: Continually. But I notice nothing.

ELIZABETH: What does she do for you?

MRS. BASIL: She heats my Bovril and washes my clothes. It's so difficult to keep clean.

ELIZABETH: A *personal* maid!

MRS. BASIL: Haven't you heard of them? But she doesn't

mind washing up. Out of all the sets of china there are only a few left. And the bowl for the Bovril. She has sold all the rest. But what are possessions? Other people buy them. Her shop is a great success. (*Wagging a finger at* NIGGIE.) I know what you are thinking! But take care! I am not senile.

NIGGIE: I wasn't thinking ...

MRS. BASIL: Yes, you were. I am as subtle as ever, but, like Elizabeth, *involved.* Living alone I have this miracle—*myself.* I defy definition. I am interested inwards—not out of selfishness but in a frenzy! Who am I—that I should have such magnificent half-thoughts? And Who holds the other half ... (*Breaking off.*) I beg your pardon! I am lost to all discipline! And there is nobody to stop a widow talking! Could you give me, dear Elizabeth, that white wool shawl —on that chair?

ELIZABETH (*bringing it—holding it up to the light*): It has moth.

MRS. BASIL: The way one is going what is moth! The point is ... who gets there first? (*Taking the shawl—looking up at* ELIZABETH.) You wanted to be mistress here, I remember, after my death.

ELIZABETH: Niggie says we could never afford it.

MRS. BASIL (*flippant*): A freehold! No rent.

ELIZABETH: But the upkeep enormous.

MRS. BASIL: I don't keep it up. (*To* NIGGIE.) You seem very quiet.

NIGGIE: She talks for both of us.

ELIZABETH *moves off again, looking now at pictures.*

MRS. BASIL: I talk for all three! Have you cossetted the spirit in her?

NIGGIE (*following* ELIZABETH *with his eyes, low*): She hasn't cossetted the spirit in me.

MRS. BASIL: Were you weak or strong? I never knew.

NIGGIE (*low*): The stronger is the one who grumbles.

MRS. BASIL: I so adored you. I adore you still. But it takes a marriage to find out the depths of a man. Intelligence is such an easy thing. One knows at once. But the stuff that shoulders a life and a wife is harder to discern.

NIGGIE: Were you stronger than my grandfather?

MRS. BASIL: No. He made me behave. I have never behaved since. I have been more myself. But whether myself has value I don't know. (*Realizing she is not including her guests.*) Pour yourself a drink! All of you. (*To* HERBERT—*gay.*) That reminds me! Who is going to be killed *this* time?

HERBERT: One hopes no one.

MRS. BASIL (*sly*): But *Du Bois* is back.

NIGGIE: Du Bois!

MRS. BASIL: I guaranteed personal charge of her. She came back with mavellous tales of the asylum! It wasn't as dull as she thought.

NIGGIE: Good God—is she safe?

MRS. BASIL: One hopes so. After all she never killed him. She only played with the knife.

NIGGIE: She had killed before.

MRS. BASIL: I never looked up the reports in the newspapers. I thought it better not. I can't remember whether I ordered more whisky. Does anyone here drink?

NIGGIE: In what sense?

MRS. BASIL: Drink too much is that I mean.

DU BOIS (*appearing in doorway*): What time do you want dinner?

MRS. BASIL: What corpse have you in the kitchen?

DU BOIS: A chicken.

MRS. BASIL: Roast it with an onion.

DU BOIS: *Bien.* (*Withdraws.*)

NIGGIE: Why does she talk French?

MRS. BASIL: It was thought therapeutic. And it worked.

ELIZABETH: Doesn't she remember us?

MRS. BASIL: I shouldn't think so. It is part of the cure.

NIGGIE: Are you enjoying any part of your life, grandmother?

MRS. BASIL: Half.

NIGGIE: Half?

MRS. BASIL: The nights. And the mornings up till dawn. Do

look, dear Herbert—*is* there a second bottle of whisky?
I asked you before.

HERBERT: There is.

MRS. BASIL: We may need it. Most nights we have a party.

NIGGIE (*astonished*): Here!

MRS. BASIL: Why not? I was famous for my parties when I
first married! (*Turning.*) I am looking at you, Herbert, with
particular interest. You would make a butler.

HERBERT (*adopting the joke*): Have you guests tonight—
Madam?

MRS. BASIL: Only if it rains. Go outside—down the corridor
to the courtyard entrance and see if it is raining.

　He goes, but obviously hears her next words.
(*Confidential.*) I wanted to get rid of him for a moment. I
wanted to talk to you, Elizabeth and Niggie. Elizabeth . . .
(*With an effort, holding out a hand.*)

　ELIZABETH *comes up to her.*
(*Serious.*) How did it go—your marriage?

ELIZABETH: It went.

MRS. BASIL: What?

ELIZABETH: Anything there was.

MRS. BASIL: Talk to me. Both of you. I will try to keep quiet.
I want to know. But I have lost the habit of listening. You
have been through so much without me. How long did
you remain in love?

ELIZABETH: I was never in love.

MRS. BASIL (*echoing*): *Never* in love . . .

ELIZABETH: You knew what I loved! You knew all along.
It was the *house*! Its age—its manners! And perhaps you.
(*Looking at* NIGGIE.) He was too young to love.

MRS. BASIL: Do you say it before him!

ELIZABETH: There are no secrets between us—and no love.

MRS. BASIL (*with pain*): My magic grandson . . .

ELIZABETH: I have taken it out of him all these years because
I have never been in love. You should have listened to me!

MRS. BASIL: I remember you talked about social position.

ELIZABETH (*bitterly*): He lost it marrying me. I painted myself black—as black I was—to warn you! You should never have allowed it! You were fascinated by the negro in me! Shatov was right! You were fascinated by your liberality! It was a disaster! I knew it would be and it is.

MRS. BASIL: You never got that rhetoric seen to!

ELIZABETH: You talk as though it was a tooth!

MRS. BASIL: Niggie—you say nothing?

NIGGIE: I say nothing. I listen to her. I have heard it all before. There is no end of an end of an end to her discontent. She sees the worst in everything and that is the worst you can have.

MRS. BASIL: Have you never been unfaithful?

NIGGIE: Yes, but I am too tired to change.

MRS. BASIL: And you—Elizabeth?

ELIZABETH: Who with? There is no one better than Niggie. And I am not happy with that. At least he has the better part. He was once in love with me!

MRS. BASIL: Is there *nothing* between you?

NIGGIE: Yes. There is something. She is all I have in the world. She is my one throw of marriage and I have lost on it. But I *know* her. What is terrible is to know no one!

MRS. BASIL: It sounds a small comfort.

NIGGIE: It is. But I am a small man. I am a baby.

MRS. BASIL: That never changes! Something at the centre still cries those little tears of woe . . . (*Not a question—a wail.*) *Why* did you go—both of you! I have been eight years without you—without getting to know you . . .

ELIZABETH: You know why we went.

   Silence.

MRS. BASIL (*low, admitting guilt*): I wanted to die here. It was mine. (*As nothing is said she looks up.*) You could have lived elsewhere —in England.

ELIZABETH: And pushed a pram with a black child?

MRS. BASIL: Was it better in Jamaica?

ELIZABETH: I made a mistake. It was worse. (*Pause: with*

anger.) He was secretary to a golf club till they found out.

MRS. BASIL (*all but trembling*): And then?

ELIZABETH: I had a dress shop and he swept it out.

MRS. BASIL: But you had *money*! I sent him *money*!

ELIZABETH (*sulkily*): He wouldn't use it. He has brought it back.

MRS. BASIL: Why ... why ... (*Energetically*.) *Why*, Niggie?

NIGGIE: I couldn't live on an allowance. I had to grow up ...

MRS. BASIL (*interrupting, quickly*): Hush—Herbert's coming. We'll talk of this again ...

HERBERT (*returning*): You asked if it was raining and it is.

At which MRS. BASIL *glances at the ceiling, goes across to the zinc bath, slightly adjusts it to catch fresh drops that she knows will come.*

MRS. BASIL (*returning*): Where by the way is that new child of yours? If I had known I would have asked him.

HERBERT (*looking at his watch*): He is just about due.

MRS. BASIL (*frowning*): You might have told me!

HERBERT: I wanted to break it to you. I was apprehensive about his introduction.

MRS. BASIL: Why?

HERBERT (*wry*): We never lose our sense of shame.

A man comes walking down the corridor.

MRS. BASIL (*observing him*): Hardly a *boy*!

HERBERT: A ritual expression.

MRS. BASIL (*looking closer, it is the same daffodil hair, she does not shake hands*): We have met before. (*Meditating*.) I don't think I can call you Charlie. Do sit down. (*Meditating*.) Curious how I still have traces of snobbery. You thought I was selling my house, if I remember.

CHARLIE: The project is still on. They want to put more houses here ...

MRS. BASIL (*sliding it in*): ... till—like the first cuckoo—they will be writing to the papers when a blade of grass is seen ... (*Switching, frowning*.) When you are in love, Herbert, you look younger.

HERBERT (*delighted*): *Do* I?

MRS. BASIL: Yes, but not in a very pleasant way.

HERBERT: Are you intolerant!

MRS. BASIL: I can be odious. You'll see!

CHARLIE (*nervously interrupting*): ... this gentleman told me ...

MRS. BASIL (*sharp*): What do you call him?

CHARLIE (*depressed at the question*): Bertie.

MRS. BASIL: Your new relationship may have God's blessing —you can't have children. (*Second thought.*) Or have they invented that you can?

CHARLIE: (*confused*): Not yet.

MRS. BASIL: They may be right, I suppose, to breed and breed and fall into the Ditch of God like the Gadarene Swine ... What was that sum you offered at the time?

CHARLIE: I have come to offer you double.

MRS. BASIL (*absently*): ... and money is half the value ... Do you mean—*eighty* thousand pounds?

CHARLIE: Subject to this and that.

MRS. BASIL: Subject to what?

CHARLIE (*clearing his throat, taking a breath and speaking all in one breath*): Subject to taxes at compound interest—subject to contract survey, subject to confirmation by the ministry concerned—subject to a certain tax query recoverable ...

MRS. BASIL: Query?

CHARLIE: I wouldn't like to be sure it won't be blocked by the next budget.

MRS. BASIL: But there will be a little cash hanging about it?

CHARLIE: I must warn you—there is another side to it.

MRS. BASIL (*sharply*): What side?

CHARLIE: The borough surveyor has your title deeds and maps.

MRS. BASIL: Copies of them.

CHARLIE: I have seen them. Your fields are illegally enclosed.

MRS. BASIL: Since when?

CHARLIE: Since 1530—from Common Land.

MRS. BASIL: My great-grandfather bought them in 1720 from the Crown. You must arraign the King.

CHARLIE: They come under the heading of agricultural neglect. There is a wind-drift of weeds. "A dirty Lay"— they call it.

SHATOV *appears.* MRS. BASIL, *who has her back to the hallway, doesn't see her.*

MRS. BASIL (*sarcastic*): And you are *still* not the head of your firm!

CHARLIE: Not yet.

MRS. BASIL: Owing, I suppose, to that strange mask of youth that you retain ... (*Hunting for the word.*) ... professionally ... (*Not satisfied with the word.*) Or do I mean socially?

HERBERT (*not pleased*): You mean sexually.

MRS. BASIL (*not pleased either*): Thank you, Herbert. (*To* CHARLIE.) Why do you come here with this detailed information?

SHATOV (*stepping forward*): I wrote to him.

MRS. BASIL: Ah—Shatov ...! You never answered my invitation!

SHATOV: I am not staying.

MRS. BASIL: Nonsense! (*Preoccupied.*) What room can I give you. (*Impatient.*) Do sit down!

SHATOV *sits on the edge of the nearest chair. She has developed a nervous tic—always strangely avoiding the face of whoever she is speaking to.*

Besides—Elizabeth is here!

ELIZABETH *gets up eagerly, but* SHATOV *puts out a hand to stop her.*

SHATOV: Not yet. (*Discomforted, nervous.*) I am very uncomfortable, Mrs. Basil.

MRS. BASIL (*going to drinks table*): I am so sorry. Have another chair.

SHATOV: I represent a society that wants to restore the land to the people.

MRS. BASIL (*pouring sherry for* SHATOV, *vaguely*): I don't know when they had it last but not for a long time. (*Carries the glass to her.*)

SHATOV *doesn't take glass so* MRS. BASIL *is left with it.*

SHATOV (*looking slightly beyond* MRS. BASIL): Do you think you can do what you like with seven empty acres?

MRS. BASIL: I should have thought so. (*Rings hand-bell.*) Don't you like to be alone?

SHATOV: There isn't room for it! And a house—with thirty rooms . . . to which you had the sauce to ask me . . .

MRS. BASIL (*smiling pleasantly*): To which you had the sauce to come!

SHATOV: . . . when I knew there were many without a slate over their heads . . .

MRS. BASIL (*glancing up*): There are not many over mine.

DU BOIS *appears.*

Du Bois! Another bedroom.

DU BOIS: There are no more sheets.

MRS. BASIL: Use dust sheets. Who stayed here last week?

DU BOIS: I can't remember.

MRS. BASIL: Nor can I. Use the same towels. Wait! I may want you.

SHATOV (*on her feet, clasping her wretched handbag, speaking oratorically—but, oddly enough, to some other part of the room*): Five hundred families could be settled here!

MRS. BASIL (*replacing sherry in bottle—her back to her*): They would kill what they settled on. The thyme, the bees. The larks, the grass. The blackberries in September. My vixen and her four cubs . . .

SHATOV (*moving her head to look away to the other side*): Do you put them before human beings?

MRS. BASIL: They are wild life. They are still here. The mammoths have gone. The whales are going. (*With absentminded panache.*) The enormous curiosities . . . the giraffe with his neck like a question-mark—questioning his existence . . . (*Stops.*) It may be that mankind is divinely important—but why are you so passionate about *numbers*?

(*Artificially—to* CHARLIE; *really she can't bear to look at* SHATOV *any longer.*) And *then too* . . . they are kept *alive* so long!

CHARLIE (*startled. At sea*): Who?

MRS. BASIL: All the people who *used* to be children. (*Shaking her head.*) Each one . . . *such* a disappointment to someone! (*Polite—enquiring.*) Have you a family? (*Recollecting.*) But no —of course . . . (*Enunciating the word.*) . . . physio—logi— cally you haven't! (*Triumphant—to* HERBERT.) I got the right word that time!

SHATOV (*with irritation*): So much emphasis—in this house— is laid on *words*!

MRS. BASIL: As I grow older I have to catch them in a butterfly net! (*She laughs a little. To* SHATOV.) That didn't amuse you.

SHATOV (*grim*): No.

MRS. BASIL: I see it didn't! There are things I laugh at by myself. I am getting so obscure! But it alarms me when I find that I am alone to laugh at them! (*A twinkle at* NIGGIE: *who winks.*) But don't you speak in public?

SHATOV: I am happier on a platform. (*Stammering.*) . . . f . . . f . . . fer . . . instance . . .

MRS. BASIL (*mechanically*): Take a breath.

SHATOV (*taking one*): Have you heard of the population explosion!

MRS. BASIL (*objective*): Yes. That *is* a different use of words.

SHATOV (*desperate*): I mean . . . (*Shouting.*) Have you *heard* of it?

MRS. BASIL (*sweetly*): You are cross about something?

SHATOV: I can't conduct an argument when words are used like tennis balls!

MRS. BASIL: Use them like cannon balls!

SHATOV: I *will*. Do you mend your barns?

MRS. BASIL: I prefer them broken.

During the next eleven lines DU BOIS *behaves like someone watching a rally at Wimbledon, turning her head as each one speaks.*

SHATOV: Do you cultivate your fields?

MRS. BASIL: I *imagine* the cultivation!

SHATOV: If I lived here I should be *drowned* in what you haven't done!

MRS. BASIL (*suddenly twice her height*): I swim when it rains!

SHATOV (*muttering*): ... May God help God in the Last Judgment! ...

MRS. BASIL (*to* CHARLIE): Shall you pull the house down?

CHARLIE: What else?

MRS. BASIL: Am I not to be allowed to drop to pieces alone?

SHATOV: Has your body its own freedom—*not* to be buried?

MRS. BASIL: I am talking of the eccentricities of the living!

SHATOV: I am wary of the originality that the rich worship!

DU BOIS (*delighted—almost out of breath*): *Whoops!* That wasn't bad!

MRS. BASIL (*to* DU BOIS): Did you say there was a paying side to your asylum?

DU BOIS: There is a wing.

MRS. BASIL: Where one can ring for the night sister and have cocoa?

DU BOIS: One can.

MRS. BASIL: Oh those talks between sleep and sleep—with a strange person. Oh that sweet comfort in the night of the sweet cocoa! No responsibility! ... No remorse—no affection. Only the clean, stiff, *unattached* ... personality of the night sister on duty! (*Grandiloquently.*) Ring them! I may have finished with humanity!

CHARLIE (*low—to* HERBERT): Is she quite all right?

MRS. BASIL (*who has heard*): *Who* is quite all right! (*Gloriously.*) Especially "*quite*"! (*To* DU BOIS.) This is Charlie—I never introduced you ...

> *They are so astonished they bow.*

... take him with you. (*Stops.*) Wait! (*To* HERBERT—*sharp.*) No tendencies?

HERBERT: To what?

MRS. BASIL: To suicide.

HERBERT: I hope not!

MRS. BASIL (*to* DU BOIS): Take him to the kitchen till I ring.

MRS. BASIL, *who has walked to the kitchen door and shut it behind them, turns and looks at* SHATOV. SHATOV *drops her head and examines the hand that lies in her lap. A moment's silence.*

Why don't you look at me?

No answer.

All this time you have never looked at me.

SHATOV (*low*): I lose the thread. I stammer when I see a person's face.

MRS. BASIL: I like you better when you stammer.

SHATOV: No one else does! Not I myself. I hire it out—my indignation! I have a sort of dreadful eloquence—for which they pay me! On which I live.

MRS. BASIL: But you have money.

SHATOV: I don't use it.

MRS. BASIL (*gravely*): You look as though you should.

SHATOV: To live better? (*Shrug.*) To eat better? ... To dress better ... But I've never been a woman! Only a girl. And only when ... (*Looking up, stammering.*) ... h ... h ... he was here!

MRS. BASIL: A lover?

SHATOV: A lover? Yes. My father. We lived alone. I never spoke to a soul till he sent me to school. He was a widower. He counted every penny. We counted it together. It was the game he played with me as a child. As I grew I watched how he amassed it. He loved it—*we* loved it—as men build cities, temples. The extraordinary gifts he had for it, magical, foreseeing ... I was dazed! Why is a painting nobler than making a fortune? Both are arts. I was nineteen when he died and alone at his deathbed. He asked me ... (*Stops, then recovers.*) He asked me to love his money as he had loved me. How could I get rid of it? It was like trying to throw away someone's clothes ...

Pause.

MRS. BASIL: And then?

SHATOV (*turning to her—with a start*): I took ... 1 ... 1 ... (*Firmly.*) ... lessons.

MRS. BASIL: On what?

SHATOV: On how to speak in public. I was so shy I couldn't speak to people. (*The ghost of a smile.*) I could only speak to crowds.

MRS. BASIL: What did you speak about?

SHATOV: I had to *find* a subject. (*Another touch of a smile.*) That's how I got my principles. (*Moving to the hallway, hugging her bag.*) Don't see me out. I have my little car. (*Turning to look at* ELIZABETH.) Goodbye ...

ELIZABETH: Aren't you going to ask anything? Aren't you going to ask about *me*?

SHATOV: You're married. I shall never marry.

ELIZABETH: But that's about *you*.

SHATOV: I never take my eyes off—*me*—for one single minute.

ELIZABETH: I thought I mattered!

SHATOV: No. You were my "girl". That's all—I had to be normal with my crowd. Elizabeth ... Oh Elizabeth! How *sad* it is not to attract men! You never liked children. I would have given my life for a son. Black, white, pink, green—a *son*. I am sterile. What an *accident*! It all depends on whether you attract men! (*Goes.*)

MRS. BASIL (*bringing them back to earth*): Well—there is good in everyone. But it's a mistake to be too touched by it. (*Rings handbell.*)

HERBERT (*outraged for "humanity"*): Why?

MRS. BASIL: It would take the devotion of a lifetime. Are you prepared to give that once again?

To DU BOIS—*who appears.*

Charlie can come back now.

DU BOIS: He wouldn't stay.

MRS. BASIL: Gone! Herbert! See quick if there is blood in

the kitchen!

DU BOIS: I swear ...

MRS. BASIL (*urgent, to* HERBERT): But *see*!

    HERBERT *goes quickly.*

    (*Severely—to* DU BOIS.) I shall be very annoyed if anything has happened again.

    Exit DU BOIS.

MRS. BASIL: *Now* Elizabeth ... now both of you ...

    Bang, drip, drip.

ELIZABETH (*startled*): What's that!

MRS. BASIL (*indifferent*): The water dripping in the bath—it's the rain.

ELIZABETH: ... the *English* rain!

MRS. BASIL: Didn't it rain in Jamaica?

ELIZABETH: Don't talk of Jamaica! I hate and detest it! The dust and the dogs and the eruption of cacti over the broken fences—they depress and disgust me! I sit in a swing in a white dress like a woman from Chekov—and loathe the bougainvillaea!

MRS. BASIL: You have changed.

NIGGIE (*warning*): Don't say it.

MRS. BASIL (*to* ELIZABETH): What has changed you?

NIGGIE: Don't ask her!

MRS. BASIL (*to* ELIZABETH): What do you want out of life?

ELIZABETH (*violently*): This house ... (*Stops.*)

NIGGIE: Be careful.

ELIZABETH: I *won't* be careful—and Niggie has it when you die!

NIGGIE: *Elizabeth!*

ELIZABETH: I am so unhappy I am tone-deaf. I am so angry I can only think of one thing!

MRS. BASIL: That I am still alive?

ELIZABETH: I knew you were! But I thought you would be nearer ... I mean I thought you would be older ...

MRS. BASIL (*rather smugly*): One must be obstinately immortal.

ELIZABETH (*on her feet, frenzied*): But you are not immortal!

(*Stands over her like one of the Furies.*)

MRS. BASIL (*looking up, quietly*): Could you kill me?

ELIZABETH: I could! And I *am the next*!

MRS. BASIL (*rising to face her*): And do you know what *I* am?

Wind and rain are gale force. Soot falls heavily into the grate. A torn piece of ceiling paper detaches itself and hangs down. Water comes faster into the bath.

I live like a goat—in my own ruins! I crop among stones. The fire doesn't light because the chimney is broken. You came in the dark, you didn't see the porch is slipping!

A window bursts open. The wind drives the light curtains up to the ceiling, They fall again.

(*Shouting over the noise.*) You are too late, Elizabeth! The house is falling! You are too soon, Elizabeth. *I* am not falling.

NIGGIE *shuts the window. A crash of plaster is heard next door, and the rush of water.*

DU BOIS (*opening the kitchen door*): Half the kitchen is down!

MRS. BASIL (*superb*): Cook in the other half.

DU BOIS: *Bien.* (*Disappears.*)

ELIZABETH, *spent of her fury, is sobbing on the sofa.*

NIGGIE: Are you going to do nothing?

MRS. BASIL: Nothing. She will ring them—the plumber and the builder. She hates to be wet. They come every night when it rains. They dry their clothes in here. They light a fire on the hearth and we talk through the smoke. *They* are my society. We sit. We talk of life—through their eyes. They are indifferent to life through mine. We drink into the early morning . . .

NIGGIE: *You!*

MRS. BASIL: I sip. (*Absently—her eyes on the weeping* ELIZABETH.) I am old—and I like to be surrounded by men . . .

ELIZABETH (*passionately*): I didn't mean it!

MRS. BASIL (*rueful*): You did when you said it.

ELIZABETH: Yes.

MRS. BASIL (*lightly*): A murderess is only an ordinary woman in a temper!

ELIZABETH: Has it happened to you?

MRS. BASIL (*indifferently*): Yes. (*Going towards* NIGGIE, *speaking over her shoulder—as if she felt some explanation was needed*.) When I was married. About the seventh year.

ELIZABETH: You said it was so happy!

MRS. BASIL: It was a triumph. (*Moving up to* NIGGIE.) But it took doing.

    (*Putting both her hands on* NIGGIE's *shoulders, with love and grief.*)

What can I do for my married grandson . . .?

NIGGIE: We will make something of our lives. There is always something to be made of any life.

MRS. BASIL: There is the child.

NIGGIE (*gravely correcting*): There are two.

MRS. BASIL (*suddenly brought up short—on a different tone*): Is he clever?

NIGGIE: Who?

MRS. BASIL: The black one.

NIGGIE: Brilliant.

MRS. BASIL: And the white one?

NIGGIE: He is just a little boy.

MRS. BASIL (*eagerly*): You said—"brilliant"? (*Impatient.*) My black grandson!

NIGGIE: He is only seven. But he *knows*. Without learning.

MRS. BASIL: Some chess-playing, mathematical, musical infant! They are only misplaced in time!

NIGGIE: He is not like that.

MRS. BASIL: What then?

NIGGIE: He is some sort of marvel.

MRS. BASIL: I am not fond of children.

NIGGIE: He is not a child.

MRS. BASIL: Do you love him?

NIGGIE (*hesitating, then firm*): Worship—is the word.

MRS. BASIL: And you—Elizabeth?

ELIZABETH: I am afraid of him. (*Pause.*) It was not my wish.

(*Low.*) I have been used . . .

MRS. BASIL: Let me see my great-grandson! (*Flash of vanity.*) I am not as old as that sounds! I married young. When you bring him here there is an attic with two rocking horses. Two are so much better than one. And a sandy beach . . . (*She falters.*) . . . by the river in the marshes . . . I never had time . . . (*She stops.*)

NIGGIE (*leaning over her—with surprise*): Those are real tears.

MRS. BASIL (*carrying it off*): I was a worldly woman in very high society! (*Pause.*) I wasn't patient with children. Only in the night when I think of them. . . .

NIGGIE (*gravely*): In all my life I never saw you cry.

MRS. BASIL (*a violent movement of her handkerchief*): Let it be! . . . Elizabeth . . . (*Moving swiftly to* ELIZABETH.) . . . . . . you are very unhappy!

ELIZABETH (*looking up at her*): I have been obsessed. (*Pause.*) With this house. Which was my vision.

MRS. BASIL: You had only been here two hours!

ELIZABETH: I have been here through history. All through my childhood I thought of England. There is something passionate and patriotic . . . perhaps false . . . that lurks in those islands! Perhaps my clue was books. I didn't get it from life. But my eyeballs are screwed—looking back at England! I am a pillar of salt looking back at England. Oh let me come here! You have the strength and the calm. I want to be cured of the terrible responsibility of being what I am! (*Weeping.*) One of them might do better . . .

MRS. BASIL (*rising in her emotion*): "One of them"! Which? My black grandson?

DU BOIS (*entering hurriedly*): They are here from the asylum!

MRS. BASIL (*incredulously*): You *rang* them!

DU BOIS: You told me to!

MRS. BASIL: They are actually here at the door . . .

DU BOIS: Was I wrong?

MRS. BASIL: It was a figure of speech . . . No. Not wrong! (*Smiling at her.*) It was the idiotic divination of a wise

woman! So be it. Ask them to wait. The patient is nearly
ready.

DU BOIS (*in horror—mistaking her*): ME!

MRS. BASIL (*as it were idly*): Me. Shall I give her the house,
Niggie?

NIGGIE: You can't do that!

MRS. BASIL: It's the only way I *can* do it! There are things to
which I am tied that need loosening. (*Looking round the room.*)
A trumpery and tender collection. Pieces of jade—light
through corridors, odd angles, small windows . . . I can do
without them . . . (*Turning to the window and looking out.*)
I can re-invoke them! I can re-invoke the sun rising and
my sheep in shadow and their backs blazing! Dispossess me
of my house—and I can raise the bricks again with my
divine eyes!

NIGGIE (*tenderly—half understanding her*): Have you gone mad?

MRS. BASIL (*gay*): I'm glad you notice it! (*To DU BOIS.*)
Pack my books.

DU BOIS: And your clothes?

MRS. BASIL: I shall wear a nightgown.

ELIZABETH: Is there the money to set things right?

MRS. BASIL: Yes, there is the money. But not the strength.
You need youth to put order back—for a second time.

ELIZABETH: *I* would do it!

MRS. BASIL: You are more direct than I. Yes. *You* would do it.

ELIZABETH: I would fight to the last ditch! Oh let me stay
here! I will be your bricklayer, your foreman, your
messenger. . . .

MRS. BASIL: We couldn't live here together, Elizabeth. I am
too old for you. I say things . . . (*Thinks.*) . . . peripherally
cruel but not meant. There is more anger than there used
to be among the generations. The house is threatened. I don't
know its future, but such as it is I give it to you. Bring them
up here—if you can, Elizabeth! *Make* something of the black
boy.

ELIZABETH: He *is* something. He is more than I am.

MRS. BASIL (*kissing her forehead*): Now—leave me alone with my boy.

ELIZABETH *goes.*

(*To* NIGGIE, *when she has gone—with pressing excitement.*) European features?

NIGGIE: No. He has every feature of a negro.

MRS. BASIL (*murmuring*): Saxons, Romans, French, Dutch . . . The soil can stand a change . . . (*Turning.*) Has he the bumpy forehead of the black man?

NIGGIE (*smiling*): You would say he is as ugly as sin!

MRS. BASIL: No, no! That's where they keep their poetry! The front of the face—and just above the eyes. I am *tired* of the whites, Niggie! The ground is trodden sour with pallor —like a sick field. The mind of the white man has been explored to its last lair and hair! The *poets* are missing! Where are the poets? (*Pause.*) They are behind the bumpy foreheads of the black men! Let them save us! Vive my great-grandson! Let him scrap the scientists! It may be that is what he will do! (*Pause.*) Niggie! Come nearer! (*She glances behind her at the door.*) Come nearer! (*With energy, but lightly.*) I cannot *swallow* death!

NIGGIE: Who can!

MRS. BASIL: Oh, there were Romans! And such! Greeks and so on. I am not afraid. What I ask is —*not yet*! I can't take my eyes off the fate of the living . . .

DU BOIS (*entering, trance-like, carrying a wine glass*): I heard.

MRS. BASIL: Heard what?

DU BOIS: That you cannot swallow death.

MRS. BASIL: You *mis*heard. I said "not yet".

DU BOIS (*ecstatic, gliding forward*): Now the hour comes—and you need me. (*Her face lit by an absurd smile.*) I have packed the shroud.

MRS. BASIL (*dry*): I mentioned a nightgown. Are you drinking again?

DU BOIS (*still nearer—holding out the glass*): I have brought you your sleep.

MRS. BASIL (*with her habit of growing taller*): There used to be
a word—the Quality. Meaning people like me. I don't know
how my class had the impudence to coin it! But it meant
being taught courage at my grandmother's knee. Do you
believe in immortality?

   DU BOIS *nods*.

How would I dare meet her with a glass of carbolic in my
bowels! I may have difficulty in dying. But other people
do it! Look at *The Times*—every day. Spreading their
umbrellas and jumping off the globe! What they can do
I can do—the car's there?

DU BOIS: Yes.

MRS. BASIL: Have you put in my books?

DU BOIS: Yes.

MRS. BASIL: Take out the shroud. Proceed . . . Wait! Fetch
my white elbow-length kid gloves. I have to put on a front.
I am a new girl at the asylum.

   DU BOIS *goes*.

(*Waits a moment by the door—needing to be sure* DU BOIS *is
out of hearing—then turns to* NIGGIE; *fast and low*.) Only to
you, Niggie! Only to you . . .

   Door re-opens.

(*Vexed*.) *You* again—Du Bois!

DU BOIS: Shall you take me with you?

MRS. BASIL (*more vexed*): I *have* to. Who else will look after
you? Wait in the car. (*Suddenly enraged calling after her as
she goes*.) And sit in *front*. With the *driver*! (*Turning back
from the door, cross with herself, shaking her head*.) The old
trouble—too high handed . . .

NIGGIE: What were you going to say?

MRS. BASIL (*close to him, childlike*): Words—words, Niggie.
You never stop me talking! Words lead me into attitudes
I *can't* sustain! Only to you . . . only to you . . . I'm as scared
of death as anyone! And when it comes . . . But it won't!
Because I'm immortal . . .

   He puts an arm round her.

... *when* it comes ... (*Suddenly—pointing through the window.*) Oh ... *look!* There goes Herbert ...

DU BOIS *slips in again unseen.*

... his arm round Charlie. Charlie isn't worth Herbert's little finger. ...

DU BOIS *glides up behind them.*

... but what does it matter what *kind* of love it is—if it's love!

DU BOIS (*arms wide, eyes glassily shining*): I *adore* you.

MRS. BASIL *turns with a start.*

When we get there ... (*A step nearer.*) ... *won't* you call me Jacky ...

MRS. BASIL (*walking straight past her and out*): I'll be buggered if I do.

CURTAIN

STUDY & INF.